Seeking Mahādevī

Seeking Mahādevī

Constructing the Identities of the Hindu Great Goddess

Edited by Tracy Pintchman

State University of New York Press

The "Dancing Devi" image on the cover is used by permission of
The Metropolitan Museum of Art.

Published by
State University of New York Press, Albany

Printed in the United States of America

For information, address State University of New York Press
90 State Street, Suite 700, Albany, NY 12207

Production by Judith Block
Marketing by Fran Keneston

Library of Congress Cataloging-in-Publication Data

Seeking Mahadevi : constructing the identities of the Hindu Great Goddess / edited by Tracy Pintchman
p. cm. —
Includes bibliographical references and index.
ISBN 0-7914-5007-4 (alk. paper) — ISBN 0-7914-5008-2 (pbk : alk. paper)
1. Goddesses, Hindu. I. Pintchman, Tracy.

BL1216.2.S46 2001
294.5'2114—dc21 00-061223

10 9 8 7 6 5 4 3 2 1

For my daughter, Molly Alice French
born April 14, 2000
the same month as this book

the Goddess does indeed have many forms

Contents

Illustrations ix

Acknowledgments xi

Note on Transliteration and Pronunciation xiii

Introduction: Identity Construction and the Hindu Great Goddess, *Tracy Pintchman* 1

1 The Tantric and Vedāntic Identity of the Great Goddess in the Devī Gītā of the Devī-Bhāgavata Purāṇa, *C. Mackenzie Brown* 19

2 Mahādevī as Mother: The Oriya Hindu Vision of Reality, *Usha Menon* 37

3 Ambiguous and Definitive: The Greatness of Goddess Vaiṣṇo Devī, *Mark Edwin Rohe* 55

4 The Goddess as Fount of the Universe: Shared Visions and Negotiated Allegiances in Purāṇic Accounts of Cosmogenesis, *Tracy Pintchman* 77

5 Waves of Beauty, Rivers of Blood: Constructing the Goddess in Kerala, *Sarah Caldwell* 93

6 From Village to City: Transforming Goddesses in Urban Andhra Pradesh, *Sree Padma* 115

7 Reconstructing the Split Goddess as Śakti in a Tamil Village, *Elaine Craddock* 145

8 Perfecting the Mother's Silence: Dream, Devotion, and Family in the Deification of Sharada Devi, *Jeffrey J. Kripal* 171

9 Goddesses and the Goddess in Hinduism: Constructing the Goddess through Religious Experience, *Kathleen M. Erndl* 199

10 What Is a "Goddess" and What Does It Mean to "Construct" One? *Thomas B. Coburn* 213

Glossary 223
References 227
Contributors 243
Index 247

Illustrations

Table

5.1 Variants of Bhagavati Textual Traditions 96

Figure

10.1 Diagram of the Relational Quality of Religious Life 217

Photos

2.1 Kālī Standing on Śiva 45

6.1 Hāriti 122
6.2 Erukamma 123
6.3 Pyḍamma 126
6.4 Durgālamma 128
6.5 Polamma 130
6.6 Nīlamma 131
6.7 Kunchamma 132
6.8 Kanaka Durgā 134
6.9 Ellamma 137
6.10 Kanaka Mahālakṣmī 140

Acknowledgments

I wish to thank each of the contributors for their hard work and, most especially, their patience, for this volume took shape rather slowly over the course of five years. I extend heartfelt thanks to the staff at the State University of New York Press as well, especially Nancy Ellgate and Judith Block, who have been cheerful and supportive editors. Anonymous readers made several helpful suggestions and comments, and I am grateful for their insights. My gratitude extends also to Judy Davis, who prepared the index.

Portions of C. Mackenzie Brown's chapter are reproduced from his book *The Devī-Gītā; The Song of the Goddess: A Translation, Annotation, and Commentary* (Albany: State University of New York Press, 1998).

All photographs in chapter 6 were taken by Sree Padma.

A Note on Transliteration and Pronunciation

Words from various Indian languages are transliterated in this book according to accepted conventions. We have retained the Sanskrit forms of terms and names to a great extent for the sake of internal consistency, but we have allowed for variation to reflect regional languages, such as Tamil, Telegu, and Malayalam, and to accommodate contributors' preferences. We have not used diacritical marks for contemporary geographical names (e.g., Bhubaneshwar, Visakhapatnam, Delhi). Foreign terms that recur in the essays or are used without explanation are defined briefly in the Glossary.

The pronunciation of certain letters in Sanskrit and other Indian languages represented in this volume is quite distinctive. Those that we feel are most in need of explanation are below.

Letter	Pronounced as in the English
a	c*u*p
ā	t*a*r
ṛ	*ri*m
ī	m*ee*t
ū	t*oo*th
c	*ch*eek
ś, ṣ	*sh*ip

In addition, the letter *h* after a consonant aspirates the consonant, meaning that it is pronounced as a puff of air following the consonant. So, for example, in the name "Bhairo," the *b* and the *h* are pronounced separately, resulting in an aspiration of the letter *b*. *Th,* similarly, is pronounced as an aspirated *t,* as in ho*th*ouse (*not* as in pa*th*).

Introduction

Identity Construction and the Hindu Great Goddess

Tracy Pintchman

Goddess worship has been an important dimension of Hindu religious life for many centuries, and the Hindu goddess tradition is one of the richest, most compelling such traditions in existence today. In cities, towns, and villages all over India, temples and shrines dedicated to goddesses abound, and devotees flock to these to express their reverence, concerns, hopes, and fears. Goddesses also figure prominently in many home shrines and rituals, and both men and women participate widely in various forms of goddess devotion. Although Hindus recognize and revere a variety of different, discrete goddesses, they also tend to speak of "the Goddess" as a singular and unifying presence.

The notion of a singular, supreme Goddess is crystallized in a text of approximately the sixth century C.E. called the Devī-Māhātmya, "Glorification of the Goddess." The central narrative concerning the Goddess in the Devī-Māhātmya has to do with her adventures as a great slayer of demons who leads the gods to triumph in their fight against demonic forces and vanquishes those who would subdue her. The vision of the Goddess that the Devī-Māhātmya achieves in narrating this story borrows and weaves together narrative and devotional threads already in existence at the time, but, in so doing, it produces a marvelous new picture of divinity. Thomas Coburn, who has written extensively on the Devī-Māhātmya, observes the synthetic nature of the text's vision of the Goddess:

> The synthesis that is accomplished in the Devī-Māhātmya is therefore extraordinarily and uniquely broad. It reaches deep into the Sanskritic heritage, identifying the Goddess with central motifs, names, and concepts in the Vedic tradition. It appropriates one familiar myth on behalf of the Goddess, and enfolds several less well-known tales into its vision. It locates the Goddess in relation to a full range of contemporary theistic and sectarian movements, familiar ones such as those of Śiva and Viṣṇu, and more recent ones such as those of Skanda and Krishna Gopāla. (1991, 27)

Coburn notes also the unique contribution of the text historically, observing that "the Devī-Māhātmya is not the earliest literary fragment attesting to the existence of devotion to a goddess figure, but it is surely the earliest in which the object of worship is conceptualized as Goddess, with a capital G" (1996, 16).

In the Devī-Māhātmya the Goddess is given numerous epithets, indicating that while she is unique, her forms are many. Contemporary devotees, too, often maintain that there is one supreme Goddess who has many forms or who is the unity underlying all discrete goddesses by way of accounting for the multiplicity of goddesses that persists alongside talk of "the Goddess." David R. Kinsley notes that in general, there are two primary ways in which the unity of all goddesses is envisioned in the affirmation of a single, Great Goddess in the Hindu tradition. One way is to postulate the existence of one transcendent Goddess possessing the classical characteristics of ultimate reality and to portray all particular goddesses as her portions or manifestations. Another way is for a particular goddess like Pārvatī, Lakṣmī, and so forth to be affirmed as highest with all other goddesses viewed as her portions or manifestations (Kinsley 1986, 132).

As scholarly interest in Hindu goddesses and goddess traditions has flourished in the last two decades, scholars have continued to puzzle over the "goddess(es) versus Goddess" conundrum. John S. Hawley observes quite correctly that since Indic languages observe no distinction between capital letters and lowercase letters, and since they lack the definite article, the "g/G" issue and the problem of whether to use the article "the" when naming (the) Hindu Goddess is "clearly ours, not India's." He also remarks, however, that regardless of the lack of a "g/G" problem in Indic languages, "the quandary as to singular or plural is shared," and that "sometimes the singular feels more accurate, sometimes the plural" (1996, 8). Kinsley uses the name Mahādevī or "Great Goddess" to refer to the supreme, singular Goddess underlying all goddesses. One could in fact see the use of the prefix "Mahā-," "great," in Mahādevī's name as largely analogous to the English capital *G* that Coburn points to in his description of the Devī-Māhātmya as "the earliest [literary fragment] in which the object of worship is conceptualized as Goddess, with a capital G." Hence, one way to refer to the singularity or capital *G*-ness of Devī's nature is to affix "Mahā-" to her name. In some contexts, Devī is explicitly called Mahādevī, whereas in other contexts her "Mahā-" nature is not stated but is implicit in the ways she is portrayed. In this book, we will refer to her as Devī, (the) Goddess, Mahādevī, and (the) Great Goddess, understanding all these names as indicating her supreme, singular form.

Mahādevī is both the unity underlying all female deities and a magnificent divine being. Kinsley offers a "composite sketch" of her that he compiles from a number of textual sources. He notes that generally she is homologized with the principles *prakṛti* (materiality), *māyā* (cosmic illusion), and *śakti* (power), which drive the process of cosmogenesis and sustain the created world. She is portrayed as both transcendent and immanent, rooted in the world and embodying it but stretching beyond it as well, and in some contexts she is identified with ultimate reality, Brahman, itself (1986, 133–139). She is both creator and queen of the cosmos and is often portrayed as independent of male control rather than married or subservient to a male consort (138; also Coburn 1982, 1996). Many contexts emphasize her nature as Divine Mother, too, a status that clearly reflects her gender, although she is sometimes said to transcend gender at the highest level (137).

Although many of these characteristics persist across different contexts, there is also a great deal of diversity with respect to portrayals of Mahādevī's identity. The Devī-Māhātmya has been highly influential in shaping later text-based portrayals of the Goddess, but later traditions that appropriate various themes from the Devī-Māhātmya do so in diverse ways, achieving their own, unique visions of the Goddess. And, of course, other influences apart from the Devī-Māhātmya are at work, too. In his study of the Devī-Bhāgavata Purāṇa, for example, C. Mackenzie Brown skillfully demonstrates how themes derived not only from the Devī-Māhātmya, but also male Vaiṣṇava theologies, especially those articulated in the Bhāgavata Purāṇa, are incorporated in this text's portrayal of the Goddess, resulting in a fresh perspective on her nature and identity (1990). Kinsley notes that in certain texts of the Pañcarātra school of thought and devotion, Lakṣmī is "elevated functionally to a position of supreme divinity" and is spoken of in terms that are quite consistent with other Hindu portrayals of the supreme, singular Goddess, although descriptions of her in the sections of text to which he refers—which have to do largely with cosmogony—do not bear any clear narrative resemblance to the martial goddess of the Devī-Māhātmya (1986, 30–31). When it comes to practice, as Coburn notes, Devī's identity is always shaped by local custom, and where text-based ideas about Devī weave their way into popular practice, they do so in complex ways (1996, 43–44). The qualities of the Goddess that are emphasized, the name and nature of the goddess identified as Devī, and other such factors are all subject to local interpretation. Hence, while Kinsley's "composite sketch" is a helpful starting point for talking about Mahādevī's identity, it does not—nor does it purport to—encompass the myriad variations on and departures from the themes that Kinsely identifies.

The much-invoked notion that there is one, supreme Goddess with many forms encourages the understanding not only of all individual goddesses as Mahādevī's parts, but also of all distinct Mahādevī "portraits" as so many different perspectives on the singular Goddess. It functions as a hermeneutical lens that enables us to see unity within the multiplicity of views on Mahādevī's nature and character. While not disputing the legitimacy of such a perspective, these essays turn to focus on the multiplicity itself, the many ways in which the supreme Mahādevī and her unified diversity are portrayed, understood, and experienced.

The topic of this book is "constructing the identities of the Hindu Great Goddess." As noted above, we understand the Hindu Great Goddess, Mahādevī, to be the supreme female deity who is also considered to be the unity and source of all individual goddesses. Different essays in this book may highlight one or the other of these dimensions of her being, or both. We understand "identity" to refer to Mahādevī's nature, character, and attributes as these are portrayed in oral and written texts or understood and articulated by devotees. We use terminology of "construction" to signal what we understand to be the constitutive role of interpretation in shaping portrayals of Mahādevī's identity in diverse ways in different contexts. This understanding is informed by a more general tendency in many strands of contemporary scholarship to regard certain forms of knowledge as context-dependent and inherently conditioned by interpretive activity.

In his classic works *The Social Construction of Reality* and *The Sacred Canopy*, Peter L. Berger argues persuasively that social and cultural truths are constructed through human processes of "world building." Such world building also entails the construction of religion and religious categories.[1] But, like cultures, religions themselves are internally diverse and encompass multiple, sometimes competing discourses that are conditioned by context. The various texts, communities, and individuals explored in this volume envision the Goddess through epistemological lenses that are shaped by a diversity of religious, social, textual, political, psychological, historical, and other, often local conditioning factors. Worshipers encounter the Goddess through experiential and ritual frames that are similarly conditioned. For purposes of the task at hand, therefore, we understand Mahādevī to have multiple identities that are constructed through interpretive activity occurring in particular textual and devotional contexts subject to particular conditions. This understanding is meant not as an ontological claim but as a hermeneutical framework that guides our exploration of Mahādevī's identity.

In addressing our topic, contributors tend to organize their essays around the issue of identity-construction primarily in two ways. First, some contributors focus on the "constructions" or constructed identities of Mahādevī themselves in the specific textual, devotional, and historical contexts in which they arise. Construction is a process, too, however, and some essays explore processes through which particular goddesses or women come to be identified with the singular Mahādevī in particular instances, or how and why such identification occurs. These two emphases are relatively interwoven, of course, and to separate them is somewhat misleading. However, several of the essays tend to focus relatively more on one issue or the other.

There are three primary goals of this volume. First, it aims to call attention to the great diversity of Mahādevī's identities to those who worship her. In so doing, it considers a wide variety of materials and explores a wide range of particularized contexts. We deem both textual and nontextual materials to be worthy of consideration, although most of the essays focus on Mahādevī's identity in lived devotional contexts. Second, it aims to elucidate the various ways that Mahādevī's diverse traits and attributes are interpreted, enlivened, and rendered meaningful in different ways in different contexts. And third, by ranging broadly, this collection of essays hopes to encourage further exploration of both continuities and discontinuities concerning perceptions of Mahādevī from context to context. While several studies of Hindu goddesses investigate localized portrayals of the Great Goddess (e.g., Sax 1991, Erndl 1993, Brown 1990), by juxtaposing numerous depictions of her, this book invites comparative reflection on her multiple identities and the ways these are constructed.

One important question raised by this collection is that of the characteristics or attributes that are most consistently central to Mahādevī's nature in the variety of textual and devotional environments we explore in these pages. This is a somewhat loaded question, for it suggests a desire to circumscribe a core identity that transcends specific context, an enterprise that this book ultimately resists. It is also not a question that any of the contributing authors addresses directly. I would propose, however, that themes pertaining to Devī's immanence coupled with her transcendence, her nature as *śakti*/Śakti, and her status as Divine Mother seem to recur in these essays with the greatest frequency. It is Devī's transcendence-yet-immanence, in fact, that Hawley sees as particularly characteristic, remarking: "The unity of the Great Goddess incorporates the world as we know it, as well as transcending it. In some sense, the Goddess IS our world in a way that God is not" (1996, 6). The association of the Goddess with *śakti*, too, is so strong that traditions of devotion to the Goddess in any of her forms are called Śāktism, devotion to Śakti, and devotees of the Goddess are known as Śāktas. The epithet "Mā," "mother," is commonly used for goddesses all over India. The understanding of Mahādevī as Divine Mother, an understanding that is obviously related to her femaleness, is underscored in several chapters of this book.

As many of these essays make clear, however, the various qualities associated with Mahādevī, including her immanence, her nature as *śakti*/Śakti, and her status as Divine Mother, have multiple resonances and connotations, and different emphases may come to the fore in different contexts. In Purāṇic accounts of creation, for example, the Goddess's nature as *śakti* has a good deal to do with cosmogony; in her essay, however, Elaine Craddock argues that in the devotional context she has researched, devotees understand the Goddess's nature as *śakti* as having to do less with her cosmogonic power than with her ability to do things for her devotees. In some contexts, her immanence may be related to her nature as the cosmogonic principle *prakṛti*, the material basis of creation, underscoring the point that "Mahādevī is the world, she is all this creation" (Kinsley 1986, 136). But it may also have to do with her manifestation in language as the sound "Hrīṁ," a sound to be used in meditation that is associated with the Kuṇḍalinī energy inherent in human bodies, or with her embodiment as three rounded stones or *piṇḍis* in a Himālayan cave (see the chapters by Brown and Rohe in this volume). In some Purāṇic cosmogonies, Mahādevī as World Mother is the source of all creation; in the Devī Gītā, she is also the divine Mistress of the Jeweled Island who lies beyond all relationship and "manifests herself out of the subtle vibrations of pure consciousness" (Brown's chapter). Oriyan informants, however, associate her motherhood with receptivity to the needs of her children (see Menon's chapter). While persisting translocally, therefore, these qualities are richly complex and contextually nuanced.

In pointing to Mahādevī's immanence and her nature as *śakti*/Śakti and Divine Mother as qualities that seem to persist across the range of contexts discussed in this book, we do not intend to make universal claims. In fact, these qualities do not appear to be stressed in all contexts. C. Mackenzie Brown's marvelous study of the Brahmavaivarta Purāṇa (1974), for example, reminds us that Mahādevī's nature as *śakti* is not terribly central in that text, and Sarah Caldwell points out in her chapter in this volume that the Goddess's erotic, rather than motherly, appeal comes to the fore in the Śrī Vidyā cult. Even though it invites inquiry and reflection about unifying qualities that persist across a number of diverse contexts, this book does so in the process of also highlighting diversity, difference, and particularity regarding Mahādevī's depiction and worship. Ultimately, we do not purport to resolve the tension between unity and diversity when it comes to her identity; we mean to draw attention to it. We leave readers to make their own decisions about the relative merits of emphasizing one pole or the other.

We probably should think further, too, about what aspects of the Goddess's most consistently invoked traits might be particular to her and what might be shared, especially when it comes to lived devotional experience and worship. For example, in many contexts Devī's immanence means that she "IS our world," as Hawley notes. But Hindu scriptures boast a deep history of portraying the manifest cosmos as the body of the divine, beginning with the well-known Puruṣa Sūkta of the Ṛg-Veda and flowing into contemporary devotion to not only Devī, but her male counterparts as well. The Bhāgavata Purāṇa, for example, portrays the world as the male Vairāja Puruṣa, "cosmic man," the material form of God; this emphasis is picked up in contemporary Braj Vaiṣṇavism, which holds that the entire world is Kṛṣṇa (Brown 1990, 188; Haberman 1994, 125–127, 215). Pilgrimage spots known as *śakti pīṭhas* purport to enshrine portions of Devī's body, emphasizing her embodied, immanent nature, but the pilgrimage spots in the Himalayas known as the five Kedars similarly enshrine Śiva's body, and Kṛṣṇa devotees write of and experience different regions of Braj as embodying different portions of Kṛṣṇa's body (Haberman 1994, 126–127). In what ways might the experience of Devī's immanence be unique? Is there a qualitative difference, or is it a matter of the consistency with which Devī's immanence is emphasized? With respect to *śakti*, Devī's nature as the cosmic, life-creating force that sustains the universe and everything in it comes to the fore in many contexts. But what about the nature of Mahādevī's *śakti* as her ability to act on behalf of her devotees that Craddock invokes in her essay—what dimensions of *śakti* as it is interpreted in such contexts might be unique to the Goddess? Joseph Alter and Philip Lutgendorf have argued that the male monkey-god Hanumān, too, is widely perceived to be the embodiment of *śakti* (Alter 1992, 199; Lutgendorf 1994, 240; 1997, 321–322). What might Hanumān and Devī share in this regard?

Another issue that we might raise here is to what extent Mahādevī's unmarried status seems central to her "Mahā-" nature in some contexts, since this is a quality to which a number of scholars have called attention in their research (e.g., Brown 1990; Coburn 1982; Erndl 1993). In his introduction to *Devī: Goddesses of India,* Hawley notes that Vasudha Narayanan's and Donna Wulff's essays in that volume push the limit on this issue regarding the status of Śrī/Lakṣmī and Rādhā, who, in certain devotional contexts, are coupled with a male deity but are perceived to be coequal with or even independent of their mates. Usha Menon's chapter in this volume also considers the issue with respect to Kālī as she is understood by devotees in Orissa. If a text depicts a goddess in Mahādevī-like ways, as supreme Śakti, Divine Mother, and so forth, and attributes independent agency to her, or if devotees understand and relate to her in such ways, how much does her marital status matter as a defining element of her identity?

In negotiating Mahādevī's diverse portrayals, it might be helpful to think about her "Great" or "Mahā-" nature more in terms of status than in terms of particular traits or attributes. Like the status of "Queen," the status of supreme Goddess is a position, one that is held by different goddesses in different contexts and in relationship to different individuals or communities. The various attributes frequently ascribed to Mahādevī—her nature as Brahman, *śakti, prakṛti,* or *māyā,* her embodiment as the world, and so forth—seem to function more as family resemblances, traits that tend to run in the Great Goddess "family" but have diverse forms and may be downplayed or even absent in some contexts or pronounced in others. And in some cases, features that are not generally recognized as particularly common familial traits might come to the fore. Ultimately, the identity of the Great Goddess may have more to do with how she functions in the lives of devotees than what, precisely, we are able to pin down as her particular traits and characteristics. Perhaps, therefore, it would be helpful to think of her "Greatness" as being grounded in the way a community of worshipers understands and relates to its goddess. Such a perspective on the Goddess, however, while potentially useful as a heuristic model, does not purport to reflect the perceptions or experiences of most Goddess devotees.

In arranging the chapters of this book, I have tried to take into account the emphasis of each with respect to the two main foci of this book, namely, Devī's constructed identities in various contexts and Goddess-construction as a process. The essays by C. Mackenzie Brown, Usha Menon, Mark Edwin Rohe, Tracy Pintchman, and Sarah Caldwell focus relatively more on the former issue, whereas the essays by Sree

Padma, Elaine Craddock, Jeffrey J. Kripal, and Kathleen M. Erndl focus more on the latter. The chapters are grouped accordingly.

In the opening chapter "The Tantric and Vedāntic Identity of the Great Goddess in the Devī Gītā of the Devī-Bhāgavata Purāṇa," C. Mackenzie Brown focuses on the portrayal of the Goddess in a small section of this well-known *śākta* text, a section known as the Devī Gītā (Song of the Goddess). Brown begins by contrasting the account of Devī's birth as it is narrated in the Devī-Māhātmya, with the version found in the Devī Gītā, noting that the Devī Gītā's story, while borrowing elements from the Devī-Māhātmya's account, radically redefines the Goddess and constructs her identity in a thoroughly different manner. While not denying her fierce, demon-destroying role, the Devī-Bhāgavata Purāṇa as a whole frequently emphasizes her softer, maternal side. This is also true in the Devī Gītā, where Devī plays the role of teacher rather than warrior.

Brown argues persuasively that the identity of the Goddess in the Devī Gītā as revealed in the account of her birth is both Advaitic and Tantric. Her Advaitic identity reveals itself in depictions of her as the supreme consciousness that is the non-dual Brahman of Advaita Vedānta philosophy. Her Tantric identity is revealed in her nature as the Tantric goddess Bhuvaneśvarī, "Ruler of the Universe," the benign, auspicious mother of the world. These two aspects of her identity and their essential unity are exemplified not only in the birth narrative, but also in terms of sonic symbolism: Devī's two dimensions, that of Brahman and Bhuvaneśvarī, are also embodied in two mantras, Oṃ and Hrīṃ, that are identified with her. These two mantras represent her dual nature as both the ground of existence and its manifesting and ruling power.

Mahādevī's identity as World-Mother, which Brown raises in his chapter, is highlighted in the next chapter, "Mahādevī as Mother: The Oriya Hindu Vision of Reality." In this essay, Usha Menon explores the significance of the Goddess to Oriya Hindus living in Bhubaneshwar, a city in Orissa. Menon focuses on three issues pertaining to Devī's identity in Bhubaneshwar: the belief that the Goddess is immanent in all forms of the created universe; the significance of her most common epithet, "Mā" or "Mother," to devotees; and the importance that Oriya Hindus place on male/female complementarity and its relevance to their understanding of the Goddess's identity.

Bhubaneshvar is predominantly Śaiva, and the perspectives on Devī's identity and nature that Menon articulates reflect this orientation. Devī is Śiva's *śakti*, his creative power, which not only enables the creation of the universe, but is also immanent in its every aspect.

As in the Devī Gītā, however, she becomes accessible to devotees as "Mā," the world-mother who generates and regenerates all life. Menon focuses particularly on Kālī, a form of the Goddess that is widely worshipped in Orissa and whose designation as "Mā" may at first appear problematic: Kālī is widely known to be a wrathful and indiscriminately destructive goddess with a tendency to spin out of control. Menon has found, however, that Oriya Hindus perceive Kālī as wild, but not altogether lacking in self-discipline.

In their interpretations of a popular image of Kālī standing on Śiva, devotees describe Kālī as pulling herself together and regaining self-mastery even in her most wanton moments when her attention is drawn to her responsibilities as Śiva's wife and the mother of all living creatures. When devotees address Kālī as "Mā," that simple utterance calls Kālī's attention to the needs of her "children" and makes her receptive to the needs of her devotees. Furthermore, while honoring and affirming Mā's autonomy, Oriya Hindus do not consider her to be superior to or independent of Śiva, but rather think of the two as complementary. The complementarity that exists between God and Goddess mirrors the complementary relationship between mortal men and women in the human realm. Hence, Menon argues, ordinary devotees make sense of Devī by domesticating her and defining her in terms of social roles that render her approachable.

In the first two chapters, Brown and Menon strive to clarify the core elements of Devī's identity in the contexts they explore. In the next essay, "Ambiguous and Definitive: The Greatness of Goddess Vaiṣṇo Devī," Mark Edwin Rohe emphasizes instead the ambiguity of her identity. Rohe takes us to the mountain cave shrine of Vaiṣṇo Devī in Jammu. Vaiṣṇo Devī is a relatively new goddess, but her home on Trikuta Mountain has become arguably the most important pilgrimage site to a goddess in North India. Aside from the pilgrimage itself, posters, photos, pamphlets, movies, songs, newspaper and magazine articles, and temple statues present her images and stories to the public throughout the subcontinent.

Rohe observes that while Vaiṣṇo Devī's location is quite specific—only the cave shrine in Jammu is the true home of this goddess—her theology is quite fluid. Her nature as Mahādevī, the Great Goddess, is expressed by the three rounded stones or *piṇḍis* that represent her at the shrine and are said to embody the three goddesses Mahāsarasvatī, Mahālakṣmī, and Mahākālī. In both scripture and popular usage, these three deities are considered to be the three primary manifestations of Mahādevī (cf. Brown 1990, 132–154). But beyond this, ambiguity abounds. Which *piṇḍi,* if any, is truly Vaiṣṇo Devī? Or is she all three? Is she a form of Durgā, Lakṣmī, Śeraṇwālī,

Kālī, or Satī? A mother or a virgin goddess? Rohe argues that her theology is sufficiently vague that all pilgrims are able to create a meaningful experience for themselves no matter what their own devotional orientation. He also observes that her pilgrimage is simultaneously perceived to be extremely ancient and quintessentially modern in its facilities and administration, yoking traditional values to visions of material progress and hopes for an increasingly better future. Hence, Vaiṣṇo Devī's qualities make her an exemplary deity for Hindus pressed by the desires and demands of a future-looking, modern urban society but longing to connect with their traditional religious heritage.

My essay, "The Goddess as Fount of the Universe: Shared Visions and Negotiated Allegiances in Purāṇic Constructions of the Goddess," continues to address themes of unity and ambiguity in portrayals of the Great Goddess, but it does so with a focus on the Purāṇas and accounts of creation found in these texts. The Purāṇas are encyclopedic by nature and include a variety of mythological narratives, ritual prescriptions, devotional exhortations, and other types of religious materials. By definition, however, all of the Purāṇas contain accounts of creation, and several cosmogonic narratives are often found in a single Purāṇa. My essay argues that despite differences in devotional orientation, the Purāṇas tend to portray the Goddess in a similar manner: she is a creative agent embodied as the principles *śakti* (creative power), *prakṛti* (materiality), and *māyā* (illusion).

Although the formulation of Devī as these three principles is already evident in the Devī-Māhātmya, later Purāṇas rework this formulation in a new way. *Śakti, prakṛti,* and *māyā* are portrayed as explicitly cosmogonic principles that unfold during the early stages of creation and are identified as the Goddess no matter what may be the sectarian perspective of a given Purāṇa or Purāṇic section. Hence *who* the Goddess is—her name and personal identity—changes from text to text, but *what* she is—her nature as a tripartite cosmogonic agent—persists and transcends sectarian difference. Whichever goddess is *śakti, prakṛti,* and *māyā* is the Great Goddess. Such a portrayal of Mahādevī is indicative of her multiple singularity, for her nature as a cosmic creative power transcends particular form and allows for numerous interpretations of her identity. It also points to her generative capacity as Divine Mother, for it is she who gives birth to the universe.

In the fifth essay, we turn to Kerala and even greater ambiguity with Sarah Caldwell's essay, "Waves of Beauty, Rivers of Blood: Constructing the Goddess in Kerala." Caldwell's focus is the goddess Bhagavati, whom devotees worship as Mahādevī and whose mythology is connected to that of the pan-Indian goddesses Durgā and Kālī. In Kerala, the ritual construction of Bhagavati's physical form in ritual possession performances, temple icons, narrative, *kaḷam* (portraits of the Goddess in colored powders), and so forth is a fundamental form of Hindu religious practice. Yet the way her body is formed and enlivened and the perceived nature of the Goddess thus constructed vary significantly from one social group to another and reflect differing religious, historical, and political contexts.

Caldwell focuses on the way that the Goddess's form and identity are constructed in four different social groups: Brahmins, Nayars/Kṣatriyas, low-caste and tribal groups, and women of both high and low castes. She finds that although there is a good deal of overlap, each group emphasizes different rituals, songs, and texts pertaining to the Goddess and paints a portrait of Bhagavati that tends to reflect values important to that particular social group. Hence, says Caldwell, each of these incarnations is Mahādevī herself, yet each reflects the social realities of the human community that constructs it.

Taken together, these five chapters explore some of the ways in which Mahādevī's identity is understood in a diversity of textual and devotional contexts, moving from approaches that place greater stress upon unity and clarity of definition in a given context to those that stress ambiguity, negotiation, and multiplicity. The next four chapters, however, focus more on the processes of Goddess "construction." In this section, we begin with essays that more clearly focus on elucidating particular cases and move toward those that are more centrally concerned with using particular cases as a springboard for reflecting on larger issues.

Sree Padma's chapter, "From Village to City: Transforming Goddesses in Urban Andhra Pradesh," takes a fresh look at Sanskritization by exploring its impact on village goddess cults, a process through which local village goddesses come to be cross-identified with the pan-Indian goddesses of Sanskritic Hinduism. She focuses on the city of Visakhapatnam in Andhra Pradesh and the surrounding areas, which are undergoing rapid urbanization. In searching for the Hindu Great Goddess in Visakhapatnam, Padma argues for the primacy of village goddess cults over Sanskritic traditions, maintaining that despite increasing Sanskritization, the primary protective function of village goddesses is always sustained, while Sanskritic influence adds only superficial elements pertaining to liturgy, iconography, and ritual. Such elements are, says Padma, ritual and metaphysical "window-dressings" that do not affect the fundamental, village-based ethos of goddess veneration but, at least in Visakhapatnam, serve primarily to make local goddesses "user friendly" in an urban context, where devotees come from all over India and hence are not predisposed to revere local deities. While acknowledging the importance of texts like the Devī-Māhātmya, Padma holds the Hindu Great Goddess should be identified primarily not with Sanskritic, Brahmanical formulations of her identity, but rather with the protective and nurturing powers of village goddesses, powers still venerated by much of India's rural populace—and, increasingly, its urban populace as well. Padma concludes that in the search for Mahādevī, what we find among ordinary devotees is a celebration of her abilities to protect and grant worldly boons. Hence, Padma ultimately calls for greater recognition of devotional experience in the construction of scholarly models.

In the next essay, "Reconstructing the Split Goddess as Śakti in a Tamil Village," Elaine Craddock focuses on the Tamil goddess Māriyammaṉ. Also known as Bavāṉiyammaṉ, Māriyammaṉ is the goddess of smallpox in Tamil Nadu. But, as Craddock observes, to many of her devotees she is also Devī, Goddess with a capital *G*. Craddock focuses on what she believes connects Bavāṉiyammaṉ, a local goddess, to Mahādevī. The connecting link that Craddock finds is sacrifice in terms of both its ritual and mythological dimensions.

Regular ritual offerings of buffaloes to Māriyammaṉ/Bavāṉiyammaṉ perpetuate the practice of blood sacrifice. Furthermore, the tradition of hook-swinging that is traditionally associated with her worship is a form of self-sacrifice in which devotees can participate, as are practices of head shaving and the "neem sari" ritual that Craddock describes. But mythological traditions pertaining to Bavāṉiyammaṉ also pick up, transform, and reconfigure images and themes pertaining to sacrifice. In this regard, the theme of death and regeneration through sacrifice is of particular importance. Not only is Bavāṉiyammaṉ herself the divine transformation of a woman, Reṇukā, who has been beheaded by her son and then brought back to life, but she also embodies the powers of regeneration associated with both female fertility and sacrificial action. Devī's role as Divine Mother, too, is related to these sacrificial themes: the mother that Reṇukā's son reconstructs is no longer just his own mother but now becomes, through death and regeneration, the Mother of all, the source of all life and the refuge of all beings. Devotees then continually construct and reconstruct their understanding of her as Śakti, the Divine Mother, through their ongoing experiences of her and her power.

Jeffrey J. Kripal explores the theme of woman as embodiment of Devī the Mother in his chapter, "Perfecting the Mother's Silence: Dream, Devotion, and Family in the Deification of Sharada Devi." Devotees of Ramakrishna Paramahamsa, a nineteenth-century Bengali religious leader, considered his wife Sharada Devi, whom they referred to as "the Mother" or "the Holy Mother," to be the Goddess in human form. Kripal's essay addresses two questions that Sharada herself poses about her own status—"How am I different from them (the other women of her village)? . . . And why are these people coming like this?"

Kripal proposes that Sharada's status as Devī, the Holy Mother, is constructed largely upon Sharada's silence: by either quietly accepting others' interpretations of her or by maintaining a voiceless presence, Sharada allows devotees to construct her identity as Devī without actively claiming such a status for herself. But the deification process that Kripal envisions is nevertheless dialectical, involving both what the disciples bring to this process and what they find in Sharada herself, the qualities that allow them to address her with confidence as "Holy Mother." Kripal finds that Sharada's proclaimed visions and the role her husband assigns to her in ritual signal to devotees her special status, a status that is confirmed in devotees' visions and especially dreams of Sharada, which are then recorded and passed on to others. Sharada's divine status is confirmed in many other ways as well, through psychological projection, interpretive twists accorded to particular phenomena, and so forth. But Sharada also confirms her devotees' interpretation of her identity as "Holy Mother" by her behavior and her demeanor, for Sharada offers an alternative both to hierarchical social codes then prevalent in public Bengali culture and to the humiliating conditions of colonialism. In the community that forms around her, Sharada supplants the often harsh social codes of her day pertaining to *dharma*, caste, and purity with the simple, unconditional love that a mother bestows on her children. To Sharada, her devotee-children form a single family and a single caste, and she considers all of them to share equal claim to her love and affection.

Earlier in this introduction, I raised the issue of interpretation and the ways that interpretation shapes or helps construct knowledge and experience of the Goddess. Scholars, like devotees, encounter Mahādevī through interpretive frames. The scholars who have contributed chapters to this book exercise their interpretive agency in bringing to bear on the materials they consider a variety of questions, modes of inquiry, and interpretive models that they apply to their own observations and to reported understandings and experiences. This variety raises issues regarding the scope and adequacy of interpretations that are rooted in scholarly, as opposed to devotional, perspectives on Mahādevī's identity. Kathleen M. Erndl captures some of this issue in her essay, "Goddesses and the Goddess in Hinduism: Constructing the Goddess Through Religious Experience."

Erndl emphasizes the need to take seriously devotees' experiences in considering the issue of Goddess "construction," observing that scholars may invoke scholarly models and modes of inquiry that do not necessarily reflect reported devotional experience. She notes in particular two models that scholars have brought to bear on the issue of "one Goddess versus many goddesses." The first, an historical model, frames the issue in terms of historical processes through which a variety of goddesses come to be incorporated into Hinduism and identified with Sanskritic goddesses or a Great Goddess. The second, the psychological/structural model, considers the issue of unity versus multiplicity in relation to categories of either Hindu social structure or psychology. This approach to the Goddess suggests that either social or psychological categories underlie and ultimately account for the coexistence of multiplicity and unity of goddesses. Erndl herself proposes a complementary, alternative approach that she calls the "experiential approach." Noting that ordinary Hindu devotees move with apparent ease between universal and particular notions of the Goddess in their ritual and devotional lives, she focuses on devotees' reported religious experience to make sense of the apparent contradiction. The identity of the one, universal Great Goddess is rendered concrete in the personal experience of devotees, which is conditioned by specific geographic, social, theological, and political factors.

Erndl frames the scholarly models she considers as metadiscourses about the "one (Great) Goddess versus many goddesses" issue. Although none of the other contributors to this volume purports to engage in such metadiscourse, Erndl's essay provides a helpful lens through which to view many aspects of the essays that precede it, for the models and approaches she delineates appear in different places throughout this book. The desire to convey devotees' experience of the Goddess that Erndl highlights in her experiential approach is, for example, strongly present in Menon's observations about Oriya devotees' experiences of Kālī. But one can see the influence of the historical and psychological/structural models she highlights throughout the book as well. Rohe and Padma explicitly engage issues concerning the homologization of non-Sanskritic goddesses with those of the Sanskritic pantheon, a concern that reflects the first model that Erndl identifies, the historical model, although Padma calls into question the way in which scholars have tended to look at the Sanskritization process. Caldwell and Kripal, among others, suggest that social and/or psychological realities have a lot to do with how and why the communities they focus on construct Mahādevī's identity in the ways that they do, engaging concerns and assumptions that inform Erndl's second model, the psychological/structural model. It might be helpful also to suggest a fourth model or approach, the narrative approach, which seeks to understand Mahādevī's nature and identity in relation to narrative structures that provide for multiplicity within unity, an approach that informs my own essay.

While many of the chapters in this volume are explicitly concerned with how believers experience Devī and how texts describe her, some of them also bring to bear on their analyses assumptions that people are not only religious, but also political, psychological, social, and gendered beings, and that these realities, along with history and narrative, play important roles in the construction of religious categories and religious experience. Many of the essays also assume that one task of scholarly inquiry is to explore how such embodied realities may be brought to bear upon religious questions. Most devotees, however, would probably find such concerns irrelevant to the question of Mahādevī's identity. The merit and adequacy of scholarly models in relation to a more purely experiential approach remains an unresolved question in this book, one that we pose but do not purport to answer in these pages.

Erndl's chapter raises questions regarding the very adequacy of the sort of inquiry that much of this volume represents, the wisdom of seeking knowledge about the Goddess through "objectifying" scholarly models and methods, and the potential helpfulness of an experiential approach to the issue of Goddess construction in relation to the other approaches she highlights. In the concluding chapter, Thomas B. Coburn offers some insightful reflections on the volume as a whole and on the nature of deity in his concluding chapter, "What is a 'Goddess' and What Does It Mean to 'Construct' One?" Coburn focuses on the relational quality of deity-construction, noting that "Goddess"—like "God," "deity," "scripture," and so forth—is a relational concept grounded in interaction with particular persons and communities. Coburn's ruminations on the relational quality of deity prompt him to make five observations, which in turn give rise to questions and issues that Coburn invites us to ponder for subsequent reflection and investigation. These include questions concerning gender (in terms of both divinity and human participants), the media that enliven and sustain the relationship between devotees and the Goddess, common features of Mahādevī that persist in different contexts, and the metaphysical issues involved in worshipping the Great Goddess. I think that readers will find Coburn's comments, like Erndl's, particularly helpful for thinking through both the contributions and the limitations of all the chapters in this volume.

This collective exploration of Mahādevī's multiple identities suggests that the Goddess is nowhere and everywhere at the same time. She is nowhere in the sense that one cannot point to any single text or community as the unique, pan-Hindu, authoritative source of her identity. Like water, Devī slips through our fingers and eludes our grasp. She is everywhere, however, in the sense that numerous goddesses all over India and in a variety of scriptures can claim that status, and one could point to any one of these deities and justifiably claim, "*She* is Mahādevī." Ultimately, however, no matter where one finds the Goddess, one always finds those who love and worship her, and it is through their devotion that Devī's presence is rendered vibrant and meaningful.

Note

1. Debates have surfaced in recent scholarship about the limits of "construction" language and its usefulness with respect to certain forms of knowledge and discourse. See, for example, Searle 1995 and Hacking 1999. Even those scholars who argue that "construction" language has limited usefulness, however, would agree that concepts and representations of deities, such as those explored in this volume, are socially constructed.

Chapter 1

The Tantric and Vedāntic Identity of the Great Goddess in the Devī Gītā of the Devī-Bhāgavata Purāṇa

C. Mackenzie Brown

The Birth of the Goddess and Her Identity

Around the sixth century of the common era, in the Devī-Māhātmya of the Mārkaṇḍeya Purāṇa, the Great Goddess (Mahādevī) makes her first formal appearance in the Hindu Sanskritic tradition. The Devī-Māhātmya recounts the story of the birth of this Great Goddess from the combined wrath of the gods just prior to her battle with the demon Mahiṣāsura. The story nicely reveals her awesome might and martial fury. The intense anger of the gods, arising from their defeat at the hands of the demon, issues from their bodies in the form of light. The several lights unite into a single mass, from which emerges the Goddess herself:

> The gods beheld a dazzling concentration of light, like a mountain ablaze, pervading all directions with its flames. Then that incomparable light, born from the body of all the gods, pervading the three worlds with its brilliance, coalesced into the form of a woman. . . . Honored by the gods, she roared on high with a boisterous laugh over and over, filling the entire heavens with her dreadful bellow. . . . The demon Mahiṣāsura [rushing towards the roar] then saw her brilliance pervading the three worlds, her feet trampling the earth while her crown scraped the sky. The twang of her bowstring jolted the underworlds. Her thousand arms reached out in all directions. (2.12–13; 2.32; 2.37cd–39ab)[1]

This much beloved story of the Goddess's birth has at times been closely associated with the ultimate origin of the Goddess. As such, it is seen as the defining event that molds her essential character. Thus, Lawrence A. Babb has written of the Goddess as she appears in the Devī-Māhātmya: "the only discernible emotion of the goddess is anger—black, implacable, and bloodthirsty. She is something emerging from the highest gods; she is the very essence of their anger" (1975, 221). Babb goes on to suggest that while "she seems more powerful, certainly more terrible, than her creators," she is in the end controllable by them. This control comes about especially through marriage, according to Babb, as seen in such benevolent consort-goddesses as Lakṣmī and Pārvatī. As the Great Goddess is all goddesses, she is both unmarried—in her horrific and destructive forms such as Kālī—and married—in her tamed forms—obedient to her husband and fulfilling the fully auspicious role of conventional wife.

Birth stories are significant as a mythological means for constructing the identity of a deity. The origin story of the Goddess in the Devī-Māhātmya is eminently suitable for a divine being perceived primarily as powerful and violent, and whose appeasement is seen as the best recourse for securing prosperity by enlisting her aid for the destruction of enemies. The success and appeal of this vision is attested by the countless Hindu retellings and reenactments of the myth in numerous variants.

The author or authors of the Devī-Bhāgavata Purāṇa (composed many centuries after the Devī-Māhātmya, probably sometime between the twelfth and sixteenth centuries) admired the origin story sufficiently to retell it twice (5.8.27–5.9.38, and 10.12.3–25). But the Devī-Bhāgavata sees the birth story of the Devī-Māhātmya not as an account of the origin of the Great Goddess herself, but only of the manifestation or incarnation of one of her lesser forms. Such an interpretation is already explicit in the Devī-Māhātmya, which asserts that the Goddess is eternal, but that she incarnates in the world in manifold ways (1.64–66).

Within the Devī-Bhāgavata is a long dialogue between the Goddess and her devotee Himālaya that represents the philosophical and theological consummation of the text. This dialogue, known as the Devī Gītā (Song of the Goddess),[2] is introduced by a frame story that provides an alternative birth story to the Devī-Māhātmya's. In the Devī Gītā's account, the Goddess once again emerges from a blazing orb of light.[3] But the Devī Gītā's story thoroughly redefines the Goddess, constructing her identity in a radically different manner.

The occasion for the birth of the Goddess in the Devī Gītā (at least ostensibly), as in the Devī-Māhātmya, is another dire predicament of the gods–this time harassment by the demon Tāraka. The Goddess here arises not spontaneously out of the wrath of the gods, but as a gracious response to years of their devoted praise. Finally she appears before them:

> Suddenly, on the ninth lunar day in the month of Caitra, on a Friday, that lustrous power revealed in scripture appeared before the gods. Praised on all sides by the four Vedas incarnate, it blazed like ten million suns, yet soothed like ten million moons. . . .Without beginning or end, it had no body, no hands, no other limbs, nor did it have a woman's form, a man's form, nor the two combined. The dazzling brilliance blinded the eyes of the gods. When again their vision returned, the gods beheld that light appearing now in the form of a woman, charming and delightful. She was exceedingly beautiful of limb, a maiden in the freshness of youth. Her full, upraised breasts put to shame the swelling buds of the lotus. Her girdle and anklets jingled with clusters of tinkling bells. . . . Three-eyed and four-armed, she held a noose and goad while gesturing her beneficence and assurance of safety. She was dressed in red and appeared lustrous like blooms of the pomegranate. Richly adorned in garments all suited for love, she was worshiped by all the gods. Satisfying all desires, she is the Mother of all, the Deluder of all. The Mother's kindly face, so gracious, displayed a tender smile on the lotus mouth. This embodiment of unfeigned compassion the gods beheld in their presence. (1.26–27; 1.29–32; 1.39–41)

In order to see more clearly the new identity of the Goddess manifested in this birth story, let us examine in some detail its two major motifs: the aniconic blazing orb of light, and the iconic form of the Goddess that emerges from that light. The first motif is critical for constructing the Vedāntic identity of the Goddess, the second for her Tantric identity.

The Vedāntic Identity of the Goddess as Brahman

The blazing orb of light from which the Devī emerges symbolizes and embodies not the collective anger of the gods, but the supreme consciousness that is the non-dual Brahman of Advaita Vedānta. The Devī Gītā describes the Goddess as infinite being, consciousness, and bliss *(sac-cid-ānanda)*, the three primary aspects of Brahman (2.25 and 10.4).

The central and quintessential aspect, that of consciousness, is symbolized in the Devī Gītā by this blazing light, referred to as "*mahas.*" This term, meaning "greatness, power," as well as "light, luster," appears in the Taittirīya Upaniṣad (1.5) as the fourth *(caturthī)* mystic syllable, beyond *bhūḥ, bhuvaḥ,* and *suvaḥ.* Specifically, it is identified with Brahman *(maha iti brahma),* and as the power by which the various worlds and entities "become great." The notion of *mahas* as the fourth also suggests the idea of the fourth state of consciousness *(turīya),* beyond waking, dream, and deep sleep, and thus further evokes the transcendent form of the Devī as pure consciousness.

The Devī Gītā does not simply utilize Upaniṣadic terminology in establishing the Advaitic identity of the Goddess. The text also assimilates features of an important mythic drama from the Upaniṣads that discloses an ancient association between the Goddess (or rather, originally, a goddess), and Brahman. The myth, appearing in the Kena Upaniṣad (3.1–4.3), concerns the famous story of the humbling of the gods Agni, Vāyu, and Indra. This same story appears in an elaborated version in the Devī-Bhāgavata itself (12.8.12–86) and serves as mythological background for the manifestation of the Goddess in the frame story of the Devī Gītā.

The basic myth as told in the Kena Upaniṣad concerns the arrogance of the gods in claiming for themselves a victory that was actually achieved by Brahman, the supreme power, on their behalf. To curb their false pride, Brahman appeared before the gods in the form of a spirit or *yakṣa.* The gods were curious to know who or what this spirit was and sent the fire-god Agni to find out. Agni, approaching the spirit, was suddenly asked by the *yakṣa* what power he possessed. The fire-god replied that he had the power to burn anything on Earth. The spirit then placed before him a blade of grass, which Agni was unable to burn. Humiliated, Agni returned to the gods, who then sent the wind-god Vāyu, who has the power to blow away anything on Earth. But Vāyu was unable to blow away the blade of grass placed before him by the spirit. Finally Indra was sent to the *yakṣa,* but it disappeared in front of him. Then, in that same space in the sky, Indra came across a woman, the brilliant and beautiful Umā Haimavatī, who revealed the identity of the *yakṣa* as Brahman, to whom the victory was due. In the subsequent tradition, Umā Haimavatī came to be identified with Brahmavidyā, the knowledge revealing Brahman.

The Devī-Bhāgavata, in its elaborate recounting of the Kena story, explicitly identifies the Goddess with the *yakṣa,* and thus with Brahman itself rather than just with a mediator of Brahman. Further, the Devī-Bhāgavata adds a number of other details. The *yakṣa,* when it first appears, is described as a mass of light *(tejas)* like ten millions suns, without hands, feet, or other limbs. This spirit is also referred to as the supreme lustrous power *(paraṃ mahas)*. When it disappears before Indra, it instructs him to recite the single mantric syllable Hrīṃ, the significance of which we shall consider later. For one hundred thousand years Indra devoutly carries out the repetition of this mantra. Then suddenly, on the ninth lunar day in the month of Caitra, the light reappears, in the midst of which manifests a beautiful young woman, referred to as Umā Haimavatī Śivā. Her iconic description is the same as that of the emergent maiden in the frame story of the Devī Gītā: she is three-eyed and four-armed, holding a noose and goad in two hands while gesturing her beneficence and assurance of safety with the remaining two.

The manifestation of the Goddess in the Devī Gītā is closely parallel to the Kena myth (as interpreted by the Devī-Bhāgavata), which further helps to explain the Devī Gītā's reference to the "lustrous power revealed in scripture." That lustrous power, the *mahas* of the Taittirīya Upaniṣad, is also the Umā Haimavatī of the Kena Upaniṣad. Clearly, then, the Goddess is understood to be both the supreme revealer Brahmavidyā and the supreme Brahman that she is to reveal.

There is another interesting mythic parallel to the Devī's birth from the blazing light. The emergence of the Goddess out of the brilliant orb is reminiscent of Śiva's self-manifestation in the famous myth of the origin of his infinite Liṅga.[4] As told in such Śaivite texts as the Śiva Purāṇa (Vidyeśvara Saṃhitā 1.68) and Liṅga Purāṇa (1.17), Śiva appears before the quarreling Brahmā and Viṣṇu as a shaft of light (Jyotir-liṅga), a massive pillar of fire with no top or bottom. Then, as the syllable Oṃ (the sonic symbol of Brahman/Śiva, as Hrīṃ is of the Goddess) reverberates through space, from out of that blazing column steps forth Śiva in his iconic form as Maheśvara, five-faced and ten-armed. The aniconic Jyotir-liṅga represents Śiva as the supreme Brahman without parts *(niṣkala)* and without marks *(aliṅga)*; the iconic form represents him as with parts *(sakala)* and as the qualified Brahman that oversees the cosmic processes of creation, maintenance, and destruction, as well as liberation. This Śaivite myth clearly serves, among other things, to identify Śiva with the supreme reality taught in the Upaniṣads and elaborated upon in the later schools of Vedānta.

The Goddess's own myth of emergence functions, on the one hand, as a counterpart to the famous origin myth of the Jyotir-liṅga, belonging to one of her major male rivals, Śiva. On the other hand, in a manner parallel to the Śaivite myth, it establishes in dramatic fashion the Devī's own transcendent, aniconic identity with the supreme Brahman of the Upaniṣads, an identity enhanced by her ancient association with Umā Haimavatī/Brahmavidyā.

At this point we are ready to consider in specific terms the second motif in the Devī Gītā's birth story: the particular nature and identity of the Goddess who arises out of the blinding light of pure consciousness, and whose sonic symbol, the syllable Hrīṃ we have already encountered.

The Tantric Identity of the Goddess as Bhuvaneśvarī

Of special importance in the Tantric understanding of the divine is the notion that all deities along with their powers are manifested in monosyllabic symbols or sonic condensations called "seed-mantras" (*bīja-mantras*). The seed-mantra Hrīṃ, often referred to as the "Hṛllekhā" or "Heart-Sign" Mantra (*hṛd* = heart, + *lekhā* = mark or sign), has traditionally been associated with the Tantric goddess Bhuvaneśvarī, "Ruler of the Universe." Hrīṃ embodies Bhuvaneśvarī's heart or essence, and the syllable is recited when the essential core power of the Goddess is invoked. It is the recitation of this syllable by the gods that brings forth the Goddess, precipitating, as it were, her visible form out of the subtle sound vibrations of Hrīṃ that permeate the universe.

This visible precipitation of sonic energy, as we have seen, occurs in two stages: first in the aniconic manifestation of blinding light, followed by its resolution into the iconic form of a young maiden. The iconographic descriptions in the Devī-Bhāgavata of the woman emerging out of the orb of light accord with the typical visual meditations *(dhyānas)* of the Goddess Bhuvaneśvarī found in such ninth- to fourteenth-century Tantric works as the Śāradā-Tilaka Tantra (9.14) and the Devī Upaniṣad (verse 24). The former text almost certainly was known to the composer of the Devī Gītā, the latter definitely, as we shall see.[5]

All the descriptions of Bhuvaneśvarī clearly emphasize her benign and auspicious nature. As a modern devotee affirms, her "four hands represent *dharma, artha, kāma,* and *moksha,*" that is, her powers to bestow the four chief ends of human existence: virtue, wealth, pleasure, and spiritual liberation (Ayer 1988, 46). Bhuvaneśvarī's specific role in the Devī Gītā is not to fight demons, but rather to bestow spiritual wisdom upon the gods. She teaches them the mysterious nature of the universe with its attendant sorrows, and the yogic disciplines that will lead to liberation from those sorrows. Regarding Tāraka, Bhuvaneśvarī simply promises the gods that she will send a manifestation of herself, Pārvatī, to bear Śiva a son, who will slay the demon. As Bhuvaneśvarī, the Goddess is no longer primarily the implacable warrior, but rather a spiritual preceptor.

Who, then, is this Bhuvaneśvarī? Whence does she come? The Tantric Goddess Bhuvaneśvarī may well have first appeared in the late Purāṇic pantheon (probably after the eleventh century) not as a separate individual figure, but as a member of a company of female deities known as the ten Mahāvidyās.[6] The ten represent, on an esoteric level, the various forms of knowledge *(vidyā)* and power that constitute the universe. On a mythological level, they are ten facets or aspects of the Great Goddess. The group in some ways represents a late medieval Śākta counterpart to the Vaiṣṇava notion of the ten main avatars of Viṣṇu, whose role frequently is to maintain cosmic order through the destruction of demons.[7] The Mahāvidyās at times function in a similar role, as in the Śiva Purāṇa (Umā-Saṃhitā 50.28–29) where they come forth from the body of the Great Goddess as she fights against the demon Durgama.[8] But unlike Viṣṇu's avatars, the Mahāvidyās usually work in concert, and their primary role is not necessarily the preservation of cosmic order (Kinsley 1986, 161–164; 1997, 21–22).

The mythic origin of the ten is recounted in the Mahābhāgavata Purāṇa (8.62–71), a late Śākta Purāṇic text perhaps belonging to the fourteenth or fifteenth centuries.[9] Here the Mahāvidyās are said to arise out of a fearsome form of the goddess Satī in order to frighten Śiva into granting her permission to go and disrupt Dakṣa's sacrifice.[10] In addition, Satī herself portrays these emanations as a means of providing her devotees with various worldly and other-worldly benefits. The ten Mahāvidyās procure these benefits in large part by exercising their terrifying and destructive powers to subdue or defeat enemies. Nonetheless, despite the fierce nature of the Mahāvidyās as suggested by their origin, they also have a more benign potential that is emphasized in later texts, where at least some of them are described as beautiful in appearance.

While the early myths and texts generally do not specify the particular functions of the individual Mahāvidyās, the relatively late Uddhārakośa (sec. 1, last five verses) expounds the efficacious nature *(guṇa)* of the ten as follows.[11] Tripurā gives liberation *(mukti)*, Lakṣmī prosperity *(lakṣmī)*, Vāgdevī (Sarasvatī) wisdom *(vidyā)*, Tārā knowledge and release (*jñāna* and *mokṣa*), Bhuvaneśvarī sovereignty *(aiśvarya)*, Mātaṅgī freedom from fear of female demons and enemies *(rākṣasīśatrubhīti)*, Śārikā happiness *(śam)*, Rājñī royal authority (*rājyam*), Bhīḍādevī all-pervading expansiveness *(santati viśvavyāpinī)*, and Jvālāmukhī wealth *(dhanam)*. These functions are somewhat repetitive and overlapping, but what is noteworthy in the present context is the association of Bhuvaneśvarī with sovereignty.

The word *aiśvarya* (sovereignty), deriving from *īśvara* (lord), suggests a supreme divine power that oversees the universe. It is linked not only with wealth and affluence, but also with omnipotence and omnipresence. *Aiśvarya* is thus a quite natural property of Bhuvaneśvarī, "She who is Lord (Queen, Mistress) of the World." Further, *aiśvarya* subsumes most of the efficacious qualities of the other ten Mahāvidyās, with the exception of those relating to liberation, associated especially with the goddesses Tripurā and Tārā. Bhuvaneśvarī, as we shall see, developed fairly early a certain affinity and synergism with Tripurā (Tripurā-Sundarī or Lalitā, as she is also known) that led to an apparent convergence of the two.

In the Devī-Bhāgavata, Bhuvaneśvarī assumes the roles of all the other Mahāvidyās, including those of liberating knowledge and ultimate release. She is the source of all female manifestations or Śaktis, including the Mahāvidyās. In the Devī-Bhāgavata's version of the slaying of Durgama, for instance, various of the traditional Mahāvidyās are named among the Śaktis emanating from her body, but–unlike in the Śiva Purāṇa's version–Bhuvaneśvarī is not included (7.28.54–56). Emphasizing that she is no longer just one of the ten Mahāvidyās, the Devī-Bhāgavata regards her as Mahāvidyā (Great Wisdom) herself, whose avatars include many of the earlier members of the standard ten, along with other renowned incarnations of the Goddess. Accordingly, in another demon-slaying story involving the *asura* Aruṇa, the gods address the Goddess as Mahāvidyā, who assumes various forms to favor the gods. Among these forms are named several of the usual Mahāvidyās, plus other incarnations such as Śakambharī and Raktadantikā from the Devī Māhātmya (Devī-Bhāgavata 10.13.87–103). As in its story of the slaying of Durgama, the Devī-Bhāgavata here does not include the name of Bhuvaneśvarī among the forms. Rather, the gods in concluding their hymn of petition use the name Bhuvaneśvarī to refer to the one, supreme World-Mother, who dwells in the Jeweled Island of Maṇidvīpa.

The supremacy of Bhuvaneśvarī in the Devī-Bhāgavata is marvelously evoked in a detailed description of this paradisial island home of the Goddess, highest of all heavenly realms (12.10—12). The island, lying in the Ocean of Nectar, is forested with a great number of fantastic flowering trees, perfumed with the scent of divine blossoms, and resplendent with ornamental lakes and rivers. The palatial structures include a number of walled enclosures, concentrically arranged. Within each enclosure dwell various classes of celestial beings, gods and goddesses, and their incarnations. In the enclosure just outside the central circle reside the closest associates or helpers of the Goddess, her great divisions *(mahā-bhedās)* referred to as Mahāvidyās (12.11.106). In the innermost enclosure dwells Bhuvaneśvarī herself. Her distinctness from, and transcendence over, the Mahāvidyās is hereby amply demonstrated.

Within the final enclosure is the Goddess' own mansion, a magnificent dwelling constructed of wish-fulfilling gems *(cintāmaṇi)*. Inside the mansion are situated four halls *(maṇḍapas)*, in which she conducts four different sorts of business: amorous sport, delivering souls from the bondage of rebirth, discoursing on truth, and consulting with her ministers on running the universe. Within the palace also is a great couch of remarkable design, composed of five *preta*s, ghosts or corpses. The four legs are the lifeless bodies of Brahmā, Viṣṇu, Rudra, and Īśāna (the latter two being forms or aspects of Śiva), and the seat is the outstretched corpse of Sadāśiva (the eternal Śiva). Upon this throne Bhuvaneśvarī rests in ease. This conception of Bhuvaneśvarī seated on her Pañca-Pretāsana (Seat of Five Corpses) reveals her supreme sovereignty, especially over masculine pretensions to cosmic power. Brahmā, Viṣṇu, and Śiva are the three male deities traditionally associated with creating, overseeing, and destroying the universe. But here, as elements of Bhuvaneśvarī's throne, they represent her latent cosmic energies, unconscious and inert, residing under her feet until aroused by her desire.

Sitting on this great couch in the midst of her jeweled palace, Bhuvaneśvarī manifests herself in a manner remarkably similar to that of the goddess Tripurā in the South Indian Tantric text, the Tripurā-Rahasya (Jñānakhanda chap. 20, p. 135), and of Lalitā in the Brahmāṇḍa Purāṇa (3.4.37). Indeed, the Devī Gītā's Bhuvaneśvarī seems especially to fuse the characters of her own self as ruling queen with that of Tripurā, who as mentioned above is associated with the granting of liberation. Of all the Mahāvidyās, it is Bhuvaneśvarī and Tripurā who are generally the closest iconographically. Like Bhuvaneśvarī, Tripurā/Lalitā is charmingly beautiful, clothed in red, three-eyed and four-armed, bearing a noose and goad, though her other two hands hold a sugarcane bow and flower arrows, rather than gesturing Bhuvaneśvarī's beneficence and assurance of safety. The easy fusion of these two Mahāvidyās reinforces the Tantric ideal that the Goddess is the giver of both *bhukti* and *mukti* (worldly enjoyment and liberation).

The convergence of the two goddesses is found already, in implicit fashion, in the Devī Upaniṣad, an important Tantric text referred to above and probably composed sometime between the ninth and fourteenth centuries. It is one of several Śākta Upaniṣads dedicated to one or another particular goddess conceived as supreme, or to a form of the Goddess. The Goddess in the Devī Upaniṣad is addressed in the most general and universal of terms, as Mahādevī, and is thought to be all goddesses. The Upaniṣad provides two brief iconographic descriptions of the Great Goddess. According to the first, "She is the power of the Self; she is the enchanter of all, holding a noose, a goad, a bow, and arrows; she is the auspicious Mahāvidyā" (verse 15). This is a concise description of Tripurā/Lalitā.[12] According to the second depiction, "She resides in the middle of one's lotus heart, shining like the rising sun; auspicious, bearing the noose and goad while gesturing her beneficence and assurance of safety, she is three eyed, dressed in red, granting all wishes to her devotees" (verse 24). Here, of course, is Bhuvaneśvarī. The author of the Devī Gītā was greatly indebted to the Devī Upaniṣad—his conception of the Goddess is clearly inspired by the fusion of the two great Mahāvidyās responsible collectively for all worldly and spiritual well-being.[13]

The Tantric character of Bhuvaneśvarī in her early career is apparent. By the time of the Devī-Bhāgavata, she has undergone a process of thorough Vedicization, a development already well underway in the aforementioned Devī Upaniṣad. The Devī Upaniṣad is a Śākta Tantric work that understands itself as fully within the domain of Vedic (Vedāntic) truth, indicated by the very fact of presenting itself as an Upaniṣad. Its Vedic pedigree is further affirmed by its quoting the famous "Devī-Sūkta" from the Ṛg Veda (10.125). Its concern with various root and seed mantras of the Goddess, including Hrīṃ, attests to its Tantric nature. The Devī Upaniṣad thus points to an important step in the evolution of the Great Goddess: the fusion of her Tantric and Vedāntic personalities, a fusion that becomes fully elaborated in the Devī Gītā. The Vedicization of the originally Tantric Bhuvaneśvarī had considerable appeal to the composer of the Devī Gītā. He was aware of the Devī Upaniṣad, as he quotes five verses (8–12) of its "Devī-Stuti" (hymn to the Goddess) (quoted in Devī Gītā 1.44–48). It is no wonder, then, that the Goddess herself in the Devī Gītā (10.22) mentions the Devī Upaniṣad as one of those texts whose recitation is pleasing to her.

This synthesis of the Vedic and Tantric within a Śākta perspective stresses the identity of Bhuvaneśvarī with Brahman and her absoluteness and complete independence from any male consort. As Bhuvaneśvarī, the Great Goddess is wholly auspicious and benign. As the supreme Brahman, she is one alone without a second. As both Bhuvaneśvarī and Brahman, she is paradoxically the benign World-Mother beyond all relationship, identical with all and subject to none.

The Sonic Synergism of Brahman and Bhuvaneśvarī: Cosmogonic and Soteriologic Functions of Oṃ and Hrīṃ

The story of the birth of the Goddess in the Devī Gītā is a dramatic narrative that reveals her Tantric and Vedāntic personalities and their essential unity. The fusion of these two aspects is further indicated on a more subtle level by the integration of the mantric embodiments of Brahman and Bhuvaneśvarī, the seed-syllables Oṃ and Hrīṃ, respectively. The explicit identification of the Goddess with both sacred syllables is presented in the hymn of praise offered to her in the first chapter of the Devī Gītā: "Hail to her in the form of the syllable Oṃ;[14] hail to her embodied in the syllable Hrīṃ" (1.53). The importance of this double identification is underscored by its repetition, in slightly altered form, two chapters later: "Hail to you, Ruler of the Universe [Bhuvaneśānī, synonymous with Bhuvaneśvarī]; hail to you, composed of the syllable Oṃ. Hail to you established in the whole of Vedānta, embodied in the syllable Hrīṃ" (3.45). The cross-correspondences here (the Tantric Bhuvaneśvarī with the Vedāntic Oṃ, and the established truth of the Vedānta with the Tantric Hrīṃ) attest to the thorough commingling of her two fundamental aspects.

The identification of the Goddess with both Oṃ and Hrīṃ represents a sonic encryption of her dual nature as the essential ground of existence and as its manifesting and ruling power. The author or authors of the Devī-Bhāgavata/Devī Gītā elaborated upon the interplay between the two symbols in various cosmogonic and soteriological contexts. In the process, the Tantric and Vedāntic functions of the Goddess as Mahāvidyā, the powerful and benevolent World-Mother, and as Brahmavidyā, the revealer of ultimate truth and the truth itself, are incorporated into each other, her dual nature integrated.

The Cosmogonic Interplay of Oṃ and Hrīṃ

According to Advaita Vedānta, Brahman is not only one alone without a second, but also absolutely unchanging, beyond all modification. Thus, the world of duality or multiplicity is, in some sense, an illusion, less than fully real. Otherwise, the absolute oneness of Brahman would be compromised. Yet Brahman is somehow the source of the world–it brings forth the world through the mysterious power of Māyā, neither real nor unreal. Associated with Māyā, Brahman appears in three successive forms or bodies, causal, subtle and gross, which represent stages of manifestation of the material universe.

The Devī Gītā, in accord with this Advaita perspective, sees the Goddess as the one alone without a second, associates her creative power with Māyā, and affirms the three bodies as manifestations of her own highest Self. Thus, both ontologically and cosmologically, the Great Goddess fully implements her "Brahman-nature." Yet, unlike in Advaita, she not only wields Māyā, she also is Māyā. Māyā in the Tantric perspective is not so much an illusory power, but rather is the mysterious, generating force, feminine in nature, by which the Goddess transforms herself into the various psychophysical energies and entities that constitute the manifest world. Māyā is the measuring and constructing force (related to the verbal root *mā*, to measure or measure off) which forms out of itself the material universe. This material power is thereby readily linked to maternal creativity, a link made evident in the Sanskrit noun *mā*, meaning both "mother" and "measure."

Māyā is intimately connected to Bhuvaneśvarī, the World-Mother of the Devī Gītā, as revealed in the common Tantric name for her sacred syllable Hrīṃ: *māyā-bija* (Māyā's seed-mantra).[15] Hrīṃ represents in a cosmogonic context the initial sonic vibration and dynamic point from which all the material world arises. It contains within itself the master plan and patterns for all manifest forms. Hrīṃ is the sonic essence of the World-Mother reverberating throughout the universe and within the hearts of beings (cf. Kinsley 1997, 134–136). Thus, Hrīṃ embodies the power of Māyā, whose essence is embedded in the very structure of the syllable itself, in its letters and parts, according to various esoteric, Tantric explanations. The Varadā Tantra, for example, provides the following esoteric correspondences: "The letter *'h'* signifies Śiva; *'r'* means Prakṛti (Nature); the *'i'* indicates the Great Māyā; the *nāda* (the nasal sound of the *'m'*) represents the Mother of the universe; and the *bindu* (the dot of the *'m'*, the silent reverberation of the syllable following its audible recitation) signifies that she is the remover of sorrow."[16] We shall consider the salvific aspects of such esoteric etymologies below, but will here focus on the cosmogonic.

The Varadā Tantra's explanation encodes a basic Tantric conception of creation. Tantra in general presupposes a bipolar, gendered view of ultimate reality, of the One unfolding into Two as God and Goddess, associated with various other complementary opposites, also gendered in their symbolic associations. Especially important among such pairs are spirit (Puruṣa, masculine) and nature (Prakṛti, feminine), consciousness (masculine) and energy (Śakti, feminine). Both creation and liberation are seen as the result of the union or reunion of the two co-ultimate principles/deities, a process usually expressed in terms of the interaction between Śakti (the Goddess as Power) and Śiva. The relationship may be one of dependency or codependency (in the strict meaning of the term), or it may be one of radical independence, or something in between. Śākta Tantrics, focusing on Śakti and her relationship with Śiva, stress to greater or lesser degree her supremacy. According to the Varadā Tantra, Hrīṃ contains within itself both the masculine and feminine creative principles, Śiva and the World Mother, including her aspects as both Māyā and Prakṛti.

The Varadā's interpretation of her sonic symbol suggests that the Goddess is inclusive of all the "masculine" qualities and attributes embodied in Śiva, who becomes simply a lower manifestation of the Devī herself. Such, in any case, is the position of the Devī-Bhāgavata as a whole. According to the latter, the Goddess is both male and female, and only for the sake of *her own* amusement, and for the sake of creation, does she bring forth out of herself her masculine side as a separate entity, to sport with it in the form of Śiva (12.12.13–14, 17, 39). As ultimate reality, the Goddess is beyond gender differentiation, and thus the sexual, bipolar symbolism of the general Tantric perspective is somewhat muted in the Devī-Bhāgavata. It is primarily in a cosmogonic context that the Goddess manifests her female form alongside the male principle that derives from it.

The Goddess herself in the Devī-Bhāgavata presents this cosmogonic motif in familiar sonic terms. Śiva is subsumed into the supreme Brahman, thereby taking on a neuter rather than masculine appearance, though the gendered aspect echoes in the background. Brahman is represented by the *brahma-bīja* (seed-mantra of Brahman, Oṃ), corresponding to Bhuvaneśvarī's *māyā-bīja*. The account appears in the story of the humbling of Agni, Vāyu, and Indra referred to previously. After the Goddess has revealed herself to Indra in her iconic form as Umā Haimavatī (Bhuvaneśvarī), the perplexed and humbled god asks her about the identity of that blazing light or spirit *(yakṣa)* in whose midst she has appeared. She responds that the spirit is none other than her form as Brahman. This Brahman, she goes on to explain, has its sonic manifestation as the single syllable *(ekakṣara)* Oṃ, which is composed of the syllable Hrīṃ *(hrīṃ-māyā)* (12.8.64). These two seed-syllables are her chief mantras, and she assumes these two aspects or parts in order to create the world. She concludes: "The former part is called infinite being, consciousness, and bliss. The second part is known as Māyā and Prakṛti—that Māyā endowed with supreme power is I, the Īśvarī (Ruler/Queen)" (12.8.65–66).

Interestingly, it is the second part, Hrīṃ, which appears as the underlying substrate or inner essence of Oṃ (defined as *hrīṃ-māyā*). While the Goddess bifurcates herself into the two syllables, Hrīṃ seems in one sense to be prior, and to include within itself both itself and Oṃ. The dominance of Hrīṃ becomes even clearer in the soteriology of the Devī Gītā.

The Soteriological Assimilation of Oṃ by Hrīṃ

Since the time of the ancient Upaniṣads, Oṃ has played a significant soteriological role. In the Muṇḍaka Upaniṣad, the final goal of union of the Self with Brahman is likened to hitting a target (Brahman) with an arrow (Self), shot by the bow of Oṃ (2.2.4). The Muṇḍaka adds: "Meditate on Oṃ as the Self; may you fare well in crossing to the far shore beyond darkness" (2.2.6). The Devī Gītā acknowledges the salvific, meditative role of Oṃ, as it quotes (in 6.6 and 6.9) these same passages from the Muṇḍaka. But it grants a far greater soteriological role to Hrīṃ, at times even supplanting Oṃ entirely.

In the esoteric etymology of Hrīṃ from the Varadā Tantra given above, its salvific sense is suggested by the silent reverberation at the end of audible recitation, signifying that the Goddess is "the remover of sorrow." An alternative etymology develops the same basic motif: the letters of the syllable embody the mother who shines within, or pervades (from *ī*, to shine, and to pervade) the heart of beings, removing (from *hṛ*, to carry away) their pain (Brooks 1992, 103). Or, still differently, the *h* represents Śiva, the *r* Śakti, and *i* their union that produces tranquility (Beck 1993, 138). This latter alludes to a major Tantric conceptualization of the salvific process, Kuṇḍalinī Yoga.

According to this yoga, the divine is not something merely external to humans, but is also the inner guiding force and psychospiritual energy within an individual. This force is symbolized in the figure of the coiled serpent, or Kuṇḍalinī Śakti. In the unenlightened, she lies dormant in the root center *(mūlādhāra)* at the base of the spine. When aroused by the practice of Kuṇḍalinī Yoga, she ascends the central mystic channel (the *suṣumnā*) parallel to the spine, passing through various energy centers *(cakras)* to the crown of the head, uniting with her male counterpart (Śiva), and then descends. In the process of ascent and descent, she bestows both worldly powers and the bliss of liberation.

The Devī Gītā closely associates, or rather implicitly identifies, this Kuṇḍalinī with Bhuvaneśvarī and the salvific power of Hrīṃ, in accord with general Tantric views. As a contemporary Hindu explains: "In Tantric lore, Bhuvaneswari is called, among others, by the name of Hrillekha [Hrīṃ]. It means the Power which is resident in the heart of man in the form of a creeper holding fast to him and guiding him. . . . Now, competent authorities identify this Hrillekha with the *Kundalini Sakti* resident in man" (Ayer 1988, 45; cf. Kinsley 1997, 135–36).

The Devī Gītā in its final chapter describes a Tantric form of worship that begins with various internal visualizations of the Goddess. The worshiper calls to mind the Kuṇḍalinī form of the Goddess, wandering in the internal central channel (the *suṣumnā*). She is to be meditated upon as the embodiment of being, consciousness, and bliss (the primary characteristics of Brahman). Then, by an inner visualization process, the meditator installs the letters of Hrīṃ along the energy centers of that channel, and contemplates the Devī within the lotus heart. There she is seen as sitting on the Sofa of Five Corpses, the traditional seat of Bhuvaneśvarī in the Jeweled Island. The five deities lie under her feet, while she herself transcends them, being in the form of pure consciousness. Through such worship and meditation, the practitioner comes to realize the essential oneness between him or her self and Bhuvaneśvarī.

The installment of the letters of Hrīṃ along the mystic centers of the *suṣumnā* in the above Tantric worship serves to embed the psychophysical energies of the Goddess within the meditator. As the central channel represents an *axis mundi* in Tantric thought, the centers embody different levels of the universe, which in turn are correlated with different levels of consciousness. Such correspondences have long been associated with the component letters (or sounds) of Oṃ, as in the Māṇḍūkya Upaniṣad, and utilized in contemplative practice.

One such meditative practice, briefly outlined in the Pañcīkaraṇa attributed to Śaṃkara, involves first a comprehension of the correspondence between the three parts of Oṃ (Auṃ)[17] and the three bodies—gross, subtle, and causal—of the Self, with their individual and cosmic counterparts, as well as their correlative states of consciousness. In a cosmogonic context, the three bodies are seen as progressively evolving one from the next: the gross from the subtle, the subtle from the causal, and finally—though not explicitly stated in the Pañcīkaraṇa—the causal from the pure consciousness of Brahman/Ātman.

The second phase of this meditation, known as Laya Upāsanā (resorptive meditation), consists in reversing within oneself the cosmogonic process. This is accomplished by dissolving or reabsorbing in due order the three bodies, states, and so forth, back into their source, until the meditator finally merges into the supreme, non-dual Self. This resorption is actualized in the contemplative practice by regressively dissolving the letters of Oṃ (*a*, *u*, and *m*) back into their origin: *a* into *u*, *u* into *m*, and *m* into Oṃ, and finally Oṃ into the supreme (the Ātman or Brahman). In such fashion the meditator is able to realize fully the identity of the individual soul with Ātman/Brahman.

This Laya Upāsanā of the Pañcīkaraṇa, especially as explained and elaborated upon by Sureśvara in his commentary thereon, serves as a model for the Goddess' own concluding discussion of Jñāna Yoga (Knowledge Yoga) in the fourth chapter of the Devī Gītā. However, it is not Oṃ but Hrīṃ that is regressively dissolved, and she refers to Hrīṃ as the Devī-Praṇava. The word *praṇava*, meaning "humming," was originally used as a name for Oṃ. Here, then, we find the complete sublation of this prime Advaitic, sonic symbol by its Tantric counterpart.

Sonic, Aniconic, and Iconic Identities: The New Birth of the Goddess

We began with the famous birth story of the Goddess, or more accurately, her manifestation, as told in the Devī-Māhātmya. On the level of mythic narrative, we saw a transformation of the Goddess as her iconic emergence from the aniconic blazing light was radically reinterpreted in the Devī Gītā. Crucial to this reinterpretation was the fusion of the Tantric and Vedāntic identities of the Goddess. Complementing the mythic transformation was the mantric elaboration of the Devī's identity. Her visible, luminous forms, the aniconic as well as the iconic, were seen in one sense as derivative from yet a more subtle germ, the quintessential seed-syllable Hrīṃ. The new birth of the Goddess in the Devī Gītā is thus a multiphased process, her two luminous manifestations, one iconic, one aniconic, both arising ultimately from the sonic.

The development of the sonic dimensions of Bhuvaneśvarī/Brahman allowed for the integration of the various cosmological, cosmogonic, and soteriological concepts of Advaita and Tantra. In the process, the Vedāntic aspects were thoroughly assimilated by the Tantric Bhuvaneśvarī, so that on the sonic level, the former are often sublated by the latter. The sonic essence of the Goddess makes clear that her truest, most sublime nature, is not the implacable and bloodthirsty warrior of the Devī-Māhātmya, born of the anger of the gods. Rather, she is the benevolent World-Mother, manifesting herself out of the subtle vibrations of pure consciousness that is the transcendent fourth *(turīya)*, referred to by Vedāntists as Brahman, but by those who know her real creative and salvific power, as the Goddess Bhuvaneśvarī.

Notes

1. All translations from the Sanskrit are by the author. The translations are sometimes slightly condensed. Translations from the Devī Gītā are based on the author's translation of the text, published by the State University of New York Press, 1998.

2. The Devī Gītā constitutes chapters 31–40 of the seventh book of the Devī-Bhāgavata Purāṇa. Thus, references to Devī Gītā 1–10 equal Devī-Bhāgavata 7.31–40.

3. The Devī-Bhāgavata presents the alternative birth account in two versions, the first occurring in the frame story of the opening chapter of the Devī Gītā. The second, and almost certainly earlier, version of the Goddess' birth in the Devī-Bhāgavata appears in 12.8. This second account will be considered in some detail in the next section on the "Vedāntic Identity of the Goddess as Brahman."

4. While the term *liṅga* is often taken in a phallic sense, its most literal meaning is "mark" or "emblem." Since the mark of a male is the penis, the phallic significance is natural enough. However, such an interpretation is often overemphasized in the case of Śiva, where his primary defining quality or mark is that of pure consciousness, symbolized by an infinite column of light, the Jyotir-liṅga or emblem of light.

5. The Devī Gītā was composed in all probability after the Śaradā-Tilaka Tantra (ca. twelfth century), as the Devī Gītā almost assuredly quotes from it (see Brown 1998, 162–164). The Devī Gītā also quotes from the Devī Upaniṣad (ninth to fourteenth centuries) and actually refers to the latter text itself. For the dating of the Devī Upaniṣad, a critical text for understanding the historical context of the Devī Gītā, see Farquhar 1920, 266–267; Winternitz 1927, 239–240; Dasgupta 1922, 1:28; and Brooks 1990, 12–13.

6. The specific ten goddesses named vary in different lists, and sometimes there are more than ten. Bhuvaneśvarī appears in most lists, often as the fourth, fifth, or sixth Mahāvidyā (Chakravarti 1963, 85–86; Bhattacaryya 1974, 135–136; Pal 1981, 9–10, 57–59; Kinsley 1997, 9).

7. In certain late Tantras, there is an explicit correlation made between the Mahāvidyās and Viṣṇu's ten avatars (Bhattacaryya 1974, 136; Kinsley 1986, 161; 1997, 20–22).

8. The ten named in the Śiva Purāṇa are:
1. Kālī
2. Tārā
3. Chinnamastā
4. Śrīvidyā
5. Bhuvaneśvarī
6. Bhairavī
7. Bagalā
8. Dhūmra
9. Tripurasundarī
10. Mataṅgī

9. Hazra (1963, 282) dates the text as probably from the tenth or eleventh century. Kinsley (1997, 22) suggests that it, along with the Bṛhaddharma Purāṇa which provides a similar origin account of the Mahāvidyās, was probably composed after the fourteenth century.

10. The occasion for Satī's desire to disrupt her father's (Dakṣa's) sacrifice arose when he insulted her by refusing to invite her husband Śiva to the great rite. This famous story is told in countless versions.

11. The Uddhārakośa also refers to six other "Daśavidyās," who often appear in other lists: Bhadrakālī, Turī, Chinnamastakā, Dakṣiṇakālikā, Śyāmā, and Kālarātrī. The Uddhārakośa is a late collection of quotations from forty-seven other Tantric works.

12. The Sanskrit subheading in the text refers to the Goddess as Ādi-Vidyā (Primal Wisdom), similar to the name Śrī-Vidyā (Auspicious Wisdom), an alternate designation of Tripurā.

13. The Devī Upaniṣad, in its description of Ādi-Vidyā, specifically says she grants both *bhukti* and *mukti* (verse 19).

14. The text here refers to Oṃ by the term *"praṇava,"* (humming). It is a common designation of this sacred Vedic syllable. The Devī Gītā also uses the term *praṇava* to refer to Bhuvaneśvarī's seed-mantra Hrīṃ, calling it the "Devī-praṇava" (4.41). But here in the first chapter it clearly refers to Oṃ.

15. The Devī Gītā refers to Hrīṃ as the *māyā-bīja* in 5.32.

16. The Varadā Tantra text (from chapter 6) is quoted and translated in Woodroffe 1922, 244. The translation is mine.

17. The *o* is a diphthong, composed of *a* and *u*, and thus the three elements are *a*, *u*, and *m* (disregarding the fourth element represented by the dot, symbolizing the silence following the *m*).

Chapter 2

Mahādevī as Mother

The Oriya Hindu Vision of Reality

Usha Menon

In this essay, I examine the contemporary significance of Mahādevī, the Great Goddess, to Oriya Hindus living in the temple town of Bhubaneshwar in the state of Orissa in eastern India. I focus on three issues pertaining to her identity in Bhubaneshwar: first, the belief that the Goddess is immanent in all forms of the created universe; second, the meanings that Oriya Hindus attach to her most common appellation, Mā, or "Mother"; and third, the stress that Oriya Hindus place on complementarity between the male and female principles. In elaborating on these three points, I draw on several popular stories about the Great Goddess and her powers. Although these stories may be based on textual sources, it has been my experience that individuals who narrate these stories are often unaware of such sources. In some cases, narrators explicitly attribute their stories to a particular text, but such attributions are usually inaccurate. For the purpose of this essay, the lack of authoritative textual sources for these stories is relatively unimportant.

The temple town of Bhubaneshwar is predominantly Śaiva, and the Oriya Hindus who live here belong, for the most part, to families of hereditary servants *(sevaka)* of Liṅgarāj, the form in which Śiva is worshiped here (For a more complete description of the community, see Seymour 1983; Mahapatra 1981; Shweder 1991). This temple is an important pilgrimage site for all Hindus. Pilgrims from North India, Assam, and Bengal, in particular, make a point of praying here before going on south to worship at the Jagannātha temple in Puri.

Despite the temple town's largely Śaiva orientation, symbols of Mahādevī, the Great Goddess, abound. While the Oriya Hindus who live here acknowledge and worship numerous manifestations of Mahādevī, it is predominantly as Kālī and Pārvatī that she is represented in the numerous temples that dot the landscape of Bhubaneshwar. For instance, the small temple located in the middle of the temple tank is dedicated to the divine couple, Śiva and Pārvatī, with Śiva massaging Pārvatī's feet in a curious and intriguing reversal of local custom. And on the main road leading to the Liṅgarāj temple, there is a granite temple, the Kapālī Mandir, that is dedicated to the Goddess in her form as Kālī. She is represented here adorned with a garland of skulls and a girdle of severed heads and arms, her tongue protruding, and her right foot placed squarely on the chest of a supine Śiva. There is also an open air Tantric temple to the south of Bhubaneshwar that is dedicated to the sixty-four *yoginīs*, each of whom is associated with a particular yogic ability. It is said that people still worship the sixty-four *yoginīs* here on new moon *(amāvāsya)* nights.

The Great Goddess as Śakti: Immanent in the Embodied Universe

When asked, Oriya Hindu men and women of the temple town ascribe to the Śiva Purāṇa the story they tell about the origin of creation. The story, which they repeat to their children and to interested strangers, is remarkable for the prominence it gives to the female while also acknowledging the creative role of the male. John S. Hawley has observed that in certain contexts, the Goddess is understood to be "the condition that makes structure possible . . . the soul of relation. She connects, she communicates, she is warp to the woof" (1982, xi). Such a perspective on the Goddess is also evident in this Oriya story:

> We believe in one God, Bhagavān. We say there is only one God, there is no second. All the gods are just the various forms of Bhagavān. At the beginning of creation, Bhagavān looked around and was not content. Bhagavān wanted to be a creator *(sṛṣtikartā)* and so articulated the sound "Oṃ," and Mā emerged out of the round shape of the "Oṃ." And then Mā desired a male *(puruṣa)*. When she wanted to unite with a male, Bhagavān split, and the three forms of divinity *(trimūrti)*—Brahmā, Viṣṇu and Maheśwar (Śiva)—came into being. But Brahmā feared Śakti;[1] just seeing her, fierce and

glowing, was enough to age him, and his hair turned grey. Viṣṇu, too, wary of unadulterated Śakti, moved away, refusing to accept her. And so he said "Namaskār" to Śakti, bowing his head and greeting her as a mother. And Śakti said, "I need a male *(puruṣa)* to unite with. Who is the male here?" Turning to Śiva, Viṣṇu asked him to accept Śakti. And so Śiva did. Then, Viṣṇu smiled to himself, thinking, "Śiva has desired Śakti all along, and he has pretended indifference." But Śakti, who is present in everybody, was present in Viṣṇu, too, and she realized that he was mocking Śiva. So she cursed Viṣṇu. She said, "Leave me to Śiva. You withdrew, so he will be immortal *(amara)*. He is Time itself *(mahākāla)*; there will be no birth or death for him, but you will be condemned to being born again and again on this earth. Śiva is filled with my energy/power *(śakti)* and so is immortal, but you have only a little of my energy/power *(śakti)*. Since you are devoid of energy/power *(śaktihīn)*, you will have to have to replenish your energy/power through your many births." Then Viṣṇu replied, "Mā, you have cursed me in this way, but I have no power of my own. I will need you if I am to preserve this world." So Viṣṇu has his many incarnations *(avatāras)*, his ten incarnations, one after the other; and each time he is born, he destroys demons *(asuras)*, and when he cannot, he calls upon Mā, and she comes and kills them. He could not kill Mahiṣāsura (the buffalo demon), so Durgā came and killed him. In this pilgrimage center *(tīrtha sthāna)*, this Liṅgarāj temple, there used to be a pair of demons named Kṛttīvāsa and Kṛuttīvāsa whom no one could kill. Again, Mā came as Pārvatī and killed them. Even Viṣṇu can do nothing without praying to Mā for strength.

In this story, the Goddess, Mā, emanates from the power or *śakti* that springs from Bhagavān's auspicious and all-powerful sound "Oṃ" (the seed-mantra). After she appears, the three male gods—Brahmā, Viṣṇu, and Śiva—are created out of the genderless Bhagavān. Mā does not create parthenogenetically; she needs to unite with a male in order to create new life.[2] A. K. Ramanujan (1993) has recorded a Kannada creation myth that has many similar themes, but in his version, there is an element of incest; the male gods and Mā are siblings. In the version I heard, however, the theme of incest is missing. Furthermore, the female is not "destroyed, divided and domesticated"(120) among the three, as occurs in Ramanujan's version; rather, as befits a Śaiva temple town, only Śiva is given the ability to absorb her power *(śakti)* so that he never dies. He is time itself, Mahākāla. The *śakti* of Śiva, unlike that of Viṣṇu, does not have to be replenished by constant rebirths in various incarnations. Furthermore, Viṣṇu recognizes and defers to Devī as the source of his *śakti.* In any of his several incarnations, whenever he fails to kill a demon, he prays for her assistance, and she comes to his aid. Śiva is not dependent on Devī in this way.

In describing the awesome power of Mā that enables the universe to come into being, the intellectual elite of the temple town play on the resemblance between the name "Śiva" and the term *śava* (corpse). In Oriya, as in Sanskrit (Zimmer 1946, 206), the only audible difference between *śava* and Śiva is the vowel element "i." Without this vowel element, Śiva the god becomes *śava,* a corpse. Most significantly, Oriya Hindus assert that this life-giving vowel symbolizes *śakti,* the power and vital energy of the Goddess. Hence, if Śiva has any power, it is because the Goddess has given it to him.

While this kind of meaningful punning may be confined primarily to a small intellectual elite, less sophisticated residents in this neighborhood are not short on stories that identify the Great Goddess similarly as the power and vital energy that not only enable the creation of the universe but are also immanent in its every aspect. One of the most commonly told stories has to do with a Sabaro who worshiped only Śiva.[3] Mamatā, an articulate Oriya Hindu housewife well-versed in the stories of her community, recounted the following version of the story:

> This Sabaro never did goddess worship *(śakti pūjā).* He only worshiped Śiva; he only wanted Śiva. In this way many, many days passed. But by praying just to Śiva you will get no fruits, because he is Bholanātha, an ascetic *(yogī).* One day, as this person was doing his worship *(pūjā)* to Śiva, Mā came toward him dressed as an ordinary woman. She brushed past him and went by. She did this three times. Now everyday, this Sabaro would get an earthen pitcher and fill it with water to use in his worship of Śiva. Now what Mā did was, after brushing past him three times, she went and touched the pitcher filled with water. The Sabaro saw her do it, and he became upset. First he bathed; then he went to the pitcher and tried to empty it of the water, but he couldn't lift it. He tried and tried, but he couldn't. Now here was an insuperable obstacle *(vighṇa)* in his worship of Śiva. Finally, he went to Śiva and hit his head again and again, saying, "Let me end my life today. I am

> not able to do your worship in the proper way. A woman touched the pitcher of water I use for your worship, and now I can't even lift it to empty the water and refill it. Look at my condition, all because of a woman! There is no point in living like this. I'm going to end it all." Then Śiva told him, "Arre! No, you are making a mistake! You don't understand. That was Mahādevī who came and touched the pitcher." But the Sabaro didn't believe Śiva. He said, "What power *(śakti)* does this woman have that because of her touch, I am unable to lift the pitcher? What power *(śakti)* do women have?" He didn't understand. Then Śiva asked him, "Where have you come from [i.e., how were you born]?" But this man had never seen his mother and father after his birth, so he brushed aside what Śiva said, saying, "Mother and father? No, there is no such thing. I was born, so I was born." Then Śiva made him understand, saying, "Go! Just say 'Oṃ Śakti,' and then lift the pitcher." The Sabaro went from there, said "Oṃ Śakti," and lifted the pitcher. He had asked what *śakti* was, and he now knew—*śakti* was Mā. Everything around him, everything that moved, that breathed, that lived, that gave birth, that died, did so because of Mā. And from that time on, he established an image *(mūrti)* of Mā and began worshiping her.[4]

In this story, Śiva takes it upon himself to inform a faithful devotee about the true nature of reality—that it is feminine. Although the presiding deity of this temple town is Śiva, most of his servants have a faintly disrespectful attitude towards him. Like Mamatā, they call him "Bholanātha," the "Lord of simpletons." They describe him as intoxicated, stupefied, forever consuming hashish, disinterested in the world and its activities, unwilling to listen to his devotees, and utterly dependent for his very existence on Mahādevī, who is not only his *śakti*, but the universe's *śakti* as well. Therefore, Oriya Hindus say that if one desires effective intervention in the affairs of this world, it is pointless to appeal to Śiva—only Mā, the Great Goddess, can help.

It is worth noting that the story directly addresses the issue of female pollution. Śiva's devotee, the Sabaro, is a misogynist who believes that females are both inherently polluting and irrelevant to any worthwhile enterprise. But the lesson he finally learns is that, pollution notwithstanding, ultimately everything is a manifestation of the feminine principle, Mā, who is herself *śakti*. Everything in this world is ultimately dependent on her.

Mahādevī as Kālī: Social Responsibilities and Their Power to Calm

When Oriya Hindus address Mahādevī in worship or when they talk of her, the term they use most frequently is Mā, or "Mother." There is little indigenous debate regarding the appropriateness of this usage. After all, Oriya Hindus recognize her as present in every aspect of creation. Whatever her particular manifestation, whatever her particular actions, she generates and regenerates all life. Consequently, she is Mother.

Even when a particular manifestation of Mahādevī—for instance, Durgā or Kālī—is not explicitly associated with any male god nor any progeny, she is still thought of and addressed as Mother. Oriya Hindus see nothing incongruous in this usage, although many scholars are uneasy with it, tending to see in the motherhood of Kālī, for example, an irresolvable paradox. Some even go so far as to say that the labeling of Kālī as Mother is an inadvertent "mistake" made by Kālī's devotees, a mistake that should be discounted by those who seek consistency in their interpretations (see Allen 1976, 315; Gross 1983, 224–225; Kinsley 1986, 126–128). In fact, Hindus tend to perceive the defining feature of all females as the embodied potential for reproduction. Hence, an infant or a prepubescent girl, a married mother, and an old widow are all "mother" and are all addressed as "Mā." The use of this term points to their reproductive potential rather than any actual experience of motherhood.

There is also another, perhaps more instrumental, reason for the use of the term "Mā" for goddesses who are explicitly violent and do not appear to be maternal. This has to do with Oriya Hindu perceptions regarding Mā's power to destroy. Indigenous discourse clearly distinguishes the Goddess's ability to apply her destructive capacity in ways that are deliberate from those that are indiscriminate. Thus, as Durgā, for example, Mā is never indiscriminate in her destruction. Oriya Hindus tend to portray Durgā as a mighty warrior who is invincible and invulnerable. Whenever the gods are unable to destroy their enemies, she enters the fray, and she is always successful in securing victory for the gods. She never targets the innocent, for her victims are invariably arrogant demons intoxicated by their own ability to destroy. Furthermore, she is rarely wrathful but carries out her destructive duties with measured control.

Kālī, however, is a different goddess altogether. The defining characteristic of her nature is wrath *(krodha, rāga)*, and in her anger she destroys indiscriminately, giving no thought to her victims, be they demons or men, deserving of death or not. To a large extent, David R. Kinsley is quite accurate when he says that Kālī is "antisocial," threatening "stability and order" (1982, 148). In his fascinating essay on her and the meanings she holds for her devotees, Kinsley describes her as becoming "frenzied on the battlefield, usually becoming drunk on the blood of her victims, [so] that she herself begins to destroy the world that she is supposed to protect" (148). He recognizes that despite her tendency to spin out of control, her devotees regard her as the highest manifestation of the divine. In Bhubaneshwar, too, articulate residents describe her in very similar ways, as dark-skinned, wild-eyed, dishevelled, panting for blood. They say she can never be worshiped within the household, for symbolizing as she does blood, death, and indiscriminate destruction, she is highly inauspicious. She could never insure the material prosperity of the household nor the maintenance of the lineage. The appropriate place to worship her is the cremation ground, with jackals howling and funeral fires burning; and the appropriate time to worship her is on the night of the new moon.

In at least one significant respect, however, indigenous thinking about Kālī does not conform to Kinsley's persuasive interpretation of what she means to Hindus. Kinsley suggests that Kālī is "uncontrollable" (148); she is never subdued, not even by her husband Śiva. Oriya Hindus, however, regard her as tending to spin out of control but never *un*controllable per se. While she does lose her self-control at times, there are ways to compel her to contain her wrath, regain self-control, and exercise self-restraint. Devotees I spoke with always described this regaining of self-control as entirely voluntary—Kālī chooses to exercise self-control. If she did not choose to do this, there would be no way of ending her indiscriminate destruction. No one can force her to become subdued—and how could it be otherwise? As the *śakti* that sets the universe in motion and the ultimate ground of all Being, she transcends creation; hence, she is subject to no one's control. But Kālī is understood to regain her self-control when she is reminded of her responsibilities, especially those pertaining to her role as Śiva's wife and/or mother of all living creatures. Such an understanding is evident in local interpretations of a popular icon that depicts Kālī standing on Śiva. It is said that Śiva draws Kālī's attention to her responsibilities when he lies in her path, allowing her to step on him. Placing one's feet on another person's body is thought to be highly disrespectful, and a wife should never show disrespect to her husband. When Kālī's foot touches Śiva's body, she remembers her wifely duties. Similarly, human devotees can always gain Kālī's attention by addressing her as "Mā," thereby reminding her of her maternal duty to protect them, her children.

Some years ago, another scholar and I investigated the meanings that Oriya Hindus of Bhubaneshwar attach to the Goddess's facial expression in a widely disseminated icon of Kālī standing on her husband, Śiva (see Menon and Shweder 1994). In this icon, the Goddess is shown wearing a garland of skulls and a girdle of severed heads and arms. She holds a bloody sword in one hand and a freshly decapitated head in another; her tongue is red and protruding, and her right foot is placed squarely on the chest of a supine Śiva (see photo 2.1).[5] We asked ninety-two informants to interpret her expression. Not all informants were equally knowledgeable or articulate, but almost all of them identified the two figures in the icon as Śiva and Kālī. And, in sharp contrast to many scholars' emphasis on Kālī's independence from males, almost all of them also said that Kālī is Śiva's wife. This marital relationship is crucial for understanding Kālī's facial expression in the representation, which about 75 percent of the people interviewed claim illustrates Kāli's *lajjā* (modesty, deference, respectful self-restraint) for having stepped on her husband, Śiva.

Briefly, in that study (Menon and Shweder 1994, 252–266), we broke down informants' narratives into twenty-five constituent elements of meaning. We grouped these twenty-five elements into three narrative clusters, each of which constitutes a complete story in and of itself. These three clusters form a nested hierarchy of cultural knowledge about the icon. The simplest, least elaborate story is encompassed by the next, more elaborate narrative cluster; both of these clusters are, in turn, encompassed by the most elaborate and detailed narrative, which includes additional elements as well. We found that a large percentage of informants, 40 percent (thirty-eight individuals), were familiar with the basic, least elaborate version of the story. Another 13 percent, twelve of those interviewed, recounted the moderately more detailed narrative, and 23 percent (a total of twenty-one individuals), recounted the most elaborate version. This means that over 75 percent of those interviewed knew the most basic version of the story, since it is also encompassed by the two more elaborate versions. Hence, this most basic narrative is, in a sense, the "core" narrative, that is, the most widely known narrative associated with the icon.[6]

According to this "core" story, the icon represents the divine couple, Kālī and Śiva, in a way that appears at first to reverse the common hierarchy of domestic status relationships, in which the husband is the personal god of his wife. Narrators claim that the defining characteristic of Mahādevī as Kālī is her indiscriminately destructive anger. Completely absorbed in this anger, unaware of her surroundings, destroying whatever came in her path—both good and evil—Kālī once stepped on Śiva. But she did so accidentally. She then experienced acute *lajjā* at having been so outrageously immodest and disrespectful, leading her to restrain herself, get a hold of her anger,

Photo 2.1 Kālī Standing on Śiva

and cool down. It is noteworthy that when narrators comment on the manner in which Kālī is recalled to a sense of her wifely duties, nearly three-quarters of them insist that it happens by her reining in her own power, not through any external control exercised by Śiva. They point to Śiva's passivity and argue that if she wished, Kālī could have trampled him and gone on. That she chose to recognize him and contain her power for destruction rather than let it spill out is interpreted as an act of voluntarily exercised self-control, an autonomous act of self-restraint.

As previously noted, this story about the icon is both the best-known, most familiar version told in Bhubaneshwar and also the least detailed of our three narrative clusters. The slightly more detailed version of the story elaborates on the magnitude and indiscriminately destructive nature of the Goddess's anger. Briefly, this version of the story portrays the Goddess as a tremendously powerful force created by the male gods for the express purpose of killing the buffalo demon Mahiṣāsura. The Goddess is said to have become so enraged after her battle with the demon that she turned into Kālī and lost all sense of her surroundings, as well as her ability to distinguish right from wrong. This had disastrous implications for the survival of the world. In order to save the world and all its creatures, Śiva deliberately positioned himself in her path so that Kālī would step on him and experience *lajjā*. The most elaborate and detailed version of the narrative seeks in addition to explain the source of Kālī's wrath, depicting Kālī's rage as the result of a boon that the male gods had given to the buffalo demon (for more on these stories, see Menon and Shweder 1994). This boon made the demon invulnerable to death, except at the hands of a naked female. Thus, before she could kill him, the Goddess had to strip and stand naked before the demon. The extreme humiliation she experienced in doing this is said to have led to her destructive wrath. In the words of one temple town resident,

> After killing Mahiṣāsura, a terrible rage entered Durgā's mind, and she asked herself, "What kinds of gods are these that give to demons such boons, and apart from that, what kind of gods are these that they do not have the honesty to tell me the truth before sending me into battle?" She decided that such a world with such gods did not deserve to survive, and she took on the form of Kali and went on a mad rampage, devouring every living creature that came in her way.

Thus, the humiliating boon, the Goddess's nakedness, and Kālī's justifiable rage at the situation are narrative elements that are added into this version of the story of the icon.

Undoubtedly, the significance and popularity of this icon lies in the way it crystallizes several themes important to Oriya Hindu culture: female power and shame; anger as socially disruptive and destructive; the disjunction between a male-dominated social order and the potential power of women; and finally, self-control and self-discipline as the only effective means of regulating destructive anger. But these issues are not directly relevant to our present purpose. What is of particular concern here are the circumstances that lead to Kālī's experience of *lajjā* and the consequences of that experience, the cooling down and containing of her anger. On these points there is remarkable consensus amongst the ninety-two Oriya Hindus I spoke with: roughly three-quarters assert that it was through being recalled to her duties and responsibilities as a wife that Kālī succeeded in controlling herself. Interestingly enough, the details of the ruse that Śiva employs to enable her to regain self-control—his lying down in her path to get her to step on him—are only found in this local, orally transmitted story about Kālī's *lajjā*. As far as I have been able to determine, there does not appear to be any textual variant of this particular element in the story.

Before turning to discuss further this particular narrative element and its importance, it is helpful to first provide some context. While describing the events that lead up to the moment portrayed in the icon, twenty-six of the storytellers authenticated their stories by pointing to a canonical version that they attributed to Sanskritic or Oriya texts. These storytellers were evenly distributed in terms of degrees of cultural competence.[7] Sometimes spontaneously during their narration, sometimes when pressed, informants named as sources of their knowledge the Liṅga or Kālīkā Purāṇas, both Sanskrit texts, or the Caṇḍī Purāṇa, a fifteenth-century Oriya extrapolation of classical literature attributed to Sāralā Dāsa, an Oriya devotee of the Goddess.[8] Despite such explicit attribution, it is interesting to note that the most elaborate version of the story we documented contains many more elements of meaning than are found in either Sanskritic versions of the Goddess's exploits or the fifteenth-century Oriya recapitulation alone. Contemporary awareness of the Goddess in Bhubaneshwar appears to be a blend and reworking of some elements from the Devī-Māhātmya and the Devī-Bhāgavata Purāṇa, many more elements from Sāralā Dāsa's interpretation of Durgā's destruction of Mahiṣāsura, and new, provocative elements introduced by contemporary storytellers.

The second story in the Devī-Māhātmya, which is retold in a more elaborate form in the Devī-Bhāgavata Purāṇa (Brown 1990; Coburn 1991), provides most of the Purāṇic elements found in current interpretations of Kālī's icon in Bhubaneshwar. In the Devī-Māhātmya's narrative, Devī and Mahiṣāsura, the main protagonists, are pitted against each other. The demon has proven himself invincible against the gods, but the Goddess finally succeeds in destroying him. However, unlike the most elaborate version of the story told today in Bhubaneshwar and presented above, there is no boon, no humiliation of the Goddess, and no account of the Goddess's wrath transforming her into Kālī bent on indiscriminate destruction. This basic story is retold in the Devī-Bhāgavata Purāṇa but with some additional themes added to it. The most pertinent for our present purpose is that Brahmā grants Mahiṣāsura a boon that makes him invulnerable to death, except at the hands of a female. But even in this later version, despite the inclusion of this new detail, the Goddess never strips naked. She displays no indiscriminate destructive wrath, and the survival of the world is not threatened. Śiva does not make an appearance, but then he is not needed to save the day.

Several key elements of the contemporary Oriya story, however, can be found in the Caṇḍī Purāṇa, the fifteenth-century Oriya text mentioned above and attributed to Sāralā Dāsa. Here, the demon fighting Devī receives a boon from Brahmā that makes him invulnerable to death except at the hands of a *naked* female. In this account of the story, too, the Goddess strips naked in order to kill her adversary, experiences humiliation and wrath, and threatens to kill all the gods (see Shweder and Menon, forthcoming). But, Sāralā Dāsa has the Goddess regain her equilibrium not by experiencing *lajjā* (because her husband Śiva allows himself to be stepped on by her) but by succumbing to her suitor Śiva's seductive wooing. She is enchanted by his magical dancing, finds herself unable to resist his demands, and ultimately accepts his proposal of marriage.

The contemporary Oriya narrative, however, has its own particular twist—one that is remarkably different from that of Sāralā Dāsa. The story we recorded does not rely on Śiva's seductive powers to bring the still-unmarried Goddess back to her senses; instead, Śiva and Devī are assumed to be already married, and Śiva employs quite a different strategy, one that is meant to remind his wife of her wifely duties. He lays himself down in her path, allowing her to stomp on him. I have not found any version of the story in either classical Purāṇic or fifteenth-century Oriya literature that includes this crucial detail. However, this particular element is deeply significant when it comes to contemporary discourse on the Goddess. Oriya Hindus hold that, given appropriate circumstances, the Goddess is perfectly capable of exercising self-control, as she does in this instance.

While the intellectual elite in Bhubaneshwar follow Sāralā Dāsa in attempting to provide a reasonable explanation of the source of the Goddess' wrath, the majority of the residents are little interested in this exercise. They are much more concerned with the nature of the

Goddess's wrath and the ways that she can be enabled to reestablish her self-control. The consensus appears to be that the most effective way of doing this is to remind her of her obligations as not only Śiva's wife, but also mother of the universe.

Kālī as Nurturing Mother

The need to appeal to Kālī's nurturing sensibilities to cause her to regain self-control is echoed in another familiar and fairly commonplace story told in the temple town. In this story, too, Kālī regains self-control when she is recalled to a sense of her maternal responsibilities. The story as I heard it from one of Liṅgarāj's priests, is as follows:

> There can never be a bad mother (*kūmātā*). Mothers always want the best for their children, they will sacrifice anything, even their own lives, for their children's welfare. Look at Kālī Mā ("Mother Kālī"); she is fierce and terrible, but even she wants only the best for us, her needy children. And how do we worship her? We worship her as Mā ("mother"); we address her as Mā, and there is a reason for this—because only then does she listen to us. Only then will she not consume us. Let me tell you a story about the poet Bhañja.[9] Bhañja was, as everyone knows, born a fool *(bokkā)*, a simpleton. One evening, late, he went to defecate in the fields, and when he was returning Caṇḍī (another name for Kālī) pursued him. He turned around and saw her wild-eyed and dishevelled, with loose hair, and he stopped. He asked her, "What do you want?" And she replied, "I want to drink your blood. Give me your blood." And Bhañja was such a fool, he didn't recognize Mā, but he took a sharp pebble from the ground and cut his finger and gave it to Devī. Mā began sucking on the finger, and she drained all the blood from Bhañja. When life was finally ebbing from Bhañja's body, he moaned, "Oh, Mā!" That was enough! Mā heard her son call her "Mā," and she stopped drinking his blood. Instead, she gave him back all his blood, brought him back to life, and said, "My son, you were willing to give me your life; now ask me for a boon, any boon, and I will give it to you." And Bhañja asked that he be given the power to create poetry, the power to imagine (*kalpanā korībā śakti*). Mā asked him to open his mouth, and she wrote the alphabet on his tongue. From that day forth he became the silver-tongued poet that we know of today. Do you see now?

> When he called her Mā, she couldn't resist him. Even though she had this terrible desire to consume blood, she forgot herself and thought only of him.

This story articulates a fundamental Oriya notion: the impossibility of being or having a "bad mother" (*kūmātā*). Oriya Hindus believe implicitly that as a mother, Kālī can do no harm to her human children. Admittedly, Kālī represents that which is chaotic and unpredictable; yet for the Oriya Hindus I spoke with, she does not represent the unmanageable. By all accounts, Kālī is a terrifying goddess, but her devotees are not afraid of her. They seek and find reassurance in her by approaching and addressing her as "Mother." In so doing, the human devotee taps into sensibilities that cannot help but be nurturing. However out of control she may be, the cry of "Mā!" (mother!) calms her down, makes her receptive to the needs of her children, and makes her want to satisfy their prayers.

Thus, many would echo Mamatā when she describes the various manifestations of Mahādevī as different but not necessarily contradictory aspects of the Goddess. She says,

> Mā is tender and loving; she is also cruel and harsh to us, her children. How can a mother be one and not the other? If she genuinely desires the best for her child now and in the future, she has to be both harsh and demanding as well as indulgent and forgiving; only then will her child come to know what the real world is like.

Interestingly enough, while addressing Mahādevī and her various manifestations as mother, Oriya Hindus also use *tu*, the most familiar of the three forms of second person address in Oriya. Here, they are following customary practice in Oriya Hindu households where one's father and other senior males are always addressed distantly, and very formally, as *apano*, but one's mother is addressed most intimately and with great familiarity as *tu*.

The Complementarity of Male and Female: Obvious and Inescapable

There is another meaning about Mā and her relationship with Śiva that can be culled from these stories. Oriya Hindus recognize Mā's immanence and her power, and they assert her autonomy and independence of action when she is required to regain self-control, but such recognition and such assertions do not evolve into considering her to be either superior to, or in any way independent of, the male gods. Rather, those who recount these stories understand them to highlight the necessary complementarity that they, the narrators, see as existing between male and female principles. Consider, for example, the remarks of a seventy-four-year-old Brahmin man I interviewed. Unquestionably competent and articulate regarding Mā and her significance to her devotees, he stated the following in response to the question, "Who do you see as dominant, Kālī or Śiva?"

> If he [Śiva] is water, then she [Kālī] is the wetness of the water; if he is the fire, then she is the fieriness of the fire. So it is foolish to talk of him being stronger or her being stronger. They need each other, and we can't talk of one without talking of the other.

He is not alone in conceptualizing the relationship in this way. There is broad consensus on the subject; almost two-thirds of the participants interviewed in the study on Kālī's icon agree with him. Consider, for instance, the following response to the same question, articulated by a fifty-year-old married Brahmin woman, the mother of a son and a daughter:

> You ask who is dominant, Kālī or Śiva. I can't answer that! Neither is dominant, but both are necessary for each other. So it's impossible to say who dominates and who doesn't. In this picture, for instance, Kālī seems dominant. She is unbridled energy, but that is at the beginning of the story; toward the end, however, after she has touched Śiva, energy flows from her to him. She who was destructive becomes creative and he who was lifeless comes alive.

A forty-four-year-old Chassā[10] father of four sons expresses similar views:

> It is important to realize that while *śakti* is absolutely necessary for the creation and evolution of the universe, by itself even *śakti* cannot achieve anything. *Śakti* has to combine with consciousness for the process of creation to take place, and so consciousness as symbolized by Śiva has a unique position. Just as it is only through the union of a man and a woman that a child can be conceived, so too, only when *śakti* and *cit* (consciousness) come together does creation occur.

Clearly, these devotees of Mahādevī do not see her as dominating Śiva, even in her most violent and aggressive manifestation. To them, she does not transcend conventionally understood gender roles. She does not even stand for gender equality. On the contrary, they emphasize the complementary nature of the relationship between Kālī and Śiva. For them, her awesome power is channeled most productively when she is joined with her husband: through their union, creation occurs.

Oriya Hindus view this complementary relationship between Mahādevī and Śiva as reflecting the complementary relationship between mortal men and women that exists in the human realm as well. In conversations devoted to discussing a woman's duty to her husband, a man's responsibilities towards his family, or a mother's care of her children, they move between the world of gods and that of mortals smoothly, explaining divine action in terms of human needs and failings and using divine examples to express human ideals.

Oriya Hindus do not conceive of men and women as being opposed to each other, competing with each other, or having conflicting goals or interests. They do not split society along gender lines. Instead, they conceive of male and female as being the only two castes in the world whose differences can never be transcended. Men and women are different. They are also unequal—an inequality that is "context-sensitive" (Ramanujan 1990), moving in favor of women and then against them depending on particular circumstances. Simultaneously, and perhaps not surprisingly, each is also conceived of as the natural complement of the other. And it is only when they complete each other that biological and social reproduction occurs, matters that, in local thinking, are the primary tasks of all human groups.

Mahādevī as Mother: The Critical Identity for Oriya Hindus

In these pages, I have attempted to present the meanings that Mahādevī, in all her various manifestations, has for her Oriya Hindu devotees. I have tried to remain as faithful as possible to indigenous conceptions and interpretations. The voices heard and the opinions presented have been those of ordinary Oriya Hindu householders and their wives—the majority, as it happens, of the residents of the temple town of Bhubaneshwar. These men and women have few pretensions of being philosophically sophisticated. As far as I know, few would claim that they consider Kālī to be their divine mother "because she gives birth to a wider vision of reality than the one embodied in the order of *dharma*" (Kinsley 1982, 152). Neither would most suggest that she should be understood as beckoning them towards a final release *(mokṣa),* because people rarely speak of their chances of achieving such release. In fact, there are those who are sufficiently astute, mentally, to argue that even to talk of such a possibility is itself a kind of attachment and one more indication of being still bound to this world of enchantment and illusion *(moha-māyā).*

Instead, these men and women affirm life in this world, describing the life of the householder as most blessed *(dhanya),* most excellent *(śreṣṭha),* and happy (*sukhamaya*). In their estimation, it embodies "the good life" (cf. Madan 1987). They see the experiences of this world—to be born, to live, to eat, to make love, to procreate—as worthy and valuable experiences worth repeating in future lives. They unhesitatingly recognize Mahādevī as "the power that makes possible not only the creation, but also the maintenance and destruction of the universe. She transcends the universe and controls its rhythms. Yet she is also immanent, for it is said that she abides in all beings in the form of *śakti* and is described as the *śakti* of all that is" (Pintchman 1994, 120–121). But, simultaneously, and perhaps because of their positive evaluation of life in this world, they also recognize the futility of ordinary humans trying to apprehend her all-encompassing nature. Hence, they make sense of her by domesticating her, by socializing her, by defining her in terms of a particular role, that of mother. When they acknowledge her immanence, it is as Mā, Mother. As Mā she becomes accessible to them, and they can approach her without fear, doubt, or hesitation.

Therefore, most ordinary folk in Bhubaneshwar going about the everyday business of living unqualifiedly identify Mahādevī in all her manifestations, the benign and the terrible, as Mother. As a mother, they claim, she may be terrifying, but she can never be terrible to her children. As that which makes everything possible, she transcends the embodied universe; she is beyond all moral and social norms. Nevertheless, by approaching and addressing her as "Mā," her devotees reclaim her. They contend that identifying Mahādevī as mother compels her, powerfully and irresistibly, to remember her maternal, nurturing responsibilities to her children, and to never refuse their requests.

Notes

1. Oriya Hindus routinely interchange the names Mā, Devī, Śakti, Mahādevī, often in the same sentence.

2. According to Oriya Hindus, only when she is in her form as Kālī, her most destructive aspect, do bloodthirsty demonesses like Caṇḍī and Cāmuṇḍī tumble out of her body, devouring all life forms that come in their path.

3. The Sabaros are a Mundari-speaking group of tribals who live in the hills of Ganjam district in southern Orissa. The icon of Jagannātha in the temple at Puri is supposed to be of Sabaro origin and is said to have been stolen from the Sabaros by an emissary of the king of Puri.

4. Interestingly enough, the role of the one who is ignorant of the "truth" is cast upon the Sabaro, someone who could be technically categorized as the Other. As it happens, however, Sabaros, though recognized as *ādivāsis* (autochthonous people), are well-integrated into Liṅgarāj's worship. The Badus, a subcaste that claims Brahmin status and participates in ritual activities at the Liṅgarāj temple, are said to be descendants of the union between a Sabaro woman and the ascetic Siddhabhūtī, a devotee of Śiva. In fact, the woman who told me this story is herself a Badu.

5. The popularity of the icon is hardly surprising considering that the Goddess is worshiped in precisely this form in the Kapālī Mandir that I mentioned toward the beginning of this essay.

6. In addition, twenty-one informants adduced very few of the twenty-five meanings and were able to do little more than identify the figure in the icon as Kālī.

7. On examination, neither the Liṅga Purāṇa nor the Kālīkā Purāṇa appears to be the appropriate text. Rather, the Mārkaṇḍeya Purāṇa, including as it does the Devī-Māhātmya, seems to be what these people had in mind.

8. Sāralā Dāsa is the name taken by Sidheśvar Pariḍā, a *śākta* who lived out his days as the Goddess's servant at the temple dedicated to Sāralā at Chattiā in Cuttack district in Orissa. As a *śākta*, Sāralā Dāsa elaborates a highly female-oriented perspective. Two other texts, the Adhbhuta Rāmāyaṇa and the Bilaṇka Rāmāyaṇa, are also attributed to him. In the latter, as befits a devotee of the Goddess, he portrays Sītā as assuming the blindingly radiant form of Mahādevī and killing the thousand-headed demon Rāvaṇa while her fearful husband, Rāma, stands by helplessly in the shadows and watches (see Mishra 1980; Banerjee 1986).

9. Bhañja is a medieval Oriya poet who belonged to the ruling family of Mayurbhañj in northeastern Orissa.

10. A caste of cultivators, locally ranked as a "clean caste."

Chapter 3

Ambiguous and Definitive

The Greatness of Goddess Vaiṣṇo Devī

Mark Edwin Rohe

> The abode of Trikta Devī, who is also called Baishno Devī,[1] is situated near Hansal on the top of a mountain difficult of access within a watery cave, and people go on its pilgrimage with lighted candles and lamps. Every year crowds of people come here in parties and groups from far and wide, beating drums and cymbals, and go dancing and singing praises of the Devī. The ringleader is called sant.
>
> According to the belief of most of the Hindus "Devī" is the name of the omnipotent divine power, and according to some it is the manifestation of essence/principle, the primal unity which is capable of creating bodies at the behest of the Almighty. Some say it is the aggregate of the potential of all the gods. But God knows the truth.
>
> —Charak, *Ganeshdas Badehra's Rajdarshani*

The cave shrine of goddess Vaiṣṇo Devī lies nearly six thousand feet up at the end of a nine mile path on Trikuta, a three-peaked mountain located in the Jammu region of the state of Jammu and Kashmir. Ganeshdas Badehra, author of the royal chronicle Rājdarśanī (compiled in 1847 C.E. for the Dogra king, Mahāraj Gulab Singh), attributes the above description of Vaiṣṇo Devī to the time of Raja Jas Dev, who succeeded to the throne of Jammu in 996 C.E. If the reference is accurate,

This paper is based on dissertation research in India in 1989–1991. Research was supported by Fulbright-Hays and the American Institute of Indian Studies. The basic ideas of this essay were first presented at the Twenty-First Annual Conference on South Asia in Madison, Wisconsin, November 1992.

then Vaiṣṇo Devī was already being visited by pilgrims coming "from far and wide" as much as a thousand years ago. No matter what the historical reality, however, the cave shrine of Vaiṣṇo Devī has emerged today as one of the most important pilgrimage sites in all of North India.

In an important sense, Vaiṣṇo Devī is both a place and a goddess. The cave shrine in Jammu arguably *is* Vaiṣṇo Devī, for it is here that she becomes accessible to pilgrims both day and night as a living presence, physically manifest in three natural *piṇḍis* or rounded stones, residing in a home that is said to be eternal and of her own making. As a deity, Vaiṣṇo Devī transcends the particular place where she is enshrined. She is widely believed to be an ascetic, vegetarian, virgin goddess (*kanyā*), although—like all Hindu goddesses—she is also called "mother." Devotees also speak of Vaiṣṇo Devī as the all-inclusive, all-powerful goddess superior to any other deity, identifying her as Mahādevī, the great goddess incarnate.

While her location is marked with great specificity, Vaiṣṇo Devī's identity and nature are ambiguous and subject to varied interpretation. This ambiguity in some ways typifies the problem of identifying Mahādevī in popular usage. The Devī-Māhātmya asserts that the one reality of the universe is *the* Devī: her oneness is paramount; her manyness is endlessly nuanced. Her multiplicity and singularity coexist not only in her forms, but also in the singular integrity of the *śakti* who she is, even as that *śakti* takes on the particularities of specific works (Coburn 1996). The paradigm of Mahādevī's manyness and oneness is visible in the manyness and oneness of Vaiṣṇo Devī, made possible through the ambiguity of Vaiṣṇo Devī's nature contrasted with the specificity of her location. From one viewpoint, particular manifestations of Mahādevī are always partial, but a specific form may be elevated by devotees as the highest goddess, with all other goddesses seen as derivative (Kinsley 1986, 132). In her ambiguity, with her particular characteristics, Vaiṣṇo Devī tends to be elevated to such supreme status.

Authoritative descriptions of Mahādevī are located in texts such as the Devī-Māhātmya, the Devī-Bhāgavata Purāṇa, and the Mārkaṇḍeya Purāṇa. But there is no single, authoritative source of knowledge concerning Vaiṣṇo Devī, for no particular text is recognized as indisputable when it comes to her particular form, identity, and origin. Rather, information about her nature is diffused largely into matters of opinion, both personal and shared, and into the various public representations of her that are motivated by devotional and economic considerations. Personal and institutional interests in devotion and worldly needs, government and politics, business, tourism, and supporting technologies also converge in the pilgrimage to Vaiṣṇo Devī. Word of mouth, transportation technology, an efficient administration, and the increasing presentation and availability of information and images of Vaiṣṇo Devī have all contributed to the increasing popularity and positive reputation of both the goddess and her pilgrimage. Vaiṣṇo Devī's social presence in north India is readily encountered in texts, songs, pictures, statues, temples, movies, newspaper and magazine articles, tourist advertisements, billboards advertising all night devotional sessions (*jāgaraṇs)*, religious discourses, devotional activities, and holy persons believed to embody her.[2] For her devotees, she is also accessible in subtler forms as feelings, visions, and the boons that she bestows upon the faithful. The ambiguous nature of her identity functions as an asset that permits the individual devotee to enter into a meaningful relationship with her regardless of that devotee's own devotional preferences. In this regard, Vaiṣṇo Devī serendipitously incorporates many identities and powers, illustrating Mahādevī's singular-but-multiple nature.

The Pilgrimage

The Vaiṣṇo Devī cave shrine, also known in the past as Tarkota, Traikakud, Trikata, or Trikta Devī, has been a sacred place for local people—primarily Rajputs and Brahmins—for perhaps a thousand years; for Panjabis, at least a few hundred. In recent times the annual number of visitors, mostly urban in origin, has reached five million. A number of Dogra kings of Jammu have been associated with Vaiṣṇo Devī. The most important patron was Maharaj Gulab Singh who was appointed *rājā* of Jammu by Ranjit Singh, the Sikh ruler of Lahore, in 1822. When the Lahore court fell to the British in 1846, Gulab Singh paid to the victors a part of the war indemnity they demanded from Lahore. In exchange, Gulab Singh was given control of Kashmir and other territories. To support Hinduism in his enlarged kingdom, he founded an organization, eventually named "The Dharmarth Trust," to build and manage temples, schools, *dharmśālās* and charitable institutions. Its sole trustee is Dr. Karan Singh, the current successor to Gulab Singh's lineage. Although Vaiṣṇo Devī was formally placed under the management of The Dharmarth Trust by Gulab Singh, in practice, control of the shrine was held by local Brahmin and Thakur families known as the *bārīdārs*. The *bārīdārs* did not have a good reputation with pilgrims.

At the end of August 1986, when Jammu and Kashmir was under emergency governor's rule, Governor Shri Jagmohan initiated the Shri Mata Vaishno Devī Shrine Act, forcefully taking complete control of the shrine and its properties from the *bārīdārs* and from the Dharmarth

Trust. Very rapidly, Jagmohan transformed the pilgrimage from a physically difficult and dangerous path managed on the basis of greed into what appears to be currently one of the most efficiently run temples in all of India.

The climb up to Vaiṣṇo Devī's cave shrine is not easy, despite superb maintenance of the path and the ready availability of food and drink, as well as lavatory and rest facilities. Trains go as far as Jammu City, and most pilgrims rely on a bus or automobile to get them to the town of Katra at the base of Trikuta mountain. Katra is on a plateau about two thousand feet high in elevation and lies about thirty-five miles north of the city of Jammu. The Chenab River and the Pakistan border are visible at only about twenty miles distance. The Pir Panjal mountains separate Jammu from the Kashmir valley. Arriving at Katra, pilgrims proceed directly to the footpath up the mountain after obtaining a *parcī,* or ticket, from the Shrine Board. The *parcī* controls pilgrims' access to both the path and the cave itself so that the crowds overwhelm neither and everyone has an equal chance at getting *darśan* within the cave.

Walking the route up usually takes between four and six hours, although many people take longer, stopping midway overnight at the temple named "Adi Kumari" (primal maiden). Here there is also a tunnel-like cave named "Garbh Joon" (womb-vagina) through which pilgrims squeeze as a sign of their faith and sinlessness. Pilgrims freely interact with one another on the path, singing and shouting the refrain "*Jai Mātā Dī!*" (Victory to the Mother!). There are spectacular views and cool forests all along the way. Eventually, pilgrims reach the main temple complex nestled within a small valley. Here are located administrative buildings, *dharmśālās,* a bank, restaurants, stores that sell offerings, book stalls, souvenir shops, a Shri Ram temple, a medical office, bathing areas, and a lending depot for free blankets. A line usually forms for pilgrims entering the cave.

A pilgrim entering the ancient cave must squeeze through a narrow opening over a smooth boulder that is considered to be the petrified, headless body of Bhairo, a *sādhu* whom the goddess is said to have killed after he pursued her up the mountain. His "head" is preserved in a temple on a ridge a mile distant. Past the boulder, a pilgrim can stand only at an angle in the ankle-to-calf-deep stream, the Charan Ganga, which flows from the covered base of the *piṇḍis*. Proceeding forward in the stream for about one hundred feet and after a few turns and steps, the pilgrim stands in front of a platform where priests are seated. Ahead and to the right is the goddess herself, who is *svayambhū* (self-manifest) as three stone *piṇḍis,* which are surrounded by other small images. The three *piṇḍis* at Vaiṣṇo Devī are usually described by the priests as the goddesses, Mahāsaraswatī, Mahālakṣmī and Mahākālī.[3] It is here that pilgrims have their most heartfelt experiences. It is here, too, where confusion over Vaiṣṇo Devī's identity often begins.

Who Is Vaiṣṇo Devī?

Ambiguity and even confusion over the identity of Vaiṣṇo Devī are apparent in the many ways people define her in association with preexisting cosmologies. To a lesser extent there is some confusion in how people variously define the *piṇḍis* that constitute the primary *darśan* of Vaiṣṇo Devī. Existing stories vary in content and in general circulation.[4] The two most common stories are about Vaiṣṇo Devī's birth and appearance to local people at Trikuta, and even among these two, there are variations in different texts and in recountings by devotees. Nonetheless her primary attributes and role as a divine incarnation are to a degree delineated in the first type of story, and the second type locates her residence at Trikuta Mountain. The second story explains how she came to be known to local people, how the path up the mountain and the sites of its major temples came to be, and how her shrine came under the care of a lineage of local Brahmins. These stories plus her representation as Śeraṇwālī provide some of the bases for variant interpretations that in the aggregate give Vaiṣṇo Devī a variable identity. I present brief versions of these two most common stories below as a background against which to compare other interpretations.

The Origin of Vaiṣṇo Devī

> It is said that long ago in Treta Yuga, demons were destroying *dharma* on earth, so the three *devīs*—Mahāsaraswatī, Mahālakṣmī and Mahākālī—combined their power or *tejas* and formed a young girl, whom they named Vaiṣṇavī. They told her that her work was to protect *dharma,* and they sent her to take birth in south India and to do *tapas* on the seashore in order to gain as her husband Lord Viṣṇu, who was at that time incarnated as Lord Rāma. Rāma met her on the way to Lanka and told her he would marry her—even though he was already married to Sītā—if Vaiṣṇavī recognized him the next time he came to her. He returned later as an old *sādhu* whom she, of course, did not recognize as Rāma. He then promised her that she would be his *śakti* at a future time when he returns as Kalkī Avatār at the end of Kali Yuga. He also told her

to go to the holy cave in Trikuta Mountain and continue her *tapas* until his return. Rāma then sent Hanumān to accompany her.

The Appearance of Vaiṣṇo Devī to Shri Dhar

About nine hundred years ago Vaiṣṇo Devī appeared in the form of a young girl and commanded a Brahmin named Shri Dhar from the village Hansali (next to present day Katra) to hold a feast (*bhanḍārā*) for local people at the nearby Bhumika stream. At the time of the feast, Bhairo, a disciple of Gorakh Nath,[5] appeared and demanded meat and liquor. But Vaiṣṇo Devī told him he would get only vegetarian food, since this was a Brahmin's feast. Seeing her, Bhairo lusted after her. To escape him, she ran away, stopping at various places on the trail up Trikuta mountain. These places are now known as Banganga, Charan Paduka, Adi Kumari—the place where she is said to have remained for nine months in a cave—and finally Bhavan, the cave that is now known as her home. There, taking the form of Cāmuṇḍā (a form of Kālī), she beheaded Bhairo. His body fell at the entrance to the cave, and his head landed further up the mountain at a place where a Bhairo temple is now located. Bhairo then repented, and the goddess granted him future salvation. In so doing, however, she laid down the condition that unless pilgrims coming for her *darśan* did not also get his *darśan*—that is, *darśan* of his head—their pilgrimage would not be fruitful. Shri Dhar began doing *pūjā* to the *piṇḍis* at the cave, and his descendants continue to do so even today.

The common story of Vaiṣṇo Devī's origin is the foundation for identifying the *piṇḍis* in her cave as the goddesses Mahāsaraswatī, Mahālakṣmī and Mahākālī, who together were the source of Vaiṣṇo Devī. But there is considerable variation in publications and in personal opinions over just which set of goddesses or gods created Vaiṣṇo Devī and just which *piṇḍi* is which goddess. Vaiṣṇo Devī is variously described as a coalescence of the *tejas* (power) of some combination of Saraswatī, Lakṣmī, Kālī, Gāyatrī, Sāvitrī, Pārvatī and other goddesses. Or she is described as formed from the *tejas* of Brahmā, Viṣṇu and Śiva just like Mahiṣāsuramardinī, the goddess who slays the demon Mahiṣāsura in the Devī-Māhātmya. One author (Nargis 1967) even writes a story that the three goddesses Mahāsaraswatī, Mahālakṣmī and Mahākālī chanted a *mantra* and created Vaiṣṇo Devī. Thus, pilgrims were at times confused over who they were seeing when they received *darśan*. I have heard devotees say that actually one gets *darśan* of Mahāsaraswatī, Mahālakṣmī and Mahākālī but that Vaiṣṇo Devī herself is not the *piṇḍis*, and that Vaiṣṇo Devī lives somewhere "around" the cave and does her *tapas* there unseen. Or that Vaiṣṇo Devī is actually the unseen form (*svarūp*) of the three. Some devotees think that the *piṇḍis* are the very body of Vaiṣṇo Devī, who resides there doing difficult *tapas*. Some versions of the origin story above support the assertion that she is not the *piṇḍis* because Saraswatī, Lakṣmī, and Kālī were already in the cave before Vaiṣṇo Devī arrived. The priests will often say that the *piṇḍis* are the three faces (*mũh*) of Vaiṣṇo Devī, who is the totality of the three, or that the middle *piṇḍi* is Mahālakṣmī, who is Vaiṣṇo Devī, or even that the middle *piṇḍi* is the goddess Durgā. An ex-priest once told me that interpreting the *piṇḍis* and other forms in the cave is really a matter of "whatever you like."

Many pilgrims I spoke with were confused about the nature of the *piṇḍis*, wanting to know which one, if any, specifically is Vaiṣṇo Devī so that they might look upon her and she might look upon them. When large crowds of pilgrims are present, they are rushed single file through the two artificial tunnels as quickly as possible, so they hardly have time to absorb what they are seeing and do not gain the experience of the natural cave. Given that up to twenty thousand pilgrims pass through the cave each day, the average *darśan* lasts only about four seconds.[6] A Kashmiri pilgrim told me, "I looked down to see where to put my feet. The priest said 'Vaiṣṇo Mātā! Go!' And I was rushed out." A pilgrim from New Delhi put it this way:

> No one understands where the *piṇḍi*s are. [We hear] only "Vaiṣṇo Mātā"—push! "Vaiṣṇo Mātā"—push! After coming out of the cave friends ask each other, "Where is the *piṇḍi* of Mā Vaiṣṇo?" Some laugh and some get angry over this system of *darśan*.

Darśan consists not only of seeing the deity, but of being seen by the deity, too, creating an open channel for requests and blessings to flow. But the *piṇḍis* are aniconic; there is no anthropomorphic representation of the Goddess with eyes to look at the pilgrims, nor are any eyes painted on the *piṇḍis* as at some other temples, such as the temple of Vajreśwarī Devī in Himachal Pradesh. To partially compensate for the lack of mutual visual contact, pilgrims' desire for the Goddess's personal attention is extended into the idea that no pilgrim can come to the *piṇḍis* without having received her personal "call." Pilgrims readily give examples of their own or others' fruitless efforts to come to Vaiṣṇo Devī; it is only if and when she wishes to see you, they say, that one is actually able to enter the cave. Others tell of how they were apparently whisked away to the cave by Vaiṣṇo Devī. An office clerk in New Delhi told me the following:

> Once I was sitting in my house after work watching television when suddenly I just felt I had to go. I felt the Mother was calling me! I jumped up and ran out of the house in my bare feet. "I'm going to Vaiṣṇo Devī!" I yelled to my wife, and went straight to the train station.

Pilgrims to Vaiṣṇo Devī can find evidence of her constant awareness of them in a well-known story. It is said that some teenage boys were approaching Sanjhi Chat, the last main stop on the path before the Bhavan, when instead of chanting *"Jai Mātā Dī!"* (Victory to the Mother!), they mischievously shouted *"Jai Pitā Dī!"* (Victory to the Father!). Out of a clear blue sky, lightening struck them dead.[7] Pilgrims' desire for *darśan* is even extended to Trikuta Mountain itself, which pilgrims describe as having its own pull upon them, and one gets the impression that the entire physical and emotional journey is one big experience of *darśan*, increasing in focused intensity until finally culminating in the cave in front of the *piṇḍis*. Pilgrims report that while inside the cave they completely forget the rest of the world, remaining absorbed in concentration on the cave, the stream, the *piṇḍis*, and the experience of being in Vaiṣṇo Devī's presence. The *darśan* of Vaiṣṇo Devī is an experience for some of oneness where there is only the relationship of the devotee and the goddess.

Of the three main Hindu sectarian orientations—Vaiṣṇava, Śaiva, and Śākta—only Śākta devotion promotes a single, Great Goddess, standing alone, as the highest creator. Vaiṣṇavas subordinate the Goddess, known in such contexts as Lakṣmī or Śrī, but with other forms as well, to Viṣṇu, their first-ranking god; Śaivas subordinate the Goddess—known in such contexts as Umā, Pārvatī, Gaurī, and so forth—to Śiva, even though they acknowledge her to be Śiva's essential complement in the creation and maintenance of the cosmos (Śiva-Śakti).[8] Different people incorporate sectarian variations of the Goddess's identity into their descriptions of Vaiṣṇo Devī, although they might not profess exclusive adherence to any of the three main devotional orientations.

Vaiṣṇo Devī is associated with Vaiṣṇava or Śaiva worship via her identifications with goddesses normally connected with Viṣṇu or Śiva.[9] Because both Vaiṣṇo Devī and Durgā are *triguṇā* (possessing the three qualities of *sattva*, *rajas*, and *tamas* and thus capable of creation, preservation, and destruction), Vaiṣṇo Devī is also said to be a form of Durgā. In books on Vaiṣṇo Devī, passages culled from Purāṇic, Vedic, or Śākta texts that refer to the creation of a goddess from the *tejas* or power of other deities become potential resources for inventing a Shastric lineage for her, as are all references to the name Vaiṣnavī and references to any goddess said to be *triguṇā,* such as Triklā Devī and Durgā.

Pilgrims identify Vaiṣṇo Devī with Durgā—whom Panjabis (and others) also name Śeraṇwālī, "the Lion-rider"—more than with any other goddess. Popular posters of Vaiṣṇo Devī produced by S. S. Brijbasi and Sons, Jain and Company, and others have been available since at least the 1950s; they all depict Vaiṣṇo Devī in anthropomorphic form as a young woman dressed in a mostly red sari, wearing a crown, and riding a lion or tiger. She usually is depicted as having eight arms, although she sometimes is portrayed with four or eighteen arms; in these she holds an assortment of weapons—a sword, trident, discus, club, and bow—as well as a lotus and conch. One of her right hands is raised in a "fear not" or blessing *mudrā*. This form is readily identified as Durgā. Furthermore, many Hindus that I have met have asserted or have agreed that Vaiṣṇo Devī is a form of Durgā. Often it has been pointed out to me that Vaiṣṇavī is one of the one hundred and eight names of Durgā. Indeed, Vaiṣṇo Devī's human form is so strongly identified with Durgā-Śeraṇwālī that any other representation is suspect.

At the Mansā Devī temple in Haridwar, for example, the most famous wealthy devotee of Vaiṣṇo Devī, the late Gulshan Kumar, had a "Vaiṣṇavī temple" constructed.[10] The icon for this temple was sculpted according to the description of Vaiṣṇavī in the Devī-Mahātmya, that is, with four arms and with Garuḍa portrayed as her vehicle. When I was visiting this temple, the management announced that the "Vaiṣṇo Devī" temple was about to open. People went eagerly inside, stared at the image, and exclaimed, "Who's that? That's not Vaiṣṇo Devī!" The priest defended the icon to visitors by quoting the Devī-Māhātmya, but to no avail: this was simply not Vaiṣṇo Devī as many devotees know her to be represented.

Since Durgā is usually associated with Śiva (Kinsley 1986), I found this equation of Vaiṣṇo Devī with Durgā puzzling; her most common origin story (recounted above) associates Vaiṣṇo Devī with Viṣṇu (as Rāma). One Śaiva priest answered the question of Vaiṣṇo Devī's identity saying, "She is Śakti. There is only Śiva and Śakti; who else could she be?" But I also continued to meet both Śaivas and Vaiṣṇavas who stated emphatically that Durgā and Vaiṣṇo Devī are "completely different."[11] I was told, for example, that "Durgā is a great demon killer. Vaiṣṇo Devī is Lakṣmī who is a giver of wealth, she is not such a great *śakti.*" I was also told that "Durgā has nine forms. Vaiṣṇavī is Lakṣmī and rides Garuḍa; she gives wealth. Durgā rides a lion." Differing opinions often only became apparent among devotees upon my asking questions. For instance, when interviewing two pilgrims at the Vaiṣṇo Devī Bhavan, pilgrims who had come together to Vaiṣṇo Devī many times, I remarked that some devotees insist that Vaiṣṇo Devī is a form of Durgā. One pilgrim responded, "Yes, she is Durgā." The other looked at him in disbelief and cried out, "What are you saying? Durgā is one thing; Vaiṣṇo Devī is Vaiṣṇo Devī!" Several times I encountered informants who were scornful about equating Vaiṣṇo Devī with Durgā and who told me that people claiming such things are not "properly initiated" into Hinduism, or that "they don't really know anything; they don't go into the background." A Vaiṣṇava *sādhu* who serves as the ritual officiant *(pujārī)* at a Viṣṇu temple in Almorah, Uttar Pradesh, and who had visited the Vaiṣṇo Devī shrine during the 1940s, laughed when I told him that Vaiṣṇo Devī is depicted in the form of Durgā. He insisted that properly speaking, she looks more like Lakṣmī, and her vehicle is Garuḍa. Yet another devotee from New Delhi negated the importance of any differentiation, telling me, "You can go into all those details, but no one really cares for that." Several resident *sādhus* in Katra told me that in fact, no one knows her true story.

I found only one reference to Vaiṣṇo Devī as a Tantric goddess that also connects her with Durgā. Baljinnath Pandit (1983) places her in traditions of Kashmiri Śaiva and Śākta *āgamik sādhana* or "secret practices" as an aspect of Durgā, who is depicted as the "perfect" incarnation *(avatāra)* of the highest Śaiva goddess, Parmeśvarī Śakti. The author of this treatise cites as proof the fact that across from the *piṇḍis* in the cave of Vaiṣṇo Devī in a hidden crevice is a small stalagmite referred to as a Śiva *liṅga*. He defined Vaiṣṇo Devī as the power in the service of Śiva that creates multiple Viṣṇus and is above Lakṣmī.

Satī, a consort of Śiva, is frequently identified with Pārvatī, who is also identified with Durgā. The story of Satī's self-immolation and subsequent division of her body is well known. Most of the other major goddess temples in the north are said to be *śakti pīṭh*s, "seats" of the Goddess imbued with Her energy, with each having a particular part of Satī's body (see Erndl 1993). Jwālāmukhī is her tongue, Nainā Devī is her eyes, Mansā Devī her forehead, Cintapūrnī her feet, Vajreśwarī her breast, and so on. At each of these temples there is a material form identified as the body part, either simple stone icons, rock formations or at Jwālāmukhī, natural gas flames. The *piṇḍis* at Vaiṣṇo Devī prompt pilgrims, priests, and authors of books either to include or exclude the *piṇḍis* as one of Satī's *śakti pīṭh*s. Different sources claim in turn that Vaiṣṇo Devī is Satī's arms (Prasad n.d.a), backbone (Kaviraj Badrinath of Painthal), full body (Manager of Jhaṇḍewālī Mātā Mandir, Delhi), or head, placed in the cave by Śiva (Shastri 1976). At Jwālāmukhī temple in Himachal Pradesh, the Gorakh Nath *sādhus*, who manage an upper floor of the temple, have depicted the *śakti pīṭhs* in paintings on the interior walls. According to their paintings and statements, Vaiṣṇo Devī is located where Satī's breast fell, a claim that was also repeated to me by a few pilgrims.

One compendium of descriptions of pilgrimage sites repeats "old folklore" that it was actually Vaiṣṇo Devī who was born as Satī. The story is that Satī became curious about Lord Rāma and took the form of Sītā to observe him, but Rāma immediately knew who she was. Śiva found out what Satī had done and became enraged that she had any interest in another male. Satī then performed terrible penances to gain Śiva back. Eventually she became Pārvatī, and it is said that she still continues to perform *tapas* at the cave of Trikuta (Rajiv 1988). I also heard the same story recounted in connection with another cave shrine in Jammu, Śiv Khoṛī.[12] Some elder residents of Katra who claimed that Vaiṣṇo Devī was in fact Pārvatī had been told this by their parents.

A variation of the story concerning Satī's dismemberment was told to me by a Joint Secretary of the Ministry of Education, who was from Bengal. The story he heard was that Bhairo had chased Satī from Assam across the Himalaya to Trikuta, cutting her with his sword as he chased her. Her body parts fell at different places (which comprise the *śakti pīṭhs*) until finally at Trikuta, Satī again took her full form and killed Bhairo. Vaiṣṇo Devī is thus the full form of Satī. Some authors have noted that in the list of *śakti pīṭhs* found in various Purāṇas, Vaiṣṇavī is listed as in the "middle of the mothers," a phrase usually understood to mean that she is included as one of the "seven mothers" (*saptamātrika*). One source, however, interprets the claim that she is in the "middle of the mothers" to mean that she lies between the *piṇḍis* of Saraswatī and Kālī at the Bhavan (*Śrī Vaiṣṇo Devī kī Sampūrṇ Kahānī,* 5). There are many ways, therefore, that devotees argue for Vaiṣṇo Devī's inclusion in the lists of *śakti pīṭhs*.

Different sources construct Vaiṣṇo Devī's identity in still other ways as well. Not everyone agrees that Vaiṣṇo Devī is a *śakti pīṭh* of Satī. Others claim that Vaiṣṇo Devī is instead a *prasiddh pīṭh,* a renowned place, or a *siddh pīṭh,* a seat of supernatural powers. A *siddh pīṭh* is a place made powerful by the *tapas* of an ascetic—in this case understood to be Vaiṣṇo Devī herself—or a place discovered to be powerful when some ascetic performed *tapas* at the place. In fact one can purchase souvenir photo sets that contain photos of "Mātā's ten *siddh-pīṭhs*" including Vaiṣṇo Devī, Pārvatī Pīṭh (the ice form at

Amarnāth in Kashmir), and other goddesses of Jammu, Himachal Pradesh and Haridwar.

Both textual sources and devotees often cite the main goddess temples of Himachal Pradesh as *śakti pīṭhs* and may also refer to them as the "seven sisters." The standard list of these sisters includes Jwālāmukhī, Cintapūrnī, Camuṇḍā, Vajreśwarī, Śākumbharī, and Nainā; either Bhadra Kālī, Kālikā of Simla, Caṇḍī of Chandigarh, or Vaiṣṇo Devī is named the seventh and "eldest" sister. The idea of seven sisters is probably based on the *saptamātrika*, the seven Mothers (e.g., Brahmānī, Māheśvarī, Kaumārī, Vaiṣṇavī, Vārāhī, Indrāṇī, and Cāmuṇḍa) or the *sapta puri*, seven sacred cities (Ayodhya, Mathura, Haridwar, Kashi, Kanchi, Ujjain, and Dwarika). But in Jammu and Kashmir there used to exist a tradition of five sisters which, according to one informant (Professor Y. B. Singh of Jammu University) included Vaiṣṇo Devī, Kālī (Bahu Fort, Jammu), Sukrālā Devī and Khīr Bhavānī. Some of the current booklets available in markets group the eight goddesses prevalent in Himachal Pradesh with Vaiṣṇo Devī, referring to them as the nine *darbars* (courts), the nine goddesses of power, or even the nine Durgās. Pilgrims that I spoke with cited a wide variety of goddesses in such sets of seven and nine, including the goddess Kālī in Calcutta, Kāmākśī in Assam, Kālīkā and Yog Māyā of New Delhi, Mahālakṣmī and Mumba Devī of Bombay, and Kanyākumārī at the southern tip of India. By including Vaiṣṇo Devī among preexisting orders of goddesses, all of these varied claims accord her an identity much broader than that of a merely local goddess and suggest that her status is commensurate with the status of these other, well-known goddesses. In this vein, a group of teenage pilgrims that I spoke with transformed Vaiṣṇo Devī into one of the four *dhāms* of India, which they listed as Badrīnāth, Kedārnāth, Amarnāth and Vaiṣṇo Devī.

Vaiṣṇo Devī's name is frequently transformed into Sanskrit as Vaiṣṇavī, "the *śakti* of Viṣṇu," and she is thereby associated or equated with goddesses associated with Viṣṇu, especially Lakṣmī. However, some devotees used the name Vaiṣṇavī when describing her as the highest deity. Vaiṣṇo Devī is also linked to Viṣṇu through her acceptance of only vegetarian offerings, a predominantly Vaiṣṇava practice. The very terms "Vaiṣṇo" and "Vaiṣṇav" in the northwest refer to vegetarian food.

Because Vaiṣṇo Devī is said to be engaged to Lord Rāma (specifically to Viṣṇu's future *avatār*, Kalkī), some devotees argue that she is a form of Sītā. One source claims, "Bhagavatī Vaiṣṇavī was born from a part of Sītā, therefore she is the very form of Mahālakṣmī" (Sharma n.d.). Other sources claim instead that Sītā was a part of Vaiṣṇo Devī (Pt J. C. Giri, Daryaganj). The *pujārī* at the Vaiṣṇo Devī temple at Deva

Mai told me the story that Sītā, enraged that the demon Sahasrār Bahu had vanquished Rāma's army, took the form of Kālī and defeated him. Only Śiva himself could calm her by casting himself under her feet.[13] When she calmed down, she went to Trikuta mountain to do *tapas*. Therefore Vaiṣṇo Devī is Sītā, who also took the form of Kālī.

There is evidence that the story of Vaiṣṇo Devī's association with Rāma dates from at least the nineteenth century. Professor Shiv Nirmohi summarizes in *Duggar ke Devsthān* (1988) a number of books on Vaiṣṇo Devī including *Śrī Vaiṣṇavī Pīṭh* (no date) by Shri Kaka Ram Shastri. *Śrī Vaiṣṇavī Pīṭh,* wrote the professor, is a revised edition of a book published in Maharaja Ranbir Singh's time (1830–1885) and thus would be the oldest book on Vaiṣṇo Devī of which I am aware. Shri Kaka Ram Shastri defined Vaiṣṇo Devī's current incarnation as a partial *avatāra* of Sītā and thus put her directly in association with Viṣṇu and his incarnation, Rāma.

Those who emphasized Vaiṣṇo Devī's relation to Viṣṇu usually equated her with Lakṣmī, Nārāyaṇī, or Viṣṇu-Māyā. One source, for example, asserts the following:

> According to the Mārkaṇḍeya and Barāha Purāṇā this goddess (*devī*) who has many names is Vaiṣṇavī who is Viṣṇu Māyā. She is a devotee of Viṣṇu, the female form (*rūpwālī*) of Viṣṇu, and Viṣṇu's own form as *śakti* (*śaktisvarūp*). As Viṣṇu's *māyā,* she looks after the welfare of the world. (Shastri 1991)

Devotees made similar statements: "Vaiṣṇavī is another name for Lakṣmī, or Mahālakṣmī who is a form of Vaiṣṇo Devī"; "She is Mahālakṣmī in the form of a maiden (*kanyā*)"; "It is generally known that she, the goddess Vaiṣṇo Devī, is the goddess of *dharma,* and she has taken the *avatāra* of Mahālakṣmī." Many pilgrims I spoke to from Bombay also identified Vaiṣṇo Devī as Lakṣmī, equating her with the Mahālakṣmī of the famous temple there. Some even told me that the Bombay temple, like Vaiṣṇo Devī, also had three *piṇḍis* (actually there are three icons). In Katra itself, there is a temple dedicated to Lakṣmī in the "Old Serai" of The Dharmarth Trust, and the priestess there also equated Lakṣmī with Vaiṣṇo Devī.

Vaiṣṇo Devī's *triguṇā* nature is the basis for devotees' claims that she can give you whatever you want: knowledge, wealth, power, or even *mokṣa,* the granting of which was characterized by a few pundits as Vaiṣṇo Devī's special power. One pundit at the Bhavan, Prem Nath, said while delivering a discourse to pilgrims that although everything is available from her, most pilgrims approach Vaiṣṇo Devī as Lakṣmī, a giver of wealth, and forget about Saraswatī and Kālī. In a sense,

Vaiṣṇo Devī is a popularization of the attributes of Lakṣmī. Delhi markets sell Diwali festival images of Lakṣmī and Gaṇeśa for the purpose of eliciting success in business, but in the last few decades, images that depict Vaiṣṇo Devī and Gaṇeśa have also become available. That Vaiṣṇo Devī has the reputation of giving wealth is reflected in one Indian scholar's description of her as "the goddess of the nouveau riche." As one straightforward pilgrim told me, "We ask Mātā for peace. In this age peace means money, so we ask her for money."

The Devī-Māhātmya provides support for both those who say Vaiṣṇo Devī is Durgā and those who say she is Vaiṣṇavī or Lakṣmī. In the Devī-Māhātmya, Mahiṣāsuramardinī is created from the *tejas* of the gods, especially Brahmā, Viṣṇu, and Śiva. Most people that I spoke with identified Mahiṣāsuramardinī as Durgā. Some also claimed that after she is created, Durgā, who is identified as Vaiṣṇo Devī, then went to Trikuta Mountain, made three *piṇḍis* (Ādikumārī, Ādiśakti, and Parāśakti) and performed *tapas* there both before and after killing the demon Mahiṣāsura (Srivastav 1988). Others claimed instead that Mahiṣāsuramardinī is actually Nārāyaṇī or Viṣṇu-Māyā, who is Mahālakṣmī, who is Vaiṣṇo Devī. B. K. Shastri (1991), for example, cites the fifth verse of chapter five of the Devī-Māhātmya as proof (as per Coburn 1991): "Having made up their minds, the gods went to the Himālaya, lord of mountains. They then praised there the Goddess who is Viṣṇu's *māyā*." Shastri goes on to say that it was, in fact, Vaiṣṇo Devī who killed Mahiṣāsura at her cave, and that it is really his body that lies petrified at the entrance.[14] Prasad (n.d.b.) says that Durgā is the goddess who defeated the demon Durgam and is thus not Mahiṣāsuramardinī.

The ambiguous nature of Vaiṣṇo Devī's identity is further evident in the seemingly paradoxical claim that she is both a virgin girl and a mother. As per her common origin story, Vaiṣṇo Devī is defined as an immortal goddess who is both *kanyā*[15] (usually a prepubescent, premenstrual virgin) and ascetic, but her devotees also address her as "Mātā" or "Mā." Such a characterization might appear self-contradictory: how can a goddess who is a *kanyā* and is called Ādikumārī (primal maiden or virgin) also be a mother? Vaiṣṇo Devī's form as a young girl represents her status as a maiden "engaged" to marry Viṣṇu's Kalkī Avatār at the end of Kali Yuga. Indeed, vegetarianism and asceticism are also appropriate to this form in the sense that vegetarian offerings are asexual offerings, relative to blood sacrifices, and asceticism is a state of minimal transaction homologous to virginity. That is to say, blood sacrifices, which are flesh foods for deities, are considered to promote passions, including sexuality; vegetarian offerings and foods are considered to be conducive to the control of passions. Both asceticism and virginity share in the ideal of the preservation of the integrity of the body, which includes practicing celibacy and minimizing transactions with the opposite gender. The spilling of blood is sometimes considered to be equivalent to copulation and thus inappropriate for the maintenance of virginity (e.g., O'Flaherty 1980).[16] This is why in most versions of her origin story it is not Vaiṣṇo Devī in *kanyā* form who kills Bhairo, but rather her virgin form is preserved by her momentarily changing into the form of Caṇḍī or Cāmuṇḍā, both forms of Kālī known for their destructive capabilities. Vaiṣṇo Devī is also known as a mother who does not minimize her transactions but rather accepts millions of people into her own home where she is thought to give freely of herself in the form of blessings. Her reputation as a nurturing mother is reified in a well-known story of a miracle that is said to have occurred at the cave about fifty years ago. According to this story, Vaiṣṇo Devī turned the Charan Ganga into a river of flowing milk for a few hours when no milk was available for nearby children or for the food shops serving pilgrims.

The contrast between mother and virgin seems to parallel or is homologous to the Vedic and Hindu idea of creation as complementary processes of dismemberment, release, or expansion, and reconstitution, retention, or contraction. In the Ṛg-Veda, one story of creation is that the world came about by the gods dismembering and distributing the parts of the original man, Puruṣa, whose parts thereby became the different parts of all creation (O'Flaherty 1988, 25–26). In the Brāhmaṇas, the deity Prajāpati performs great austerities, then releases all his accumulated energy, a kind of dismemberment, and his energy becomes the substance and life of the world. Vedic fire sacrifices were aimed toward regathering Prajāpati's dispersed energy in order to replenish him and thereby insure further creation (Kinsley 1986, 178). Such cycles of retention and release are paralleled in creation stories in the Purāṇās. For example, in the Viṣṇu Purāṇā, the universe is described as undergoing successive expansions (*vikāsa*) into all diverse, transitory forms followed by contractions (*sankośa*) back into that which is never destroyed. The Devī-Bhāgavata Purāṇa presents the Devī as the source and seed of such cycles (Kinsley 1986, 129). Likewise a similar image is presented in the Devī-Māhātmya where dozens of goddesses come out of the body of the goddess Mahiṣāsuramardinī and are again reabosorbed into her. The goddess is presented as both the unified source and the manifest diversity of differentiated powers. For goddesses, the premenstrual *kanyā* is that form which is undivided, both in retaining menstrual blood, which is sometimes considered to be a type of female seed, and in not having joined with a male.

A *kanyā* is primal, full of the potential of creation parallel to the undivided Puruṣa and ascetic Prajāpati. Vaiṣṇo Devī as *kanyā, ādikumārī* (primal maiden), and *ādiśakti* (primal power) embodies all the potentials of creation. Pt. Devraj of Dawa, Jammu, explained to me about Vaiṣṇo Devī: "We are born to someone, but she is not born to anyone. She is *ādiśakti;* who could be her mother?" It is in the form of "Mā" that the *śakti* of the goddess (the power which is herself) is continually divided from herself into the universe giving rise to everything. All beings in the universe, from a devotional viewpoint, are her "children," born from her. Structurally, it is as the ascetic *kanyā* that Vaiṣṇo Devī is the unlimited source of blessings. It is as "Mā" that she receives pilgrims' prayers and offerings and fulfills their desires.

Vaiṣṇo Devī's engagement to Viṣṇu also places her in an ambiguous position. In Hinduism, a girl usually goes from the control and protection of her parents to that of her husband under the assumption that an unmarried woman is easily subject to harm and is sexually seductive. But Vaiṣṇo Devī is neither under the control of a consort/husband, namely, Viṣṇu, nor under parental control, although Hanumān partially fulfills the role of a protector. Rather it is by her own *tapas,* her own power of self-control, that she keeps herself from engaging in sexual relations. Her *tapas*, her vegetarianism, and her geographic remoteness, even the coolness of the cave are all considered to be conducive to celibacy. She protects herself. The only time a lustful male—Bhairo—approached her, he died. In deference to Vaiṣṇo Devī's chastity, pilgrims generally adhere to at least temporary vows of celibacy, vegetarianism, and abstinence from alcohol during their pilgrimage in order to maintain an appropriate nonsexual state. Vaiṣṇo Devī is then a virgin, a mother (i.e., *the* Mother), but not quite a wife. The ambiguity of her marital status allows her to be independent and to be considered much gentler than most single goddesses residing in remote places.

Like Durgā and Triklā Devī, Vaiṣṇo Devī has a *triguṇā* nature that makes her all-powerful, and thus she is readily considered to be the highest of all goddesses, Mahādevī or Mahāśakti. In the booklet *Srī Vaiṣno Devī kī Sampūrṇ Kahāni,* Jwala Prasad (n.d.a., 25) writes about Vaiṣṇo Devī:

> Whenever conditions in the country become hostile, then Mahāśakti herself again and again assumes various forms and destroys the wicked and saves devotees. The amalgam of tejas from out of many devtas is the Mahāśakti who is born into time. She takes the forms of Mahākālī, Mahālakṣmī and Mahāsaraswatī—whose three forms are the signs of rajas, tamas, and sāttvik guṇas.

The Devī-Bhāgavata Purāṇa and the Devī-Māhātmya both identify Mahākālī, Mahālakṣmī, and Mahāsaraswatī as primary forms of the one Mahādevī (Brown 1990, chap. 5). As an amalgam of these three deities, Vaiṣṇo Devī is justifiably recognized as Mahādevī. Thus, for example, devotees assert that Vaiṣṇo Devī is the highest *ādiśakti* (primal power), *parāśakti* (highest power), *mūlaprakṛti* (foundation matter), *jaganmātā* (universal Mother), *sarvaśakti* (the complete power), and *ādikumārī* (primal maiden), independent and second to no other god. Such assertions of her primacy may still place her in association with Viṣṇu or Śiva, but when this occurs, the male deities are clearly understood to be subordinate to her. Hence, one hears statements like, "Vaiṣṇo Devī is not Viṣṇu's wife, but his mother" (Pt J. C. Giri, Shakti Mandir, Daryaganj) meaning that Viṣṇu is a subordinate power derived from Vaiṣṇo Devī and not her consort of either equal or superior status.

When informants describe Vaiṣṇo Devī as Mahādevī, they employ several metaphors, all of which suggest that on the highest level, the Goddess is immutable, beyond change, and greater than any of her particular forms. The most common metaphor I encountered echoed a characterization of India itself as "one country, many peoples;" in relation to the Goddess, this phrase becomes "One Devī, many forms." The fact that Hindus recognize and worship numerous goddesses is reduced to an issue of nomenclature: as one informant put it to me, "There she is called Vaiṣṇo Devī, here she is called Durgā, elsewhere she is called something else." Devotees also draw on variant kinship terms and their associated stages of life to explain Devī's many-in-one nature, claiming that just as a female may be daughter, sister, wife, and grandmother but she is still only one, the same is true of the Goddess. Some of the devotees that I spoke with invoked reincarnation, remarking that as one soul may take on several different personalities in a series of incarnations, so too does the Goddess take on particular births at different times and locations. The multiple incarnations (*avatāras*) of Viṣṇu and Śiva were also used as examples. All in all, she may have different names, forms, and functions across time and space, but she is still the same Goddess. A priest in Bombay whom I annoyed by asking about the relationships between goddesses told me that time and space are irrelevant to identity. He said to me, "Listen, you were in Jammu, then you were in Delhi, now you are here. But you are still you, right?"

Vaiṣṇo Devī is therefore identified as Durgā, Lakṣmī, Śeraṇwālī, Kālī, the One Mahādevī, or someone else. Her unique identity dissolves into and merges with various other deities' identities. Most of the people that I spoke with agreed, however, that there was really only one Vaiṣṇo Devī and that Vaiṣṇo Devī's cave in Trikuta mountain is her only genuine temple. They insist that there is only one distinctive place that is her true home.

Concluding Remarks

Mahādevī is abstracted and subtle in her oneness; her manifestations are individuated in particular temples, forms, and the experiences of devotees. In Vaiṣṇo Devī, Mahādevī's oneness is particularized in the manifest mountain, pilgrimage path, cave, and *piṇḍis*; her manyness is visible partially in the tripartite *piṇḍis* but more fully in the abstracted identities devotees construct. At her mountain cave, Vaiṣṇo Devī as a singular being is hidden from view as the trunk of the three *piṇḍis* is hidden under a silver plate. Only her forms as *piṇḍis* and small statues are visible. It seems that those who accept her as Mahādevī, or those who have identified some one of the *piṇḍis* as Vaiṣṇo Devī, understand the problem of recognizing her *darśan* among the many forms before them. The first problem of *darśan* is always recognition (*pahacān karnā*). Recognition makes possible realization. "If we recognize, we accept" (Suraj Singh, Shardha, Old Delhi, 24 February 1991). The solving of the problem of recognition, the ability to recognize the divine, the object of devotion, even in an unfamiliar form or substance is a large part of what makes the divine an imminently "empirical" reality in Hinduism. Sensible reality may be deceptive or ambiguous. Judgments must be made as to the reality behind the forms. Is that a stalagmite or Lord Śiva? Is that a river or Gāyatrī? Is an apparently fortuitous event a coincidence or divine intervention? Pilgrims look for the singular deity behind the forms of Vaiṣṇo Devī homologous to understanding the singular Mahādevī behind her manifestations. The judgments they make, though often private, support the coexistence of her oneness and manyness.

The definiteness of Trikuta contrasts with the variety of ways in which Vaiṣṇo Devī is portrayed and represented, thereby giving the pilgrimage its greatest asset: Vaiṣṇo Devī is sufficiently specific in her location and sufficiently ambiguous in her cosmology that pilgrims are able to create a meaningful relationship with her no matter what their devotional traditions or personal beliefs may be. The definiteness of Trikuta Mountain—as the one true home of Vaiṣṇo Devī—also contrasts with the increasing uncertainties of life for many urban as well as rural Hindus. The pilgrimage to Vaiṣṇo Devī is not only a quest for the blessings the Great Goddess (however Vaiṣṇo Devī may be variously defined), but it is also an attempt by pilgrims to locate themselves in the changing landscapes of their country's society and culture.

Vaiṣṇo Devī's qualities make her an exemplary deity for Hindus pressed between the desires and demands of modern urban society and a longing for continuity with the culture of their ancestors. The pilgrimage to Vaiṣṇo Devī is perceived as extremely ancient and at the same time, because of its excellent administration and facilities, as a prime example of modernity.[17] As such, the pilgrimage is one partial answer in modern Hindu culture to a tension between a feeling of loss or diminishment of ancient glory, and of hope for a progressively better future—a future promoted by government, education, science, mass media, and consumerism. This tension is partially resolved in a religious context by a construction of the distant past and the future as qualitatively simultaneous, a conclusion consistent with the theory of *yugas* wherein, for example, Sat Yuga is both in the past and in the future. Simply stated, the formula is that the ancient equals the modern in which both are superior to the post-ancient and the pre-modern. In establishing the Shrine Board, Governor Jagmohan articulated such a vision of the glories of the past and future coming together with Vaiṣṇo Devī as his practical example. His idea was to combine the virtues of ancient Hinduism with modern technology and administration to create a "rejuvenated" Hinduism (Jagmohan 1991, 626).

The homologizing of past and future accommodates for both a desirable past and a desirable future coexisting and growing in the present while breaking with a kind of undesirable and lingering "middle" past, a past marked by foreign domination. Deities are appropriate to this equation because they are by definition naturally present throughout all times, marking a direct continuity from ancient past to present to future. Devotees also tend to homologize the cosmological history *(itihāsa)* of deities—and thus also the "ancient" past of India—with the history of the modern nation of India, thereby providing the country with a kind of retro-historical narrative. If history is indeed a sign of the modern (Dirks 1990), then this popular conflation of cosmological history and history by Hindus extends backward the modernity of the nation-state well beyond the periods of its myriad colonizers.

In the Devī-Māhātmya, Mahādevī promises to take incarnations to break with periods of difficult conditions to reestablish a righteous order. Vaiṣṇo Devī fulfills that promise not only by reversing the undesirable conditions of her devotees, but as the *śakti* of Kalkī Avatāra, by ultimately reversing the conditions of Kali Yuga. When breaks with the past are felt or calculated to be needed, then it is appropriate for new or invigorated forms of deities—like Vaiṣṇo Devī and Rāma—to be foregrounded.[18] Goddesses have a special appeal in this regard because they are foremost protectors and nurturers, and Vaiṣṇo Devī, as a kind of gentle Durgā or a Lakṣmī with weapons, aptly fulfills these roles. India itself is promoted as "Mother India," the goddess Bhārat Mātā, and for many pilgrims, Vaiṣṇo Devī participates in Bhārat Mātā's image as an accessible manifestation of that ageless, but changing, Mother. India's increasing industrialization, participation in the world economy and consumer culture, and growing population creates a society of greater economic competition, dispersion of families, and little opportunity for participating in lengthy religious practices. Vaiṣṇo Devī promises to alleviate these problems by easily granting desires (mainly for wealth), by providing pilgrims with a sense of a pan-India devotional community coming together at the permanent "home" of their Mother,[19] and by demanding little from pilgrims in the way of ritual participation or time. Promoted as a tourist destination, the pilgrimage is also very enjoyable, such that some people have called it a "holy picnic" undertaken by "pleasure pilgrims."

Simultaneously distinct and ambiguous, Vaiṣṇo Devī is Mahādevī. She contains all *śaktis*, all beings, and all creation; she is broadly inclusive, connecting deities, sects, times, places, and a diversity of devotees. Through her blessings, Vaiṣṇo Devī recreates the lives of her devotees, and they continually recreate her according to their own beliefs. Hence, the construction of Vaiṣṇo Devī as Mahādevī remains an ongoing process.

Notes

1. "Baishno" is Dogri and "Vaishno" is Panjabi for Vaiṣṇav. Vaiṣṇav or Vaiṣṇo food denotes vegetarian fare. Vaiṣṇavī is Sanskrit, usually meaning the feminine power personified from Viṣṇu.

2. Vaiṣṇo Devī's presence on the internet is also growing. Her official site is <www.maavaishnodevi.org>.

3. In popular usage Saraswatī, Lakṣmī and Kālī are respected as the "Mahādevīs," because they are often considered to be the primary manifestations of *the* Mahādevī (cf. Brown 1990, chap. 5), and, hence, their designation as "great." No one would argue that there is actually more than one Mahādevī.

4. There is an apparent homogeneity among most of the popular pamphlets available in the markets, a characteristic noted by Kathleen M. Erndl (1993, 40). Different authors have apparently borrowed material from each other. Although the Devī-Māhātmya is cited as a definitive authority, there is also no competition between presentations of the Devī-Māhātmya and local stories as reported by Cynthia Ann Humes (1996) for the goddess Vindhyavāsinī.

5. Gorakh Nath was a guru of the Kanphata Panth, a Tantric-Śaiva sect of *sādhus* known for their consumption of meat and intoxicants. Gorakh Nathis are generally feared even today. No Nath *sādhu* I asked would acknowledge the Bhairo of Vaiṣṇo Devī's story as a Nath.

6. The cave is open twenty-four hours every day except for an hour in the morning and evening for the priests to perform *āratī* (worship by passing a flame around the deity), and at times when snow or rain are excessive.

7. This story, also cited in Erndl (1993, 66), contrasts sharply with other accounts of Vaiṣṇo Devī's forgiving nature toward the transgressions of her devotees.

8. A common saying is that without Śakti, Śiva is *shava* (a corpse).

9. Erndl (1989) argues that both Śaiva and Vaiṣṇava elements are present in Vaiṣṇo Devī's common stories, evidenced especially by her connection to the *Rāmāyaṇa* and to Bhairo. To the extent that Bhairo is Śaiva, her argument is elegant and valid. But among pilgrims and local devotees, there is considerable variation about the identity of Bhairo, and even strong opinions over whether the story of his involvement is true. No Nath *sādhu* I met would acknowledge the validity of the story.

10. Gulshan Kumar, a self-made multimillionaire in the audiocassette industry, credited his wealth to Vaiṣṇo Devī. He founded a free *laṅgar* (public kitchen) for feeding pilgrims at Ban Gaṅgā on the path of Vaiṣṇo Devī. In 1997, he was assassinated by a rival.

11. Kurtz (1992) privileges the assertion of "all the mothers are one" (*ekhī haĩ*) over assertions that goddesses are completely different (*bilkūl phark*). That there is unity among goddesses in their essential identities is only one point of view. Deities can be simultaneously old, new, distinct, and continuous with existing conditions.

12. Śiv Khoṛī was taken under the management of the Shri Mata Vaishno Devī Shrine Board in 1991. It is a two to three hour bus ride from Katra plus another hour and a half of hiking into low hills. The cave has a wide mouth narrowing to winding passages that ultimately lead to a large cavern where there is a natural Śiva *liṅga* (formed from a stalagmite). In February and March, ten thousand or more devotees may visit Śiv Khoṛī during the annual night of worship of Śiva, Śiva Rātri.

13. This is a well-known story about the relation of Kālī and Śiva (see Kinsley 1986, chap. 8).

14. The Varāha Purāna lends credence to Shastri's claim, stating that "Devī Vaiṣṇavī" killed Mahiṣāsura (Brown 1990, 136).

15. For ritual purposes a *kanyā* may be between the ages of two and ten. R. S. Khare (1982), however, argues that a *kanyā* is primarily a matter of *dharma* and is not necessarily dependent on the biological condition of the female, for example, age or abstinence from intercourse.

16. There are, of course, many instances of the opposite. Goddess Kanyākumārī, at the southern tip of India, necessarily took the form of a virgin to kill a demon. Mahiṣāsuramardinī of the Devī-Māhātmya may also be considered a virgin.

17. The modernity of the pilgrimage astonished journalist Saurabh Mehandru (1996):

> The prospect of three successive holidays aroused my religious sentiments enough and I decided on a trip to Vaishno Devi . . . The trek to Vaishno Bhavan—the shrine—had me quite at a loss because it was clean, had a rest room and government priced eateries at practically every stop. It was as though religious sentiments had transformed the route into some exotic foreign land. In more senses than one, the mountain was "high above" its surroundings.

18. Santoshi Mā is a similar example.

19. Many Panjabis had to leave behind the temples of their family deity (*kula devatā*) at the time of Partition and have since chosen Vaiṣṇo Devī as their new family deity (*kula devī*).

Chapter 4

The Goddess as Fount of the Universe

Shared Visions and Negotiated Allegiances in Purāṇic Accounts of Cosmogenesis

Tracy Pintchman

> She is that Supreme Power *(paramā śakti)* absorbed in me, of the nature of Brahman, my beloved, endless *māyā* by which this universe is deluded. . . . She is all my power *(sarvaśakti)*. She is the source of the entire universe, *prakṛti* possessing the three *guṇas*.
>
> —Kūrma Purāṇa 1.1.34–38

This is how Viṣṇu describes Lakṣmī, his beloved wife, to those gathered before her. It is the dawn of a new cycle of creation, and a magnificent goddess has just emerged from the primordial ocean of milk churned by the gods and demons in ancient times. The sages and deities present are curious to find out who she is, so Viṣṇu introduces her. In describing Lakṣmī, who is identified in this text as the Supreme or Great Goddess (*parameśvarī,* 1.1.62), Viṣṇu equates her with the principles *śakti, prakṛti,* and *māyā* and lauds her as the source of the whole universe.

Within the Purāṇas (ca. third to seventeenth century C.E.), the richest descriptions of Mahādevī's nature tend to find expression in texts that are clearly Śākta in orientation, that is, those that portray the Goddess as supreme deity of the Hindu pantheon. This would include texts like the Devī-Māhātmya and the Devī-Bhāgavata Purāṇa (ca. twelfth to sixteenth centuries C.E.). But several of the major Purāṇas or Purāṇic sections that postdate the Devī-Māhātmya recognize the existence of a Great Goddess even though they are not Śākta, but Vaiṣṇava or Śaiva in orientation, meaning they extol either Viṣṇu or Śiva, respectively, as supreme deity.[1] Regardless of sectarian allegiance, in many of the Purāṇas the Goddess is portrayed as the wellspring of the physical universe and is identified with transcendent creative principles that are connected to this role.

Devī's nature as the immediate source of creation comes to the fore in a number of Purāṇic accounts of cosmogenesis, which the Purāṇas tend to portray in relation to an infinite cyclical pattern of dissolution and regeneration of the world. This does not mean that all Purāṇic creation narratives portray the Goddess's cosmogonic role in the same way or even assign her a role at all; there are a large number and variety of creation narratives in the Purāṇas, and many of them do not give any primacy at all to Devī. Yet the vision of the Goddess as the wellspring of the physical world finds expression in a number of accounts of creation in Purāṇas of differing sectarian allegiance, even when the Goddess herself is not accorded the highest place in the pantheon.[2]

The Goddess as *Śakti, Prakṛti,* and *Māyā* in Purāṇic Accounts of Cosmogenesis

In creation narratives found throughout the Purāṇas, the Goddess is portrayed as embodying the principles *śakti, prakṛti,* and *māyā,* which are in turn related to her world-generating nature. *Śakti,* "power," is the supreme, cosmic energy that produces and sustains creation. *Prakṛti* is materiality, the basic "stuff" of creation that forms the material foundation of the created world. *Māyā* is a bit more difficult to circumscribe. In some contexts, most notably the philosophical school of Advaita Vedānta, *māyā* denotes a mysterious power of illusion inherent in Brahman, the eternal, unchanging Godhead. According to Advaita Vedānta, Brahman alone is fully real; the world of multiplicity, which conceals the true oneness of Brahman, is not fully real but a kind of illusion that Brahman generates through the power of *māyā.* *Māyā* is associated, too, with spiritual ignorance *(avidyā),* the lack of perception of Brahman's oneness, which keeps one bound to the cycle of rebirth. In some contexts, however, including many Purāṇic cosmogonies, *māyā* has more positive connotations, often assuming the creative qualities of *śakti* and *prakṛti.* In such contexts, *māyā* is often equated explicitly with one or both of these two principles.

The identity of the Goddess with *śakti, prakṛti,* and *māyā* is firmly established in the Devī-Māhātmya, a text that Thomas Coburn has written about extensively (e.g., 1982, 1985, 1991, and 1996). The Devī-Māhātmya portrays the Goddess as the ultimate, highest reality and the supreme creator who wills creation and sends forth the cosmos.

She is said to be the material foundation of the universe, *mūlaprakṛti* (primordial or root *prakṛti*), the basic material from which the cosmos is formed. The world is her form, and the entire universe with all its parts is ultimately identified with her (e.g., 1.47 [64], 4.6 [7]). But she is also embodied as Devī, the Goddess, in which capacity she is portrayed as a great slayer of demons and divine protectress (Coburn 1991, 24–26). When she becomes manifest, as described at the beginning of C. Mackenzie Brown's essay in this volume, it is said that she only appears to take birth; in fact, she is eternal (1.48 [66]), ultimately birthless and deathless.

Devī is also called Śakti. As such, she is the power that makes possible not only the creation of the universe, but its maintenance and destruction as well (11.10 [11]). Transcending the universe and controlling its rhythms, she is nevertheless also immanent, for it is said that she abides in all beings in the form of *śakti* and is the *śakti* of all that exists (5.18 [32–34], 1.63 [82]). Coburn observes that in the Devī-Māhātmya, *śakti* is a singular and universal phenomenon, something that Devī *is* as well as something that each individual deity *has* (1982, 160; 1996, 38). As this universally abiding Śakti, she is present in all things everywhere. The Goddess is also extolled as Mahāmāyā (great *māyā*), and in this capacity she is said to be both creative, like *śakti*, and deluding (1.42–43 [55–56]). As Coburn has noted, too, in this text the principle of *māyā* is sometimes equated with *prakṛti* (1982, 155–156; 1996, 33–34).

The identification of the Goddess as *śakti, prakṛti,* and *māyā* continues to persist in later Purāṇic descriptions of the Goddess, including those found in Vaiṣṇava and Śaiva contexts. In materials that postdate the Devī-Māhātmya, however, these three principles are sometimes incorporated explicitly into accounts of creation. In the Devī-Māhātmya, although the Goddess is described in ways that suggest she plays important cosmogonic roles, there are no passages that describe the mechanisms of cosmogony per se. Purāṇic materials that postdate the Devī-Māhātmya, however, often portray *śakti* and *prakṛti*—with *māyā* somewhere in between—as different aspects or dimensions of a single, inherently female creative principle that unfolds from the Godhead during the early stages of creation and engenders the physical universe. In such contexts, the Goddess's role in cosmogony is made more explicit, and her identity as *śakti, prakṛti,* and *māyā* has a lot to do with her nature as the immediate source of the cosmos.

Similar patterns are delineated in several Purāṇic accounts of creation. Brahman, the supreme, absolute divinity—usually identified as Śiva, Viṣṇu, or a form of Viṣṇu, depending on the Purāṇa—exists at the beginning of creation in a formless *(nirguṇa)* state, which transcends all particular qualities. Femaleness resides within Brahman and is frequently understood to be Brahman's creative power, *śakti* or *māyā*. This feminine principle is usually personified, too, as Brahman's female consort, and the two are often said to be inseparable. Although technically beyond gender identity in this formless state, Brahman is nevertheless portrayed as male in relationship to his feminine power. Cosmogony begins when Brahman separates the feminine principle from himself; this act of divine gender differentiation often initiates the process of cosmogenesis. When the feminine principle stands apart from Brahman, it is identified in many contexts not only as *śakti* or *māyā*, but also as *prakṛti*. Like *śakti*, *prakṛti*, too, is often equated with *māyā*.

Just as *śakti* becomes embodied as *prakṛti* when male and female dimensions of the Godhead separate, Brahman becomes embodied as the male principle *puruṣa*, the male counterpart of *prakṛti*. The use of these categories of *puruṣa* and *prakṛti* reflects a particular perspective on creation that is most commonly associated with the Sāṁkhya school of philosophy. In Sāṁkhya, *puruṣa* is a principle of pure consciousness, whereas *prakṛti*, also called *pradhāna*, is the material principle from which the cosmos evolves. *Prakṛti* is said to consist of three constituent parts called *guṇas*: *sattva* (purity), *rajas* (activity), and *tamas* (lethargy). The Purāṇas tend to depict *puruṣa* and *prakṛti* as gendered, animate principles, respectively male and female, and several Purāṇas ascribe to them a role in creation, portraying the universe as arising from the interaction between *puruṣa* and *prakṛti*. In such cases, *prakṛti* is not a lifeless material principle, as it is in Sāṁkhya, but a form of the Goddess. The basic constituents of the manifest world, called the *tattvas*, flow from the three *guṇas* of *prakṛti*, and the universe takes shape from the *tattvas*.[3]

Hence, in these creation narratives, *śakti* and *prakṛti* generally represent different dimensions or manifestations, often active at different stages of cosmogony, of the same creative feminine principle, which acts as the immediate fount of the universe even when the Goddess is not herself portrayed as Brahman, the ultimate source of all Being. The shared nature of *śakti* and *prakṛti* is reflected in the fact that both are often called *māyā* as well. Together, these three principles constitute the Goddess in her capacity as fount of the universe and embody her tremendous generative power.

Several Purāṇas subscribe to part or all of this type of gendered vision of cosmogony, but there is variation from text to text. In some contexts, the identification of *śakti*, *prakṛti*, and *māyā* with the Goddess is understated; in others, it is proclaimed more forcefully. While some creation narratives stress the role of *śakti* in cosmogenesis, others stress *prakṛti* or *māyā*. In many of these contexts, the name "Mahādevī" never appears, but the portrayal of the goddess in question as the female dimension of the Godhead, supreme Goddess, and/or the source of other goddesses implies her status as Great Goddess. In all cases, the recognition persists that divine feminine energy, embodied in these three principles and personified as the Goddess, has an important role to play in generating the universe even in those contexts where a male deity is accorded ultimate status. In this regard, the Hindu creation narratives that share this vision stand in contrast to those like the biblical accounts of creation in the book of Genesis, where the participation of a female agent in cosmogony is so remarkably absent.

Vaiṣṇava and Śaiva Contexts

In describing the genesis of the world, one section of the Garuḍa Purāṇa (ca. 850–1000 C.E.)[4] describes creation in relation to a series of interactions between Viṣṇu and his spouse, the goddess Lakṣmī. On the highest level Viṣṇu is said to have both male and female forms (3.3.16). Although the precise identity of the female form described here is not revealed, one might infer that Viṣṇu's female form is Lakṣmī. Elsewhere the text proclaims that Viṣṇu can never be without Lakṣmī or she without him, for the two are inseparable, and that the form of Lakṣmī is reflected in that of Viṣṇu (3.3.19, 24–25). As his reflection, Lakṣmī is not really distinct from Viṣṇu but the feminine aspect of the Godhead (3.3.16), a status that implies her nature as supreme female deity.

As Brahman, Viṣṇu is also said to possess potency or *vīrya*, which represents his creative power. This potency is described as distinct from Viṣṇu yet also partaking of his same transcendent nature, both material in character and beyond material form (3.13–14). *Vīrya* can also mean "semen" or "male prowess," and in this account the principle of creative energy is allied more with the power of masculine virility than feminine energy or *śakti*, which plays the same role in other similar creation accounts. It is noteworthy that in this creation narrative, Lakṣmī does not seem to be identified with Viṣṇu's *vīrya*, and the principle *śakti* does not seem to enter into the discussion at all.

The creation of the universe begins when Viṣṇu places his *vīrya* in Lakṣmī. Here the term *vīrya* takes on the connotation of semen more strongly, and the depositing of Viṣṇu's *vīrya* in Lakṣmī has sexual overtones, although these are not explicitly played out. As the receptacle of Viṣṇu's semen or creative energy, Lakṣmī is equated with *māyā*, which is described in the same manner (3.3.11, 25–27, and 57–

58). When Viṣṇu places his *vīrya* in Lakṣmī/*māyā*, the three *guṇas* of *prakṛti* arise, implying an identification between Lakṣmī/*māyā* and *prakṛti* as the source of the *guṇas* (3.3.58). Elsewhere, *māyā* is said to be *prakṛti* in very subtle form (3.3.26). As supreme female deity, Lakṣmī manifests herself in three primary forms that embody the three *guṇas*:

> When the Lord created the three *guṇas* of *prakṛti*, there arose Lakṣmī in her three forms, Śrī, Bhū, and Durgā. Śrī consisted of *sattva*, Bhū of *rajas*, and Durgā of *tamas*. . . . One should not recognize any difference, on account of their mutual relation, among the forms, the *guṇas*, or Durgā, Bhū, and Śrī. (3.4.1–3)[5]

In relation to *prakṛti*, Viṣṇu is *puruṣa*. Viṣṇu enters the *guṇas* of *prakṛti* and agitates them, beginning the process of cosmogenesis (3.4.10ff). The *tattvas*, the constituent categories of creation, then begin to flow forth from the *guṇas* of *prakṛti*. Together, Viṣṇu and Lakṣmī enter the first two of these *tattvas* to stimulate the formation of those remaining (3.5.1ff).

The Nārada Purāṇa (ca. 850–1000 C.E. and later),[6] another Vaiṣṇava Purāṇa, begins an account of cosmogony by proclaiming that Mahā-Viṣṇu (Great Viṣṇu) alone exists as Brahman at the dawn of creation. He possesses supreme creative power, *śakti*, which is also referred to as his *māyā*. This creative power is described as consisting of both knowledge (*vidyā*) and ignorance (*avidyā*) (Pūrva-Khaṇḍa 3.3–3.6). In this context, *māyā* encompasses both the knowledge that can bring one to the true understanding of Brahman, thus delivering one from the cycle of birth and rebirth (*saṃsāra*), and the ignorance that can impede such understanding, binding one to the cycle instead.

> When the universe appears to be different from Mahā-Viṣṇu, then the result is only ignorance (*avidyā*), the agent of suffering. . . . (The) perception of the oneness of everything is considered knowledge (*vidyā*). Thus Mahā-Viṣṇu's *māyā* bestows birth and rebirth when seen as distinct from him, but if seen as identical to him, it destroys the wheel of birth and rebirth. (Pūrva Khaṇḍa 3.7–9)

In its capacity as ignorance, Viṣṇu's *śakti/māyā* instigates the process of world-creation (Pūrva-Khaṇḍa 3.6, 3.10). Hence, while the text ascribes ultimate control over the process of cosmogenesis to Viṣṇu, his creative power is specifically embodied as *śakti*. This *śakti* has many names: Umā, Lakṣmī, Bharatī, Girijā, Ambikā, Durgā, Caṇḍī, Girijā, Bhadrakālī, Vaiṣṇavī, Brahmī, and so forth—all names and epithets of female deities

(Pūrva-Khaṇḍa 3.13–15). By explicitly identifying Viṣṇu's cosmogonic power with goddesses, the text emphasizes its female nature in relation to Viṣṇu's maleness; and by identifying it with several goddesses, and not just one, the text communicates that the particular name really doesn't seem to matter. This *śakti* is the Goddess, and the Goddess has many forms.

This *śakti* is also equated with *prakṛti,* which embodies *śakti's* capacity to act as material cause of the universe (Pūrva-Khaṇḍa 3.15, 27). It is said that at the time of primordial creation, three forms arise from Viṣṇu: time (*kāla*), *puruṣa,* and *prakṛti.* In relation to *prakṛti,* the principle of *puruṣa* is male. Just as *prakṛti* is a form of *śakti,* which is the Goddess, *puruṣa* is a form of Viṣṇu, embodying his nature as "the Lord of the World" *(jagadguru).* Unlike in classical Sāṁkhya, however, where *puruṣa* is a passive, uninvolved witness to the genesis of the universe, here *puruṣa* takes on an active role in cosmogony, acting upon *prakṛti* to begin the process of cosmogenesis (Pūrva-Khaṇḍa 3.28–32), and the world flows forth from *prakṛti.* In this capacity the feminine principle, whose identity with the Goddess is implied in the text, acts as the material foundation of creation from which the entire universe arises. Hence, while this account of cosmogenesis acknowledges *māyā*'s nature as illusory power and its association with spiritual ignorance, it also affirms *māyā*'s creative capacity as an inherently feminine generative force that gives rise to the created universe.

In the Nārada Purāṇa's account, Viṣṇu's creative power or *avidyā śakti,* which is a form of the Goddess, is identified not only with Vaiṣṇava goddesses like Lakṣmī, but also with goddesses less habitually associated with Viṣṇu, including Durgā. The accommodation of Durgā in a Vaiṣṇava context is even more striking in a Kṛṣṇaite section of the Nārada Purāṇa.[7] These sections of the text elevate Kṛṣṇa, understood to be a form of Viṣṇu, to supreme status. Although Rādhā is the chief female deity in this context and is identified with Kṛṣṇa's *māyā* and with *prakṛti,* Durgā is also sometimes elevated to supreme status and portrayed as the source of creation. This section of the text describes Kṛṣṇa as dwelling eternally in his heavenly realm, Goloka, as supreme (*para-*) Brahman, who is beyond attributes. At this highest level, Rādhā is said to be united with Kṛṣṇa and abiding with him in the same body, just as Viṣṇu and Lakṣmī are said to be inseparable in the account cited above. The relationship between Kṛṣṇa and Rādhā is that of substance and attribute: they are as inseparable as milk and its color or earth and its smell (Uttara-Khaṇḍa 59.2–9). This level of Rādhā's identity transcends her material nature as *prakṛti* and exists in the form of pure consciousness (*cidrūpa*) (Uttara-Khaṇḍa 59.8). While Rādhā is identical to Kṛṣṇa on this highest level, this merging of identities seems to end when she separates from him. She becomes manifest as Mulaprakṛti Īśvarī, the goddess primordial Prakṛti, who is called the "Maker of the Universe" and the "Mother of All" (Pūrva-Khaṇḍa 83.10–11, 83.44, 82.214). Rādhā engenders five goddesses who are described as her five manifestations: Lakṣmī, Durgā, Sāvitrī, Sarasvatī, and a second form of Rādhā herself. Collectively these five goddesses are the cause of creation (*sṛṣṭikāraṇa*) (Pūrva-Khaṇḍa 83.32). While the mechanisms of cosmogenesis are not detailed here, the Goddess's cosmogonic role is implied in her nature as the fivefold "cause of creation."

This same section of the text, however, also portrays Durgā as supreme Goddess and source of creation. Various male deities are said to come forth from Kṛṣṇa's person and are subsequently paired with their corresponding female consorts, who emerge from the body of either Kṛṣṇa or Rādhā. Viṣṇu-Nārāyaṇa, for example, comes out of Kṛṣṇa's left side; analogously, Lakṣmī springs from Rādhā's left side, and Kṛṣṇa gives her to Viṣṇu-Nārāyaṇa. Kṛṣṇa creates Śiva by dividing himself in two, and Śiva weds Durgā, who also comes forth from Kṛṣṇa's body (Pūrva-Khaṇḍa 83.13–28). When she emerges, Durgā is lauded as the source of all other female divinities and as Māyā/Prakṛti:

> Durgā, the eternal *māyā* of Viṣṇu, suddenly became manifest from the body of Kṛṣṇa. This Mūlaprakṛti Īśvarī had the form of seed of all goddesses, perfect, with a splendid form, and consisting of the three *guṇas*. (Pūrva-Khaṇḍa 83.17–18)

Other passages use the same or similar epithets to describe Rādhā, calling her Mūlaprakṛti, the eternal *māyā* of Viṣṇu, and the inherent *māyā* of Kṛṣṇa, implying that two goddesses are ultimately identical (e.g., Pūrva-Khaṇḍa 83.44–47).

A similar accommodation of Durgā in a Kṛṣṇaite context occurs in the Brahmavaivarta Purāṇa (ca. 1400–1600 C.E.), where both Rādhā and Durgā are identified with the supreme feminine principle, *prakṛti*.[8] There are several different accounts of creation in this Purāṇa. In one account the Supreme Being, here called Ātman, splits into two parts in the beginning of creation through his yogic power.[9] The right side is called *puruṣa*, and the left, *prakṛti*. *Prakṛti*'s cosmogonic significance is explained in etymological terms:

> *Pra-* means distinguished (*prakṛṣṭa*), and *-kṛti* means creation (*sṛṣṭi*). The goddess who is distinguished in creation is called Prakṛti. According to scripture (*śruti*), *pra-* means the preeminent *guṇa sattva*, *-kṛ-* means the middle *guṇa rajas*, and *-ti* means

> *tamas*. Therefore, the one who consists of the three *guṇa*s possesses all power (*śakti*) and is preeminent in bringing about creation; hence she is called Prakṛti. *Pra-* means first, and *-kṛti* means creation. And that goddess who is first in creation is therefore called Prakṛti. (Prakṛti-Khaṇḍa 1.5–8)

Like Kṛṣṇa, Prakṛti, too, is said to be eternal, for the two are indissolubly connected, a type of description of the male and female dimensions of the Godhead that we have seen before. Kṛṣṇa cannot create without her, for she is also his creative power, *śakti*. Although the equation of *prakṛti/śakti* with *māyā* is found in the text, the Goddess's nature as *māyā* is not emphasized.

Prakṛti is both a feminine creative principle and the supreme Goddess who transcends all other female divinities and is their source. When the goddess Prakṛti is *nirguṇa*, without qualities, she is the counterpart of Kṛṣṇa's *nirguṇa* form (Brahma-Khaṇḍa 28.24). It is in fact remarkable that the Brahmavaivarta identifies a level of Prakṛti that is *nirguṇa*, since Sāṁkhya describes *prakṛti* as inherently possessed of *guṇas* and is thus usually described as *triguṇā*, "having three *guṇa*s," by nature. The postulation of a level of Prakṛti that transcends the three *guṇas* may be influenced by the equation of Prakṛti with the *śakti* of Kṛṣṇa/Brahman. If Brahman is in a *nirguṇa* state, it thus follows that his inherent *śakti* must also be *nirguṇa*. Since Prakṛti is here identified with Kṛṣṇa/Brahman's *śakti*, it would follow that it, too, must be *nirguṇa* at the highest level (see also Brown 1974, 134–137).

As *saguṇā*, Prakṛti is Mūlaprakṛti Īśvarī, the goddess primordial Prakṛti (e.g., Prakṛti-Khaṇḍa 1.12). She assumes five forms in the process of creation and becomes manifest as the goddesses Durgā, Rādhā, Lakṣmī, Sarasvatī, and Sāvitrī.[10] The most important of these five are Durgā and Rādhā, who both are often equated with Mūlaprakṛti Īśvarī. Brown (1974, 121–122) notes that the identification of both Rādhā and Durgā with Prakṛti indicates the essential identity of the two goddesses with one another, an identification that we have also seen made implicitly in the Nārada Purāṇa. In this text, the equation between the two is explicit (Prakṛti-Khaṇḍa 55.52, 65.25). The ultimacy of either Rādhā or Durgā as Supreme Goddess is said to depend on the perspective of the believer:

> She who is merged into Kṛṣṇa's breast is the goddess Mūlaprakṛti. The wise call her Durgā, the eternal Viṣṇumāyā. . . . Vaiṣṇavas call her Mahālakṣmī, the supreme Rādhā. (Prakṛti-Khaṇḍa 54.88–91)

Because of the Vaiṣṇava orientation of the Brahmavaivarta Purāṇa, it seems to favor Rādhā as supreme Goddess, but sometimes Durgā, not Rādhā, is elevated to this status. In one passage, for example, Kṛṣṇa is said to be present at the time of creation. Various beings spring from Kṛṣṇa's body, including the goddess Mūlaprakṛti, who springs from his intellect (*buddhi*). The Great Goddess, Mūlaprakṛti, is lauded as the foundational cause of the universe and the embodiment of *śakti*, but in this passage she is identified as Durgā, not Rādhā. In fact, Rādhā does not emerge until quite a bit later, when she springs forth from Kṛṣṇa's left side; she is described only as his alluring mate (Brahma-Khaṇḍa 3.1ff., 5.25–26).

The integration of Durgā into these materials may be attributable at least in part to the influence of the Devī-Māhātyma. The Great Goddess of the Devī-Māhātmya is commonly understood to be Durgā; indeed, the Devī-Māhātmya is widely known as the Durgā Saptaśati, "The 700 Verses to Durgā." But other influences might also be at work here as well. In many contexts, including the Devī-Māhātmya, the Goddess is independent of any male consort. When Durgā is associated with a male consort, it is usually Śiva. Coburn notes that although the Devī-Māhātmya does not understand Devī to be Śiva's consort, her worship and identity are probably intertwined with those of Śiva, and her identity seems to emerge out of a matrix in which Śiva functions as a prominent figure (1996, 40–41). Charlotte Vaudeville (1982), on the other hand, has argued for a historical connection between the cult of Devī and that of Kṛṣṇa Gopāla, an argument that Coburn also notes (1996, 5–6). Vaudeville suggests that there is an ancient connection between early Vaiṣṇava materials, which shaped later developments in the mythology and cults of Viṣṇu and Kṛṣṇa, and the Great Goddess in her forms as both Durgā and Kālī, Durgā's dark counterpart. Devī's original place is later usurped, Vaudeville suggests, by the more gentle and alluring Rādhā. This hypothesis is consonant with the Purāṇic passages above, which maintain Durgā's status as Supreme Goddess and fount of creation while acknowledging Rādhā's claim to this title as well.

The Śiva Purāṇa (ca. 800–1000 C.E.) recounts the process of cosmogenesis from a Śaiva perspective. Śiva alone is said to exist at the beginning of creation in his formless (*nirguṇa*) state as Supreme *(para-)* or True *(sat-)* Brahman (Rudra-Saṃhitā 1.6). The text emphasizes his unfathomable nature by using negative language reminiscent of that used in the Upaniṣads to describe Brahman as "not this . . . not that" *(neti . . . neti)*. Formless Brahman produces a second version of himself with form, which is called Īśvara (Lord) or Sadā-Śiva (Eternal Śiva).

Īśvara/Sadā-Śiva contains within himself a female power, the goddess Śakti. Śakti is Śivā, the female side of Śiva and the Great Goddess. Without altering his own body in any way, Īśvara sends Śakti forth from himself (Rudra-Saṃhitā 1.6.4–19). In another section of the text, it is said that although Śakti appears to be born from Śiva in his form as Sadā-Śiva, it is said that in fact she is not really born but simply becomes manifest—a somewhat common Purāṇic formula that echoes the Devī-Māhātmya's description of the Goddess as eternal and hence birthless.

> Hara, the most excellent lord, sent forth a goddess from a portion of his body. Those who are knowledgeable about Brahman say that this goddess, who is endowed with divine attributes, is the highest Śakti of that supreme Śiva. . . . Although (it appears that) she was born from Īśvara, in reality she is not born. (Vāyavīya-Saṃhitā 1.16.6–11)

Śiva and Śakti are the father and mother of the universe, the *nāda* (sound) and *bindu* (dot) whose union gives rise to creation (Vidyeśvara-Saṃhitā 16.87–90, 93). Śakti is identified with *prakṛti* and is called the "foundational cause" (*mūlakāraṇa*) and generator of all things (Rudra-Saṃhitā 1.6.20–21, 24). Both Śiva and Viṣṇu, whom Śiva creates from his left side, assume the identity of *puruṣa* in relation to Śakti's identity as *prakṛti,* and the union of *puruṣa* and *prakṛti* produces the first birth (Vidyeśvara-Saṃhitā 16.95–97; Rudra-Saṃhitā 1.1.2, 1.6.53). At the time of creation, the various *tattvas* that comprise creation evolve forth from Śakti/*prakṛti* (Rudra-Saṃhitā 1.6.55–59).

The Kūrma Purāṇa (ca. 550–800 C.E.), a cross sectarian Purāṇa, details the world-generating nature of the Goddess in a narrative section that merges cosmogonic elements into a lengthy eulogy. In this account, Brahmā, who has already been created, produces Rudra—a form of Śiva—from his mouth. At Brahmā's command, Rudra splits himself into male and female forms. The female who springs from Rudra is Īśānī, "Female Sovereign." She is named as Śivā, Māheśvarī, or Śāṁkarī—the female counterpart of Śiva—and as the supreme Goddess who creates the world. She is Śiva's female dimension made manifest. She is also Śakti. Although singular, she has different forms as the different goddesses, the *śaktis* inherent in creation, who represent her portions (1.11.2–13). As these various *śaktis,* she pervades the world.

> Śivā is all-pervading, endless, beyond the *guṇas,* absolutely without parts, singular but abiding in many portions, assum-

> ing the form of knowledge, extremely desirous, without peer. . . . That single Māheśvarī Śakti (becomes) many in combination with (her various) attributes. . . . This world is her creation. . . . She is Devī, sovereign over all and stimulator of all beings. (1.11.22–30)

As supreme Śakti, she is also identified with Viṣṇu's *māyā,* the power of delusion that he wields. In the form of *māyā,* Śakti is also called upon to make Śiva's universal form *(vaiśvarūpya)* become manifest (1.11.34–35). Thus, she is linked with both Viṣṇu and Śiva.

As Śiva's counterpart, Śakti is his partner in cosmogenesis, and everything is said to spring from Śiva and Śakti together (1.11.42). She is also described as the source of both *puruṣa* and *prakṛti,* here called *pradhāna.* While abiding near Śiva, Śakti, who is called Māyā in this passage, splits herself and becomes *pradhāna* and *puruṣa* (1.11.40–41). As Śiva's *śakti,* she transcends *pradhāna* and is its source, yet *pradhāna* is also a form of her (1.11.241). Śakti is the source of various other categories of creation as well (1.11.222), but the evolution of the *tattvas* described explicitly in some other accounts of cosmogony is not included in this particular creation narrative.

Śākta Contexts

Although the Devī Māhātmya's vision of the Goddess as *śakti, prakṛti* and *māyā* is maintained in both Vaiṣṇava and Śaiva contexts, her status as highest, ultimate reality is not. Assertions of equality between the ultimate male God and his consort are quite common in these texts, but in fact it is the male who is really supreme. It is said, for example, that ultimately there is no distinction between Śakti and the possessor of Śakti, who is Brahman, but it is the male who possesses the Goddess. Śakti is never described as the possessor of her consort. In the Devī-Māhātmya, the Goddess is represented in ways that portray her as Brahman, although such identification is not made explicitly in the text. This is clearly not the case in Vaiṣṇava and Śaiva contexts.

In the Devī-Bhāgavata Purāṇa, which is *śākta* in orientation, narrative patterns concerning cosmogony that we have already seen in Vaiṣṇava and Śaiva Purāṇas merge with the Devī-Māhātmya's vision of the Goddess as supreme, ultimate reality.[11] This Purāṇa celebrates the Goddess as Brahman, an identity that Vaiṣṇava and Śaiva Purāṇas would reject. Yet the same understanding of the Goddess as the wellspring of the universe, a role embodied in her nature as *śakti, prakṛti,* and *māyā* persists, although the Goddess's role as generator of the cosmos is subsumed under the Goddess's larger identity.

In the Devī-Bhāgavata Purāṇa, as in the Devī-Māhātmya, the Goddess is the eternal, omnipresent overlord of creation and support of all that exists (e.g., 1.2.4–5, 1.2.8, 1.2.19). She is both *nirguṇa* and *saguṇa,* and the text distinguishes between these different aspects (e.g., 1.8.40, 1.12.51, 3.7.4–7, 3.24.39, and 12.8.75). In her *nirguṇa* state, she has a transcendent form that surpasses the three *guṇas;* she is supreme reality itself and transcends all qualities. When her *nirguṇa* aspect is emphasized in the text, she is sometimes called Nirguṇā Śakti, Mahāmāyā, or even—as in the Brahmavaivarta Purāṇa—Nirguṇā Prakṛti (e.g., 1.5.48).

In an account of cosmogony in the Devī Gītā section of the text, which Brown explores in detail in this volume, it is said that before the universe is created only the Goddess exists as Supreme (*para-*) Brahman. Brahman possesses a single inherent power *(śakti)* called *māyā,* described in true Advaita fashion as neither real, nor unreal, nor both (7.32.1–4). Ultimately, this *māyā* is not different from the Goddess herself (7.33.1 and 12.8.67). As Brown notes above, in this text the Goddess not only wields *māyā* as world-generating power, she *is* the very *māyā* that she wields.

There are two dimensions of the Goddess's power of *māyā;* they are described as different kinds of causes that play different roles in cosmogenesis. Through its association with consciousness *(caitanya),* the Goddess's *māyā* acts as the instrumental or efficient cause *(nimitta)* of creation, that is, the agent necessary for creation to occur. By its transformation into the visible world, it is the material cause of creation (7.32.8), that is, the *prakṛti*-like substance from which the cosmos is fashioned. Given that the Goddess is not different from her *māyā,* these two causes seem to represent two dimensions of the Goddess herself as cosmogonic agent, corresponding to *puruṣa* and *prakṛti* in creation narratives from the Garuḍa and Nārada Purāṇas detailed above. It is also said that when the Goddess unites with her creative power, she becomes the "cosmic seed" (*bīja*) that serves as the source of creation (7.32.7).[12] This form of the Goddess as cosmic seed, too, seems to correspond to *prakṛti* in some of the other cosmogonies detailed above as material foundation of the visible world, except that here this cosmic seed is also Brahman, since the Goddess is Brahman (Brown 1998, 96). Both *māyā* and the Goddess are, in fact, identified with *prakṛti* (e.g., 7.31.44, 7.32.9).

While conceding to the ultimate identity of all forms of the Goddess, the Devī-Bhāgavata Purāṇa nevertheless distinguishes among her different aspects. As Nirguṇa Brahman, she transcends the *guṇas;*

she is beyond attributes. As creator, she possesses and wields creative power, *māyā śakti,* which is the impelling force behind cosmogenesis. But both this power and the *prakṛti*-like form that she takes as the cosmic seed that gives rise to the visible universe are forms of the Goddess herself. Hence, the Devī-Bhāgavata maintains the same vision of the Goddess as immediate wellspring of the created universe that the Śaiva and Vaiṣṇava Purāṇic accounts of cosmogenesis detailed above also share.

Conclusion

While portraying the Goddess's personal identity in different ways depending on the context, Purāṇic creation narratives from across the sectarian spectrum affirm her role as wellspring of the universe, a role that is embodied in her nature as the principles *śakti, prakṛti,* and *māyā.* Accordingly, these cosmogonies negotiate differences in sectarian allegiance while maintaining a shared vision of the Goddess as the foundational source of creation. The integration of the Goddess into the mechanisms of cosmogenesis and the identification of different goddesses with cosmic creative principles are inherently connected to the theology of a Great Goddess who is portrayed even in non-*śākta* contexts as powerful and praiseworthy. The vision of her that comes forth in these creation narratives also points to two larger issues concerning her identity that come forth in this book: Mahādevī's status as "Mother," and her multiple singularity.

As the source of all that exists, the Goddess is the Mother of all. Even in those contexts where male deities are ascribed ultimacy, it is the Goddess who acts as the immediate source of creation, giving birth to the world from her own nature as divine creative power or as the material matrix from which all arises. Such a vision of the female's role in creation reflects the biological realities of procreation, of course, for children emerge from the bodies of their mothers. While Devī's nurturing maternal role is emphasized in many of the devotional contexts explored in other chapters in this volume, Purāṇic creation accounts emphasize her generative capacity as the Mother of all that exists.

With respect to her multiple-singular nature, as *śakti, prakṛti,* and *māyā,* Devī embodies a cosmogonic potency that transcends particular form and personal identity. One might say that the identity of the Great Goddess in these contexts has more to do with *what* she is than with *who* she is. Who she is can and does change from text to text, depending on sectarian biases, but her identity as a creative force manifest in cosmogony and the foundation and source of all that is persists across sectarian contexts. Cultic practice further bears out her nature as a multifaceted creative power that transcends her particular forms. While *śakti, prakṛti,* and *māyā* are not individual goddesses with distinct narrative or ritual traditions—like Lakṣmī, for example—nevertheless devotees of a variety of goddesses may understand the object of their worship to embody these principles. Cultically as well, as generator of the universe, Mahādevī transcends sectarian borders and remains accessible to worshipers of all stripe.

Notes

1. The Brahmanical tradition comprises eighteen major (Mahā-) and eighteen minor (Upa-) Purāṇas, although there is some disagreement as to exactly which Purāṇas belong in which category. Even the Purāṇas themselves disagree as to exactly which texts should be included in which list. The main disagreement concerns whether the Śiva Purāṇa should be included as a Mahā-Purāṇa—replacing the Vāyu—or whether it should be classified as an Upa-Purāṇa. If we include both the Śiva and Vāyu Purāṇas, the result is a list of nineteen Purāṇas: Agni, Bhāgavata, Bhaviṣya, Brahma, Brahmāṇḍa, Brahmavaivarta, Garuḍa, Kūrma, Liṅga, Mārkaṇḍeya, Matsya, Nārada, Padma, Skanda, Śiva, Vāmana, Varāha, Vāyu, and Viṣṇu.

Many of the Purāṇas can be classified according to their sectarian perspectives. The major or Mahā-Purāṇas tend to celebrate the gods Viṣṇu (and his manifestations) and Śiva above all others, designating that god as Brahman, and several of these Purāṇas are clearly Vaiṣṇava or Śaiva in orientation. Four of the Upa-Purāṇas and portions of some of the Mahā-Purāṇas are *śākta* and elevate the Goddess to the highest position in the divine hierarchy. Several Purāṇas, like the Kūrma, are cross-sectarian, and others, like the Mārkaṇḍeya Purāṇa, cannot be classified as having any clear sectarian allegiance.

2. This chapter draws upon and revises earlier research detailed in chapter three of Pintchman 1994. Please see that work for further elaboration of the Goddess's role in Purāṇic accounts of creation.

3. There are twenty-three of these *tattvas* that flow forth from *prakṛti*: intellect *(buddhi* or *mahat),* egoity *(ahaṁkāra),* mind *(manas),* five sense capacities (*buddhīndriyas*: hearing, touching, seeing, tasting, and smelling), five action capacities (*karmendriyas*: speaking, grasping, walking, excreting, and procreating), five subtle elements (*tanmātras*: sound, contact, form, taste, and smell), and five gross elements (*mahābhūtas*: ether, air, fire, water, and earth).

4. These are the dates proposed by Hazra (1975, 144). Hazra also notes that the Uttara-Khaṇḍa is a later addition. The Garuḍa Purāṇa appears to have been compiled over a long period of time in several stages, and many scholars have proposed that the date of the text as a whole cannot be fixed.

Rather, they have dated different sections of the text separately, ranging from the first century C.E. up to the eleventh century.

5. Śrī is another name for Lakṣmī, and Bhū is the goddess Earth. See also Garuḍa Purāṇa 3.11.4–5, which states that *prakṛti* assumes the forms of Lakṣmī and the Earth (= Śrī and Bhū).

6. Hazra proposes the dating of 850–1000 C.E. for much of the text, but notes that some of the text is later than this (1975, 129–133).

7. These materials include the third *pāda* of the first part (Pūrva Khaṇḍa) and the second part (Uttara Khaṇḍa) of the text, sections that Hazra describes as "comparatively late" (1975, 132).

8. See Brown 1974, 119–122. Brown also looks at parallels between the Kṛṣṇaite sections of the Nārada Purāṇa and the Brahmavaivarta Purāṇa (26–27, 158–165).

9. Ātman is synonymous with Brahman.

10. For a detailed discussion of the five forms of *prakṛti* and the historical roots of this concept, see Brown 1974, 142–167.

11. As Brown notes, the ninth book of the Devī-Bhāgavata Purāṇa corresponds closely to the Prakṛti Khaṇḍa of the Brahmavaivarta Purāṇa, except that Devī replaces Viṣṇu as supreme deity (1990, x, 10, 145–147, and passim). Because the mythological material is substantially the same in both Purāṇas, I will not address this portion of the Devī-Bhāgavata Purāṇa.

12. I am borrowing Brown's translation here; see Brown 1998, 86, 89 n.11. In his translation of this chapter of the text (85–109), Brown discusses this account of creation and its roots in Advaita Vedānta in much greater detail than I am able to do here.

Chapter 5

Waves of Beauty, Rivers of Blood

Constructing the Goddess in Kerala

Sarah Caldwell

In the south Indian state of Kerala, the Great Goddess (Mahādevī) is generally known as "Bhagavati." As the Great Goddess, Bhagavati is Śakti, the power behind the physical world; a power that is summoned, enlivened, and worshipped in a variety of physical forms. Indeed, the construction and enlivening of the Goddess's physical form is the fundamental mode of Hindu religious practice in Kerala. In keeping with the general tendency of Mahādevī to manifest in a variety of forms, Bhagavati may be called Dēvi, Kāḷi, or Bhadrakāḷi in Kerala according to context. Yet while she remains at all times the supreme Goddess for her devotees, the way that Bhagavati's physical form is "constructed" through ritual enactments and textual recitation varies significantly from one social group to another, highlighting aspects of the Goddess's identity meaningful to each community. Different traditions of worshipping the Goddess pertain to specific segments of Kerala's erstwhile highly stratified society, who continue to own and perform distinct ritual songs. This essay will examine four such song text traditions:

1. Bhagavati Kaḷam Pāṭṭu and its relation to the Śākta text Saundarya Laharī
2. Bhadrakāḷi Māhātmyam (a.k.a. Bhadrōḷpati)
3. a palm leaf manuscript of Dārikavadham from north central Kerala
4. Brahmaṇi Pāṭṭu.

Differences among the song texts that in turn are indicative of the diverse social contexts in which these function clearly illustrate "the constitutive role of interpretation in shaping portrayals of Mahādevī's identity" pointed to in the introduction to this volume (4). In Kerala, the physical and mythic construction of the Goddess in ritual continually articulates the identity of the Great Goddess in particular cultural domains.

Throughout Kerala, the body of the Goddess Bhagavati is ritually constructed through *kaḷams* (portraits of the Goddess in colored powders), elaborately costumed ritual possession performances, or *mūrti*s (enlivened sculptural images enshrined in permanent temples), as well as through songs, meditation, tantric worship, and the telling and hearing of mythic stories (both oral and written) in which the Goddess is described in detail.[1] These texts range from songs sung by female agricultural workers during the rice harvest to Sanskrit poetic compositions recited by male Brahmin priests in temples. Each retells the Dārikavadham (The Killing of Dārika), a story unique to Kerala, though clearly sharing common elements with several Sanskrit Purāṇas and some Tamil myths.[2] Treatment of several important motifs in the Dārikavadham story varies among versions. We will explore this variation, which reveals much about the social construction of the Goddess within a shared religious domain.

Although we cannot know with any certainty the historical origins of Bhagavati, evidence seems to point to her development out of the ancient Tamil war goddess Koṟṟavai,[3] as well as fierce female deities worshipped by the mountain-dwelling aboriginal peoples. The Koṟṟavai tradition emphasizes the Goddess's intimate relation to the battlefield, whereas the aboriginal traditions seem to regard the Goddess as a fierce power (often embodied in snakes) dwelling in trees and mountain forests. In both traditions, she is said to love blood and to possess human bodies. Over many centuries, this earth-dwelling goddess, known in Kerala as Bhagavati, became assimiliated to the pan-Hindu Kālī.

Today Bhagavati is a mother goddess who is also terrifying and fierce. Her Kerala legends, embodied in the Dārikavadham, tell of her birth directly from the forehead of Śiva to fight the demon Dārika, her enormous size and ferocity, her beauty and power, her bloodthirstiness, and her military might. The story of the Goddess in Dārikavadham echoes many of the themes in the better-known texts Devī-Māhātmya and Devī-Bhāgavata Purāṇa. In fact, some of the Sanskrit versions of Dārikavadham, such as the Bhadrakāḷi Māhātmyam, claim to be taken directly from the Mārkaṇḍeya Purāṇa, the framing text for the Devī-Māhātmya, although they are in fact not present there.[4] In most of its plot details, in its rhetoric and metaphors, and in several crucial plot elements, even the most Sanskritized versions of Bhagavati's Kerala story are closer to Tamil literary style than to the extant Purāṇic texts dedicated to the Devī; and much of the story appears to be utterly unique to Kerala.

C. A. Menon, whose book *Kāḷi Worship in Kerala* (1959; in Malayalam) remains to date the only full-scale survey of the subject, emphasizes the unique orientations of Bhagavati worship in different castes. According to Menon, the form of worshipping the mother goddess "at the foot of the tree without any form of idol or icon" still practiced by the aboriginal forest dwellers is the oldest mode. The fundamental orientation of this worship is to request protection and avert harm from the Goddess, who is believed to be dangerous and capricious by nature.[5] Kings and sorcerers engaged in left-handed Śākta practices to obtain magical powers. Soldiers called upon the mother of the *kaḷari* (martial arts gymnasium) to endow them with "valor and heroism," while politicians and landowners "aspired for the blessings of the Mother to perpetuate their influence and status among the people." Agriculturalists worshipped Bhagavati to obtain a successful rice harvest; toddy-tappers worshipped her in the coconut palm to draw out plenty of white sap from the buds; and "the great Vedantis and those having spiritual knowledge worshipped the Mother as Mahamaya and Mahashakti, who controls birth, protection, and destruction of the universe" (Menon 1959).

This bewildering variety of apprehensions of the Goddess, understood in all her myriad forms to be connected to the single Great Goddess (Mahādevī) of the pan-Indian tradition, is reflected in the plethora of ritual performance traditions and texts specific to particular castes. One can go to a temple or folk arts festival today and see literally dozens of distinct ritual portrayals of the Goddess side by side. We are just beginning to unravel these complex interrelations between groups and to relate them to their social and historical contexts. We know that while there has been continual mixing and borrowing of traditions, essential values important to each social group persist and remain fairly distinct.[6] We can surmise that over the past two millenia, as the Goddess began to embody a set of common symbols, her form nonetheless crystallized around the concerns of each group. Only by examining her textual and ritual "construction" in each tradition can we begin to understand the whole religious, social, and historical picture.

J. R. Freeman's detailed study of *teyyam*[7] in north Malabar (1991) outlines a typology by which to sort out some of these complexities. Freeman suggests that there are three major ideological orientations in

Kerala ritual, which he calls the "sorcery," "martial," and "priestly" complexes, corresponding to three caste divisions (Śudra, Kṣatriya/ Nāyar, and Brahmin). These three complexes mobilize separate sets of ritual practice and express fundamentally different world views. While Freeman's suggestion about the distinctiveness of each group's form of worship is intriguing, the boundaries might not be as clearly defined as he suggests, for symbols and ideas move continually up and down the caste hierarchy, as well as across religious boundaries into Muslim and Christian communities in the same locality.[8] Furthermore, his scheme does not incorporate female-centered texts and rituals devoted to the Goddess Bhagavati that reflect a significant cultural and historical current and express the unique concerns of their authors. If we add a fourth category, the "female-centered" text tradition, to Freeman's schema of priestly, warrior, and sorcery ritual complexes, and acknowledge the flow of symbols and ideas across social groups, we may categorize the fundamental values expressed in the texts and rituals of Bhagavati as expressed in table 5.1.

Despite its limitations, such a schema highlights the different emphases actors and authors have drawn out from a common set of symbols. Although the basic plot elements remain constant in each of the texts (some oral, some written), notable differences emerge. These include differences in rhetorical style and plot, variations in motifs, such as the treatment of women or the relationship between the Goddess and her father, Śiva. In the following section, we will explore the

Table 5.1 Variants of Bhagavati Textual Traditions

Complex	*Warrior*	*Priestly*	*Sorcery*	*Female-Centered*
Social Group	Nāyar/Kṣatriya	Brahmins	Lower castes, mountain dwellers	Women of both high and low castes*
Text Example	Saundarya Laharī [hereafter SL] Bhagavati Kaḷam Pāṭṭu [BKP]	Bhadrakāḷī Māhātmyam [hereafter BM]	Palm leaf manuscript of Dārikavadham [hereafter DV]	DV; Brāhmaṇi Pāṭṭu [hereafter BP]
Values Emphasized	Erotic power and attraction; military might	War and bloodshed; Also *dharma*, restoration of order	Dangerous power, wild natural fury, carnivory	Social relatedness, affection, vulnerability, physicality

*Although I have grouped these together for analytic purposes, we must be careful to distinguish the two as we learn more about low caste women's values in Kerala.

construction of the Great Goddess's identity in these four different complexes, examining in turn texts and songs from each category: the warrior (BKP and SL); the priestly (BM); sorcery (DV); and female-centered (DV and BP).

Waves of Beauty

As the ritual artist (a Marar or Kurup male, hereditary temple artists) begins to draw the black geometric outlines of the *kaḷam,* or powder drawing, portraying the Goddess in her fierce form as Bhadrakāḷi, he imagines the representational picture he will draw to be the *bindu,* or center, of an unseen *yantra,* the Śrī Cakra. The Śrī Cakra is an abstract ritual diagram, consisting of a series of forty-three triangles, meditated upon by initiates into the Śākta cult of the Goddess to realize the fundamental structure of the universe. In 1992, Krishnan Kutty Marar, an expert *kaḷam* artist whose father was initiated into the Śrī Vidyā form of Śākta practice, described in detail the correspondences between the triangles of the Śrī Cakra and specific entrances to the Goddess's fort, guardian deities, planets and syllables associated with each part of the diagram.[9] For Krishnan Kutty Marar, the Śrī Cakra is a precise map of the military battlements of Tripurasundari, the Goddess at the center of the Śrī Cakra, destroyer of the fort of the demon Dārika. Krishnan Kutty asserts that Dārika's fort can be found at Kōlatiri, an ancient ruin in northern Kerala, where the Asura king was believed to have reigned on earth. The goddess's fortifications, however, are located in another dimension, not visible on the earth. Although Krishnan Kutty Marar was not himself initiated into the Śākta cult, he asserts that a close relationship existed in earlier times between the *kaḷam* tradition and the *kaḷari* (martial arts) training of ritual specialists (who also danced *muṭiyēṯṯu* and other ritual dances dedicated to the Goddess). For him the representational powder drawing of the Goddess, victoriously holding Dārika's bloody, decapitated head in her left hand, is an integral expression of this esoteric military imagery, extolled in her stories, and enacted in her ritual dramas.[10]

A central practice of the Śrī Vidyā cult is the recitation of the Saundarya Laharī [SL], the "Ocean [alt., waves/flood] of Beauty," a Sanskrit text attributed to the Kerala saint Śaṅkarācārya (eighth century?) describing the Goddess's physical charms as well as the esoteric powers that may be obtained by meditating on her. In Śākta esoteric religious doctrine, especially as practiced by kings and warriors in Kerala, military might has become a metaphor for spiritual attainment.[11] This spiritual attainment in turn derives from partaking of the

Goddess's mystico-erotic power. The goddess as supreme deity of the universe is conceived in this poem as a beautiful, erotic, supremely pure, mature female. The repeated emphasis on her erotic appeal is an integral part of her power and greatness. By meditating on the exquisite and erotically stimulating form of the Goddess, the most remarkable powers may ensue to the male devotee:

> If Thy gracious side glance falls on even a very decrepit old man who is ugly to look at, and whose erotic sensibilities are dead, he will be followed in all haste in their hundreds by love-lorn young women having their locks scattered, their rotund breasts exposed by the loosening of their brassieres, and their girdles suddenly broken in excitement, thus letting their wearing *[sic]* clothes slip down. (SL, Verse 13)

The goddess's physical beauty is a sign not only of her perfection, but also of her power over the mind (of men), the power to attract, to focus attention, and to provoke desire. In this central metaphor of the Śākta meditation tradition *śakti* itself is the conscious, physical force that manifests as knowledge, desire, and power. By pleasing the Goddess who possesses all these, the male worshipper himself will attain the same powers over others and will ultimately merge into her. In this highly gendered combination of "martial" and "priestly" values (to use Freeman's terminology) in a fundamentally Śākta ethos, meditation upon and incorporation of the female body's erotic power becomes for the tantric Nāyar warrior the very source of his martial potency.[12] In the social realm, the Goddess was considered the representative of Nāyar and Kṣatriya political concerns, a queen leading valiant warriors into glorious battle.

The SL describes the Goddess's beauty in typically florid Sanskrit poetry:

> Surrounded by curly hair resembling swarms of young bees, Thy face scoffs at the beauty of the lotus-flower; in which face, smiling gently, rendered handsome by the filament-like brilliance of the teeth and endowed with fragrance, the bees of the eyes of the Destroyer of Smara revel. (Verse 45)

> Oh mother! In the region of Thy breasts is a flawless necklace made of pearls got from the frontal globe of Gajasura (the elephant-demon). It rests there with its white brilliance variegated from within by the reflection of the ruddy tinge of Thy Bimba-like lips, as if it were the confluence of the (white) fame

and the (red) valor of Thy Consort, the Destroyer of the Cities. (Verse 74).[13]

As the form of the Śrī Cakra is related to the Bhagavati *kaḷam*, so is the SL comparable to the songs of praise accompanying *kaḷam* drawing. These songs are known as Bhagavati Kaḷam Pāṭṭu [BKP]. The BKP, sung in an old form of Malayalam, uses some of the same metaphors and similes as the SL, and like it, describes the Goddess's body from "foot to head and head to foot" (a form common to invocations sung throughout the Indian subcontinent). The poetic diction, however, is far terser. In the following excerpt from the BKP sung by Koratty Narayana Kurup, we can see the traditional description of the Goddess's beautiful limbs augmented by local motifs like the oracle's jingling anklets, Dārika's head, and local place names.[14]

I salute you oh beautiful Kurumbayil Bhagavati
I salute your heavy hair which has the color of deep darkness
I salute the fiery eye which is like a *bindi* on your forehead
I salute the shining doe-like eyes and the big nose
I salute your honey-oozing lips and your red teeth and tongue
I salute your two ear-drops which are two elephants . . .
I salute the big *tāli* [pendant] on your chest and the big flower garland
I salute your divine breasts, which have beauty and shape equal to the big Meru Mountain . . .
I salute with my hands your outer feet and toes
I salute your divine dance which makes the whole world shiver
I salute with my hand the anklets that shake when the oracle dances
I salute having seen your body from head to foot
Oh Bhagavati of Vayambrakkavu I salute you.[15]

Directly after this opening hymn of praise, another descriptive verse follows, using a very different set of images:

The one who wears with pleasure wild elephants in her ears
One in a state of high intoxication
One who rides on the Vētāḷa
She who cut the chest of the tormentor Dārika
With thick red blood indeed
One who gives the blood to Kūḷis as food

She who cuts to pieces the enemies
She who shoots booming arrows at the foe and catches with the sword
Oh my mother of Śrī Kurumbakavu who reigns with pleasure
One who reigns with many good qualities
I bow before you oh Terrible One.

This verse, sung in Malayalam, introduces violent images of battle in language reminiscent of Tamil poetry. This song stays within the descriptive praise genre but introduces themes developed prominently in the Dārikavadham texts.

Rivers of Blood

Tamil scholars have often noted a tendency toward the horrific in certain forms of battle poetry, particularly in descriptions of the Goddess Kālī and her ghoulish cohort.[16] The overt concern with fertility, death, bloodshed, and agriculture in much of this poetry is reflected in metaphors of blood as seed, heads as fruits, and war as harvest. Direct confrontation with death and the creation of life from its remains are truths highlighted in these texts devoted to the fierce goddess. The goddess's body is in fact the Earth itself, and her power is the life-force that brings forth food. She requires the sacrifice of blood to renew the earth.

The images of war, bloodshed, and carnivory associated with the Goddess Ko<u>r</u><u>r</u>avai in ancient Tamil poetry are reiterated in the Sanskrit text Bhadrakāḷi Māhātmyam [BM], which relates the Dārikavadham story (which appears to have been in oral circulation since the Sangam period[17]) in poetic detail. Claiming to be part of the Mārkaṇḍeya Purāṇa, the texts retell the story of the Devī-Māhātmya in a purely Kerala idiom. Though some motifs remain the same, most of the plot is entirely different. At times the texts appear to mimic the Devī-Māhātmya or incorporate language very near that of the SL and Lalitā Sahasranām in praising the Goddess.[18] But the poem also employs imagery very different from such better-known Sanskrit texts. Consider the following account of Bhadrakāḷi's killing of the demon Dārika, from chapter 8 of the BM:

> Then throwing that great sinner Dārika on the earth, that daughter of Śiva thrust her trident deep into his chest. That Kāḷi collected the frothy blood gushing out of that mountain-like body in her skull bowl vessel, drank it and roared again

> and again. As an aboriginal girl of the forest bakes a tuber plucked out of the earth, that Kāḷika plucked out his heart, and baking it in the fire of her third eye, she ate it. Then that Maheshi took out the entrails (from his body) dripping blood and wore them on her chest, waist, neck, and arms. Cutting off his huge head with her sword, she took it in her hands. The terrible one got up and roared again and again. . . . After drinking all the blood gushing out of the body of Dārika, the fire of her anger was not extinguished, and she ate up millions of his army. (Verses 39–47)[19]

The bloodshed is so great during Kāḷi's war with Dārika that the battlefield is said to shine with "rivers of blood" (5: 60). The mystico-erotic power of the Goddess which inspired the Nāyar hero in the SL has here become a force of pure destruction and terror. The reference to the "aboriginal" girl associates Kāḷi with the autocthonous "tribal" mountain-dwellers, believed by high-caste lowlanders to have magical knowledge and powers deriving from their intimacy with the forest (itself a place of supernatural potency).

Despite the preponderance of Dravidian poetic themes, however, the BM clearly reflects a Brahminical world-view. Chapter 5 interpolates a lengthy hymn of praise recited by the sages and gods in heaven to Bhadrakāḷi as she is fighting the war with Dārika. This hymn is heavily laden with Brahminical Śākta theology:

> Oh Bhadrakāḷi, you are formless but have taken a form, you are independent yet dependent, you have no birth yet you took a birth, we salute you. Though egoistic, you are a realized soul, though you have no qualities, you take on qualities, though you are tiny you have taken a great form, . . . you are the form of the primordial sound Oṃ. . . . Oh Bhadrakāḷi worshipped in *yaga*s (Vedic fire ceremonies), we salute you. (Chap. 5, Verses 13-15)

The text goes on to praise Bhadrakāḷi as "the Truth that is spoken of in the Vedas" (v. 37), the one "worshipped by all the Brahmins," and protector of "gods, men, and sages" (v. 63). Bhadrakāḷi is then equated with the Devī of the Devī-Māhātmya, who "long ago" killed Niśumbha and Śumbha, Caṇḍa and Muṇḍa, Raktabīja and Mahiṣāsura (Chap. 5, Verses 71–73).[20] Moved by their praises, the Goddess comforts them "with merciful looks" and takes up her arms to go to war on behalf of the gods and sages.

Root of all Living Things

Brahminical texts such as the BM, while acknowledging her bloodthirstiness and violence, tend to emphasize themes such as the Goddess's purity, her concern with *dharma*, her protection of Brahmins, her nurturance as a mother, and her ability to restore cosmic order. These Brahminical themes are conspicuously absent in other written and orally collected versions of the Dārikavadham [DV] story. A palm-leaf manuscript collected by the late folklorist Chummar Choondal from the Kallat family of Kurups (ritual performers) in northern Trichur District, Kerala is attached as an appendix to his (1981) volume on *muṭiyēṯṯu*.[21] We are given little information about the origin, antiquity, or context of use of this extraordinary text, but it is likely that the Kallat Kurup family used the songs as the basis for their ritual performances at the Kattakkambal temple near Kunnamkulam in Trichur District (Choondal 1981, 166). The rhetorical structure of the text strongly suggests it is an oral composition that has been written down for preservation.[22] Many of the motifs in this text refer in detail to the forest, to particular mountains within it, and to the hunting and gathering lifestyle of forest dwellers. This suggests that the text may have originated in a "tribal" tradition, or at least have been composed by people familiar with the forest life.

The description of Bhagavati's birth from Śiva's fiery third eye in the palm-leaf DV is intimate and earthy:

> Like a big mountain of antimony [eyeblack], with sixteen hands, with three eyes and ferocious fangs, making a terrible "Ha Ha" noise, this cheerful but terrror-inspiring Śrī Bhadrakāḷi, came out and was born. One, more beautiful than anyone else, wearing necklaces, good and blissful beauty, my dearest mother of Tirumandāmkunnu, the root of all living things, my Mother.[23] (Choondal 1981)

Although it plays on the same motifs, this diction is simpler, more intimate, and more naturalistic than the grandiose imagery employed by the BM to describe the same scene: "In that fierce fire of the enemy of death with a glow surpassing that of the dark clouds, rose up Bhadrakāḷi, with terrible roars, deafening the worlds, and a body to match. Her body was big and dark like the antimony mountain, her body and innumerable hands, eyes emitting out glowing embers, dazzling to the eyes, not ten thousand but one *lakh* [100,000] in number" (5: 3–4).

After creating Bhadrakāḷi, Śiva directs her to one of four forests,[24] where she will find the creature Vētāḷam, who will serve as the Goddess's vehicle in the war against Dārika:

> She started walking along the forest of Ambamahākāla, Śrī Bhadrakāḷi. Vētāḷam who was sleeping keeping her head on the sunrise mountain and legs on the sunset mountain, keeping her two hands on the northern and southern forests, woke up with a start. Who, who is bringing the decorated flag through my abode? Whoever it is, let me dress myself. Deciding thus, she killed a wild elephant in the forest and fixed it on her forehead as a decorative dot. She put two elephants as ear drops. With the head of another elephant she hung a marriage badge *(tāli)* from her neck. With two elephants she made bangles for her arms. With thirty-eight elephant heads she made a brassiere for her breast. With sixty-eight elephant heads she made jingle bells for her waist. With two elephants she made anklets for her legs. She had for her food two hundred elephants, she drank water from the seven oceans. Then she uprooted a banyan tree and kept it between her teeth and stood. . . . Bhadrakāḷi saw such a Vētāḷam.

The manuscript specifically mentions that the war between Bhadrakāḷi and Dārika takes place in an area to the southwest of the Vindhya mountain range and the Kaveri River in Tamil Nadu. The goddess Kartyāyini (sometimes called Durgā), who comes to Bhadrakāḷi's aid during the war, returns to sleep at her home in the foothills of the Vindhyas to the north. These geographic markers, plus frequent references to the "sunrise" and "sunset" mountains (obviously a valley bordered by mountains on the east and west), strongly suggest that the author(s) of this text dwelt in the Nilgiri Hills bordering Kerala on the East. The description of the forest-dwelling Vētāḷam's costume made of elephant hide and with jingle bells at the waist and ankles again suggests the oracular vestments of tribal groups referred to in the ethnographic literature. Although at present the suggestion cannot be confirmed, this text seems to have many elements that would tend to identify it as an aboriginal composition or one strongly influenced by contact with mountain-dwelling groups.

Another striking difference between the palm-leaf DV and the Sanskrit BM texts is the female-centeredness of the DV. The pregnancy and delivery of two *asura* women (one of whom gives birth to Dārika) are described in immediate and intimate detail that seems likely to have been composed by a woman (although no independent evidence as yet confirms this intuition).[25] The text includes a month-by-month account of the women's pregnancy symptoms, as well as the details of the "*pulikudy* (tamarind-drinking)" ceremony, performed in the latter months of a woman's pregnancy to ensure a successful birth.[26] This moving account of childbirth is unusually graphic:

> In the center of [the delivery room] the cot for the childbirth was made of sandalwood, things got ready for delivery, pain started, the body was gently stroked, they started weeping, the two *asura* girls. How was that? Oh my head is aching, oh Lord Damodara [Visnu], give me "*kazhi*." The neck is paining, oh Lord Kamadeva give me relief. My chest is paining, oh Lord Madhava, give me relief. Oh my breasts are paining, oh Lord Mukunda, give me relief. Oh my stomach is paining, oh Lord Vasudeva. Oh my waist is paining, oh Lord Ananda. Oh my navel is paining, oh Lord Narayana. Oh my thighs are paining, Lord Subramanya. My lower legs are paining, oh Lord Muchukunda. Oh my ankles are paining, oh Lord Karunakaran. The outer feet are paining, oh Goddess Bhumi Dēvi. My nails are paining, oh the Stars. The joints are paining, oh holy saints and Lord Indra. There is pain all over the body, oh the Lord full of good qualities. Oh Lord . . . , don't you understand the pain we children are suffering? There was pain in the vagina, the whole body was paining, it was gently stroked, and calling out to the Lords, a very dull-witted boy was delivered by the *asura* woman named Dānavati. (Choondal 1981)

Apart from the immediacy and female-centered tone of this excerpt, it would also be difficult to miss the obvious parallel to the hymns of praise to the Goddess Bhagavati recounted from both the SL and the BKP, above. From the head to the feet, the narrator enumerates the labor pains in each part of the mother's body, in exactly the same order as the Goddess's beautiful body is described. Even the nails and "outer feet" are mentioned in both texts. Here, of course, the poet is describing *asura* women, not the Goddess. The parallel ironically underscores the vast gap between human women (who undergo labor pains like these) and the impossibly perfect erotic ideal of the Great Goddess (who is never described as giving birth, although mother's milk flows from her breasts).

The female-centeredness of the text is also reinforced by the prominence of female characters (including *asura*s, goddesses, and the wife of Dārika) over males. In the BM, Śiva gives Kāḷi a male chieftain,

Nandimahākālan, to lead her army. He plays an important role, encouraging her when the battle is failing, and providing crucial strategic advice. Other male characters, such as advisers, chieftains, and soldiers, are also prominently featured in the BM. In DV, however, Nandimahākālan plays only a minor role. The goddess's army consists entirely of females, and Bhadrakāḷi is assisted by the Goddess Kartyāyini, who goes to Dārika's wife Manōdari in disguise and tricks her into revealing the secret mantra protecting Dārika in battle. An important motif in the DV story (and one that varies the most in oral transmission) is the curse that Dārika will be killed by a woman, despite having received every other conceivable boon of invincibility. In the BM, after Lord Brahma rewards Dārika's intense austerities by granting him all the boons he desires, Brahma asks Dārika why he did not ask for a boon not to be killed by women in battle. Dārika scoffs at this question, insisting that it is beneath his dignity even to consider such an eventuality. As punishment for his pride, Brahma curses him to be killed by a "divine woman" in battle, all Dārika's other boons becoming futile at that time. The palm-leaf manuscript elaborates this conversation by describing Dārika's further encounters with two supernatural females, who heap additional curses onto Brahma's:

> "Stop, stop, oh Asura King, Dārikarāja, there is a boon which you did not ask, nor did I voluntarily give it to you," so said Lord Brahma. "What is that?" asked Asura King Dārika. "You are going away without the boon that you cannot be killed by women," so said Lord Brahma.
>
> "Does cold water remain near the sun? Does the wind get smeared with dust? Then will the women who come in fear fight me and win?" said the Asura King Dārika haughtily. "You great sinner, because you have spoken with disrespect to all the women in the world, in course of time, you will meet with your death at the hands of a goddess." Saying thus Lord Brahma vanished. Hearing this Asura King Dārika started going away as if he had not heard it. Then when he was going along the Vindhya forests Goddess Kartyāyani saw him. "Who goes there? Are you not King Dārika? Are you not the one who got boons and a chariot from Lord Brahma? Then take one more boon before you go." So said Goddess Kartyāyani. "I am not a person to accept boons from women and animals." So saying haughtily, Asura King Dārika started moving on. "As you have equated me with animals I shall get you killed even if it be after telling lies." So saying Goddess Śrī Kartyāyani vanished.

> Going along as if he had not heard it, King Dārika was going through the Ambamahākāla forest, when the demoness Vētāḷa saw him. "Who goes there? Is it not King Dārika going, having gotten boons and a chariot from Lord Brahma? Then take one more boon from me." So said demoness Vētāḷam. Hearing that Asura King Dārika started walking on, replying haughtily, "I am not a man to accept boons from the demons, worms, snails, and insects living in the forests." So saying haughtily, he started walking on, Asura King Dārika. "Since you have equated me with the snails and worms and insects in course of time I shall kill you. I shall cut with my axe the most tasty portion of the thick flesh in your body and shall eat it." So said the demoness Vētāḷa and disappeared.

Both goddess Kartyāyini and Vētāḷam fulfill their promises later in the story, leading to the demise of Dārika. The characters of these female supernaturals, as well as that of the *asura* woman Manōdari, are fully and sympathetically drawn. In the DV text, Dārika's neglect of women is emphasized as the cause of his downfall.

When Dārika discovers that Manōdari has been tricked by the Goddess Kartyāyani (who appears to her as an aged Brahmin woman and obtains the mantra given to Dārika by Lord Brahma), he becomes furious and blames Manōdari for her naivete, which will lead to his demise. Her pleas (and Dārika's response to them) have a plaintiveness, realism, and vulnerability that again suggest the "female-centeredness" of the text, which seems likely to have had input at some point by a female author:[27]

> [Dārika addressing Manōdari:] "All my strength was due to the boon from Brahma. May no one else make such a mistake! Death is . . . certain to a person who tries to teach vital things to women. Take as much wealth as you can and whatever you brought with you and vacate this place. I shall go and fight with Bhadrakāḷi and attain the heaven of heroes," said Asura King Dārika.
>
> Hearing that queen Manōdari was very unhappy and started lamenting. "At the age of seven I came to you as your wife. Do I know the way to go? Do I know where to go and live; do I know how to live or to eke out a livelihood; do I know the market where they sell rice; do I know how to observe a ritual fast; have I ever worn wet clothes; have I ever slept on a wet grass mat? To whom are you abandoning this cursed self as you go away, oh my husband?" In this manner

> queen Manōdari started lamenting. Hearing her sad cries, he embraced her deeply and patted her and laid her down on the royal sandalwood cot. He untied her knotted hair, made her happy and put her to sleep, and started going, the Asura King Dārika.

This poignant domestic scene seems designed for female hearers, who would undoubtedly identify with Manōdari's pathetic state and find vicarious pleasure in her husband's motherly ministrations, although her actions will cause his certain death! This scene is much simplified in the BM. Dārika simply acknowledges that "the fruits of [his] karma have arrived" and says, "Let it be, I am not afraid of the inevitable." He sends Manōdari to her parents' house without scolding her. Manōdari's poignant speech and Dārika's tender ministrations are absent.

My Bhagavati

Another set of songs, the Brāhmaṇi Pāṭṭu (Songs of Brahmin Women) [BP], are known to be sung by and for women, although their authorship is not entirely clear. Nambissan, the compiler of the printed collection, states that these songs originated in oral tradition in the eighth century, but were standardized in "pure Malayalam" some six hundred years later by the male Nambudiri Brahmin poet Mahishamangalan.[28] Despite their attribution to a male author/compiler, Nambissan stresses that the songs have been passed on orally through the centuries by women in Brahmin families; he "copied [the songs] from the palm-leaf manuscript which was with my mother" (155). Nambissan mentions many great female singers and assures us that BP is a tradition "of the women, for the women, and rendered by the women" (159).

In this context, women would certainly have had the opportunity to make many interpolations reflecting their interests and concerns. The majority of these songs, peculiar to Kerala, are performed on ritual occasions to honor the Goddess Bhagavati by reciting her story. The songs are also sung to assure the prosperity (and success in marriage) of unmarried girls, as prayers for the long life of husbands, at the birth of children, at the giving of a girl in marriage, and as a daily act of worship. In Nāyar or Brahmin family temples dedicated to the Goddess Bhadrakāḷi, Brāhmaṇis prepare a *kaḷam* (colored powder drawing) and perform rituals to the Goddess. In public Bhagavati temples, a male of Kurup or Marar caste will be invited to draw the *kaḷam*, and a male Brahmin priest will perform the rituals of worship. Then two or three Brāhmaṇis sing a series of songs in unison. After some time, "the head Brāhmaṇi woman of the family (whose husband is alive) attires herself [well]," and stands at the entrance to the pavilion looking at the seat kept for the Goddess. In her hands, the Brāhmaṇi holds a plate with rice, while singers sing the song "The Birth of Bhadrakāḷi," beating time on a bronze vessel with a knife. Nambissan tells us that "the lady standing with a plate with rice in it may go into a trance, sometimes she may give oracular predictions."[29]

The "Birth of Bhadrakāḷi" is one of the most important songs in this tradition. As in DV, the diction of the song reflects a more intimate attitude towards the Goddess than that seen in the BM, referring to her constantly as "my Bhagavati" (an epithet that perhaps encourages the head Brāhmaṇi to identify with the Goddess, inducing possession trance):

> There arose the Bhagavati with a form as big as the space between the earth and the sky. The Bhagavati let off a roar as soon as she was born and it made all the three worlds shiver. She was adorned with ash and with anklets. My Bhagavati was adorned with bone garlands and pearl garlands. My Bhagavati was adorned with garlands of stars and garlands of intestines. My Bhagavati was adorned with big garlands of wildflowers and with *tecci* flower garlands [red flowers sacred to the Goddess]. My Bhagavati had smeared holy ash all over her body. My Bhagavati had white curved fangs as beautiful as the digit of a white moon. (Song No. 10, "The Birth of Śrī Bhadrakāḷi")

The relationship between Bhagavati and her father, Lord Śiva, is given a great deal of attention in the various songs of the BP. After giving birth to her, Śiva immediately concerns himself with Bhagavati's dress (a motif not seen in any of the other versions of the story we have considered):

> At that time, her Divine Self was naked. The Lord gave her an elephant skin to wear which was sixteen cubits in length. . . . My Bhagavati took it up and wrapped herself well. That was enough for draping once around and it did not cover below the knees. The Lord who was the enemy of Tripuras gave a good dress of dotted design. The Bhagavati discarded the elephant skin and wore the spotted dress.
>
> The Lord took her lovingly on his lap and gave her the name Bhadrakāḷi. He also called her by the pet name of

> Kandenkāḷi. In seeing Bhagavati the Lord was much pleased. Seeing the Bhagavati the Devas also felt happy. Lord Śiva felt sure that his daughter had the strength to kill Dārika. (Song 10: "The Birth of Śrī Bhadrakāḷi")

Bhadrakāḷi's uncharacteristic modesty here impels her to discard the skimpy elephant skin in favor of a more demure spotted dress. As in all the versions of DV, Bhadrakāḷi's enormous size presents a problem. She notices this fact and seeks advice from her father:

> Then, at that time, my Bhagavati saluted her father and spoke thus: "Why did you create me, oh my father? The earth is not big enough for me to stretch my legs and stand, my father. . . ."
>
> "Oh my daughter, humility is important for women, you should reduce the size of your face, eyes, and limbs, my daughter." Following her father's instructions, my Bhagavati made a thousand faces into one face, my Bhagavati made her eight thousand arms into eight. My Bhagavati made her three thousand eyes to three eyes. Then she also reduced her clothing accordingly, my Bhagavati. "Father, now what is it that I should do?" "Oh my daughter, by the Asura King Dārika, our worlds have been destroyed, my daughter. You should kill him and save all this world, my daughter." (Song 18, "The Setting Forth of Kāḷi")

This account emphasizes female concerns such as modesty, the obedience shown by the daughter toward her father, and his reciprocal affection toward her. As in the story of Manōdari's rejection by Dārika in the palm-leaf manuscript, the narrator gives as much attention to human relationships and bonds of affection as to the Goddess's glorious deeds and power. This emphasis mutes the themes of the Goddess's nakedness, ferocity, uncontrollability, and cruelty so prominent in the BM.

Upon her return to Kailāsam (Śiva's mountain home), Bhadrakāḷi's wrath is soothed by seeing the wild dance of her father Śiva and by drinking blood from a cut in his little finger.[30] Once she has cooled down, Bhadrakāḷi offers Dārika's head to Śiva in fulfilment of her duty. The problem then arises as to where the Goddess should stay, now that the war is over. Once again, the BP text emphasizes the mutual affection between father and daughter:

> My Bhagavati kept the head of Dārika at the edge of her father's seat, and stood there saluting him. "What should I do now,

> my father?" "Oh my daughter what I desire is that my daughter should always be with me here living happily. But then the people will refer to me as Mahādēva of Bhadrakāḷi temple. So you should go now to Malanād ["Mountain Land," i.e., Kerala], my daughter. In Malanād, you should live in jasmine creepers for protecting the common man, my daughter. Live there in the platforms, in the temples, in the lakes, in the gardens, in the banyan tree platforms; live in these places my daughter. . . . You should accept only the *pūjā* [ritual worship] of Brahmins, my daughter." "I shall do so." So saying, saluting her father, taking the head of Dārika and circumambulating Kailāsa mountain, my Bhagavati started walking towards Tulunad. (Song 35, "The Return of Kāḷi")[31]

It is striking that these female versions of the DV story do not seem to show "resistance" or "subversion," as so many postcolonial feminist theorists would like to assert. Nor do they elaborate on Kāḷi's ferocity, anger, or hostility toward men, the central plot motifs of the story. In fact these aspects of the story are muted in the Brāhmaṇi songs, and parts of the text that highlight women's vulnerability, resentment of male insensitivity, and desire for tenderness and support are elaborated. Even the hostile, terrifying Bhadrakāḷi is transformed into an obedient daughter. The martial aspects of Kāḷi are male concerns, as are her violence and sexuality. For human females, she is as remote as the male world that created her, since there is no room for such a violent, independent role model in a Kerala woman's social life, with its emphasis on modesty, demureness, and obedience.[32]

The Many Faces of Bhagavati

In the four textual traditions we have considered here, the Great Goddess Bhagavati reveals a different face to each group of devotees. To the martial Nāyar and Kṣatriya castes, as reflected in both the mystico-erotic SL and the more earthy BKP, it is the Goddess's beauty and power that are most worthy of praise. By invoking her as *śakti,* the source of all attraction and might, the martial castes hope to draw on her strength and imbibe her power into their own bodies. As a "wave of beauty," Bhagavati overwhelms the minds of all who come before her, rendering them vulnerable and subject to her will. For Brahmins, Bhagavati is a "river of blood," inspiring terror in those demonic, antinomian forces of darkness that dare to threaten Brahminical order and *dharma*. Ancient Tamil conceptions of the warrior goddess Koṟṟavai are martialed in the BM and related texts to preserve the purity and sanctity of the Brahminical rituals. For the forest-dwellers who composed the palm-leaf DV text, Bhagavati is the "root of all living things," the dear earth mother whose limbs are the mountains, rivers, and trees. Her fury is aroused by the arrogant Dārika, who fails to recognize the essentially female power dwelling in this material creation. This marvelous text presents familiar pan-Indian themes of the Great Goddess as *prakṛti,* the material world, in an intimate, geographically grounded language that makes her as near and dear as a mother.

Finally, for the singers of BP, the Goddess is "my Bhagavati," as close as breath, adorned with garlands of bone and pearls, stars and intestines, flowers and ash, fanged and beautiful as the moon. Though she nearly reaches the sky, she demurely tries to cover herself with a skimpy elephant skin; she sits on the lap of her affectionate father and obediently heeds his command to kill Dārika "and save all this world, my daughter." While male-dominated ritual traditions appropriate the Goddess's powers of attraction and destruction, women's versions of the rituals and texts seem to stress themes of vulnerability, a desire for protection and affection, and the importance of family relationships. The obvious motifs of vengeance, anger, and misanthropy riddling the texts are never taken up overtly as role models for female sentiment or action. Where social realities leave no room for female independence, Bhadrakāḷi must be domesticated in the contructions of (especially high-caste) women.

This collection of texts presents four faces of Bhagavati, four aspects of her divinity as seen by particular communities of worshippers. Each of these incarnations is the Goddess herself; yet each also belongs to the different human communities who construct it. In the act of interpretation involved in each retelling of the Goddess's story and each calling of her spirit to enter a particular ritual space, the Great Goddess becomes real for her devotees. The variations in her portrait make it difficult to essentialize the Goddess. When we look at Bhagavati, do we see waves of beauty or rivers of blood, a defender of *dharma* or of women's concerns? She is an amalgam and confluence of all these, created and constructed by her images and songs of praise. We can emphasize the social and rhetorical differences among these portraits, yet her devotees readily state that Bhagavati is in fact the Great Goddess of the pan-Hindu tradition. Like the luminous colors of sunlight reflected in a crystal, these aspects of the divine feminine refract according to one's angle of vision, without distorting her ultimate unity.

Notes

1. The most thoroughly studied forms of Bhagavati worship in Kerala are the *kaḷam* tradition (Jones 1982), *teyyam* dancing (Ashley 1993; Freeman 1991), and *muṭiyēṯṯu* (Caldwell 1999; Choondal 1981; Venu 1984; Vidyarthi 1976).

2. See Caldwell 1999, 18–21, for details.

3. Hardy 1983, 223; Hart 1975; Shulman 1985, 279.

4. For example, the ninth chapter of the BM (Tirumump edition) ends with the line: "Thus ends the ninth chapter of Bhadrakāḷi Mahatmyam of Mārkaṇḍeya Purāṇa." However, a glance at the Mārkaṇḍeya Purāṇa will reveal that the attribution is spurious.

5. Menon calls this the "Dravidian" mode of worship, apparently indicating its antiquity and relevance to a purported pre-Aryan religious culture portrayed in the ancient Tamil poetry of the Sangam Age (c. first two centuries C.E.). Mountain-dwelling groups such as the Kurumbas of Palghat District still worship in this way.

6. Kapadia's (1996) comparative study uncovers a similar situation in Tamil Nadu.

7. Teyyam is a ritual performance of northern Kerala in which members of scheduled castes wearing elaborate costumes and makeup are possessed by the spirits of various heroes and deities, receiving offerings from and giving blessings to their community.

8. Freeman of course recognizes this, as his subtle analysis of the *pulaya* "narrative of Pottan" exemplifies (1991, 674–681).

9. Krishnan Kutty Marar, *kaḷam* artist, Interview, Tripunithura, Kerala, June 1992.

10. For relation of martial arts tradition to Kāḷi worship, see Caldwell 1999, 27–31.

11. See Brooks 1992, 43–50 for discussion of the role of the SL in Śākta practice.

12. See Caldwell 1999, 29–31, for discussion of the tantric symbolism of breasts in Kerala martial arts.

13. Verses 45: Sastri and Ayyangar 1977, verse 74: Tapasyananda 1987?

14. The historical details of the relationship between Śaṅkara's well-known composition and the songs of praise accompanying *kaḷam* worship are yet to be explored; they suggest a rich area of future study, particularly as Śaṅkara was born in central Kerala.

15. Collected orally, Trichur, Kerala, December 1991; translated by L. S. Rajagopalan.

16. See, e.g., Shulman's discussion of the Tamil poem *Kalinkattupparani* (1985, 278ff)

17. For instance, the *Cilappatikāram* (composed in Tamil in the 2nd century) refers to the goddess "who tore apart the broad chest of Dāruka" (Ilankovatikal 1993, 188; Canto 20, lines 52–53). Choondal (1981, 157) states that the Bhadrōḷpati was composed "about two hundred years ago" in Maṇipravāḷam (a literary mixture of Sanskrit and Tamil) by Kallur Nambudiripad.

18. The Lalitā Sahasranām is another important poetic text used in the Śrī Vidyā Śākta tradition. Chapter 6 of the BM refers to Bhadrakāḷi as Lalitā and encodes the sixteen-syllable mantra of the goddess used in Śrī Vidyā worship as the first letters of verses 39–54. Although this mantra is essential to the esoteric Śākta tantric practice associated with the Lalitā Sahasranām, the mantra itself is not given in that text "either directly or indirectly" (SL 1987?, 27).

19. Compare the more restrained Devī-Māhātmya 8: 57–63 (Tirumump 1975).

20. This of course reinforces the point that the text could not have been part of the Mārkaṇḍeya Purāṇa, wherein the Devī-Māhātmya appears, but is a later composition modeled upon the Mārkaṇḍeya Purāṇa.

21. The text is attached as "Annexure 1" with the following footnote: "This is a true copy of the manuscript with Rama Kurup son of Kattakkambal Karungal Kallat Sekhara Kurup" (1981).

22. Such rhetorical markers include the constant interpolations of dialogic prompts such as "how was that?" frequently found in South Indian oral performance genres, the presence of formulaic language and epithets such as "Asura King Dārika," and brief, often ungrammatical phrases.

23. Tirumandāmkunnu is an important temple of north Central Kerala. The Bhagavati installed there is often invoked in the BKP, and was the tutelary deity of the Valluvanat Rajas (Menon 1959). All translations from the Malayalam cited in this paper were completed by L. S. Rajagopalan.

24. The "four forests" are called "Ekambam, Kanavīryam, Ambamahākālam, and Madhumattam."

25. In struggling with anonymous texts that have moved in and out of oral tradition over long periods of time, assertions about voice and authorship are exceedingly difficult to defend. Wendy Doniger has recently attended to this complexity, suggesting that no definitive statements can be made about male or female authorship, even when the subject matter and style of a text appear to be suggestively biased one way or the other (Doniger 1997). However, the work of Rao (1991) and Ramanujan (1986) (where the gendered transmission and alteration of a traditional text are definitively known) has suggested unique features of oral texts recounted by and for women (see also Raheja and Gold 1993). In attempting to characterize what I see as very striking differences in tone, subject matter, and voice in the texts analyzed here, I have opted for the term "female-centered" rather than "women's" to describe texts showing a strong concern for the female viewpoint. This term does not commit itself to asserting the gender of a given author or teller, and thus acknowledges Doniger's important point about the fluidity and composite nature of authorship in texts.

26. Obeyesekere alludes to a similar song tradition in Sri Lanka, describing the birth pains of Parvati at Ganapati's birth (1992, 129). This motif is also found in the BP song about Rama's birth (BP is discussed below). These commonalities suggest that the "description of birth pains" may be a south Indian folkloric tradition, or at least one shared by Kerala and Sri Lanka.

27. According to Rao (1991), Ramayana songs sung by Telugu Brahmin women commonly elaborate scenes such as this one.

28. Malayalam and Tamil diverged as separate languages in about the ninth century; texts from this period characteristically show a mixture of Tamil and Malayalam.

29. This practice of high-caste female oracular performance is in striking contrast to the general practice of excluding women from temple service. These female rituals are generally confined to the private temples of high-caste (Nāyar and Nambudiri) families; public temples employ only males as oracles. For discussion of gender and oracles in Kerala temples, see Caldwell 1996 and 1999.

30. This fascinating motif is one of a variety of endings employed by the texts to reduce Bhadrakāḷi's anger. Other endings include the creation of twin boys to suckle her breasts (similar to the motif found in the Liṅga Purāṇa), Śiva's dance, Kālī's stepping on her naked father, and intercourse with Śiva. Implications of these variants are explored in Caldwell 1999, chaps. 4 and 5.

31. Tulunad is the southern portion of the modern state of Karnataka, bordering Kerala to the north, and sharing much in the way of religious culture. As in the palm-leaf manuscript we have considered, the geographical location of Kailāsam here seems to be in the Vindhya mountains. The war with Dārika takes place in Kerala itself, and the goddess is instructed by Śiva to dwell in "Malanād (Mountain Land)," an early name of Kerala. Some Śākta sectarians claim that stories like this, in which Śiva creates and then sanctions the goddess's activities, are later interpolations on an indigenous goddess cult that the Śaivite Brahmins tried to control (Humes 1996).

32. See Caldwell (1999, chap. 5; 1996) for detailed treatment of this issue. Of course this lack of female interest in the goddess's independence or fury may well reflect upper-caste values. Rao's (1991) comparison of Brahmin and low-caste women's Ramayana songs in Andhra Pradesh revealed vastly different attitudes between the two groups (see also Kapadia 1995). We would have to compare low-caste songs about the goddess (especially those sung by female shamans) to see what differences might be there. At present, such texts are not yet available to us.

Chapter 6

From Village to City

Transforming Goddesses in Urban Andhra Pradesh

Sree Padma

> I alone exist here in the world; what second, other than I, is there? O wicked one, behold these my hierophanies entering (back) into me.
>
> —Devī-Māhātmya 10.3

These are the words spoken by the Great Goddess, Devī, to the power-usurping demon Sumbha when the demon ridicules Devī for relying on her retinue of *śakti*s to subdue him in his efforts to take over the world. Claiming that all these *śakti*s are nothing but disparate aspects of her own supremely powerful divine being, she proceeds to absorb all of them into her body. There she remains, alone and poised on the battleground, dominating the scene in her full glory.

The text in which this scene appears, the Devī-Māhātmya, establishes for the first time in Brahmanic Hinduism a tradition that clearly recognizes the supremacy of a unique Great Goddess who embodies *śakti*, creative power. It also attempts to bring all local goddesses under a single umbrella by identifying them as various manifestations of a unique, cosmic Goddess. One way to look at the portrayal of the Goddess in the Devī-Māhātmya as supreme Śakti embodying multiplicity within unity is to see it as an attempt by the Brahmanical tradition to absorb the numerous local goddesses of India into a theological hierarchy and a philosophical monism. For many Hindus, and for many scholars of a philosophical bent as well, the search for Mahādevī ends here. But the portrayal of the Goddess in the Devī-Māhātmya may represent but a single instance—albeit an important and theologically paradigmatic one—where local traditions concerning goddesses and the sociometaphysical agenda of Brahmanic apologists merge.

It is easy to see how these two streams could work together harmoniously. In Brahmanic traditions that resist theological attempts to identify any particular deity as the ultimate ground of existence, the "divine" is usually understood to be ultimately unmanifest, formless, and omnipresent. Such resistance to recognizing the supremacy of any one god depersonalizes the Godhead and makes possible the positing of an ontological unity of all manifest deities, including village goddesses, who are viewed in other contexts as discrete and are worshipped for a variety of this-worldly purposes. The idea of the divine as ultimately formless is expressed in Brahmanic scriptures as early as the Bṛhadāraṇyaka and Chāndogya Upaniṣads and is elaborated at great length in later philosophical traditions. But it is also common currency in the views of ordinary devotees who worship their goddesses in many forms, including that of a shapeless rock, tree, pot, snake hole, or even village. From such a perspective, the ways that the Goddess expresses herself have never been fixed; her transcendence of particular forms is common knowledge and is simply not an issue of debate. Furthermore, the Devī-Māhātmaya's portrayal of Devī as all-powerful may serve only to confirm a fundamental, widespread assumption that the Goddess represents the basic power of existence. Hence, the identification of the Goddess with *śakti* has as much to do with the protective power of local goddesses still venerated by so many of India's villagers and, increasingly, by its urbanized populace as well as it has to do with the philosophical and metaphysical musings of Brahmanic tradition.

In Andhra Pradesh, where I have undertaken research on goddess traditions, Durgā is most widely identified as Mahādevī, the Great Goddess who takes on the form of different goddesses at her own will. A recently published Ph.D. dissertation by a priest of the famous Kanaka Durgā temple in Vijayawada town in the heart of Andhra Pradesh, reflects the views of the present priestly circle.

> Since very remote times Devī has been worshipped in many different forms by both civilized and uncivilized people; Innocents worshipped village goddesses, warriors worshipped snakes and others worshipped trees. Devī is mentioned as Para Śakti (great cosmic energy) in Vedas, Brahmanas, Agamas and Tantras. All the goddesses mentioned in Vedas and Puranas are the forms of Parā Śakti. Among these many different forms Durgā occupies a prominent place. Durgā has the capacity to protect the good and punish the wicked. (Satyanarayana Murty 1989, 5, 35–69)[1]

Hence, this Brahmanical author adopts the position articulated in the Devī-Māhātmya that all individual goddesses are really emanations of a unique Great Goddess, here identified as Durgā. It is not uncommon to find this type of perspective articulated throughout Andhra Pradesh. But a definitive search for Mahādevī really must move beyond the Brahmanic assertions of the Devī-Māhātmya and other Brahmanical texts into the convictions and practices of ordinary devotees. I would argue, in fact, the impetus to perceive all goddesses as diverse manifestations of a unique and all-encompassing Goddess, as well as the tendency to identify this Goddess with power, stems largely from local, non-Sanskritic traditions.

One of the assumptions that often informs scholarly work concerning goddess cults involves the view that historically, local goddess cults became legitimate when they were "added" onto or absorbed into an evolving Hindu tradition, a process known as "Sanskritization." Such a view is usually based on an understanding of Hinduism as being centered in pan-Indian Brahmanic Hinduism that predominates in Sanskritic textual and cultic environments. Yet even today the population of India—despite unprecedented urbanization—remains at least 70 percent rural and located in villages where veneration of local goddesses dominates religious life. It is without question the most widespread form of religiosity expressed in the Hindu tradition. Sanskritization of local goddess cults, therefore, needs to be seen not so much as something added onto an evolving Hindu tradition, but rather as a process by which an ancient, predominant form of religious practice comes to be incorporated into textual traditions.

In the cultic consequences of Sanskritization that I explore in this essay, the primary protective function of local goddesses tends to be always sustained, and Sanskritization, for the most part, tends to add only elements of liturgical elegance, anthropomorphic iconography, and ritual elaboration. In other words, elements of Sanskritization in the goddess cults I examine function primarily as ritual and metaphysical "window-dressings" that do not alter the fundamental ethos of goddess veneration. While some scholars interpret the Sanskritization of local goddesses as reflecting the absorbent nature of the "great tradition" of Brahmanic Hinduism, I would argue that veneration of local goddesses is actually the "great tradition" in question, given its historical longevity, geographical ubiquity, and cultic predominance. Sanskritization is simply a means of making these cults "user friendly" in urban contexts where congregations are not homogeneous, as they tend to be in villages, but draw devotees from a variety of different castes and ethnic backgrounds. In many instances, Sanskritic goddesses are transformed in character to become more like local goddesses, an adaptation that makes them more powerful or more appealing in the eyes of devotees. This process of "de-Sanskritization" makes the goddess in question more accessible in some social contexts and is quite characteristic of urban religiosity.

Setting the Context

The present chapter forms part of a major project on local goddess cults, for which I have conducted fieldwork in different rural and urban parts of Andhra Pradesh. The eight goddess cults discussed in this study are found within the confines of Visakhapatnam, a major coastal port city of Andhra Pradesh located midway between Calcutta and Madras on the Bay of Bengal.[2] From archaeological evidence, we know that Visakhapatnam has great antiquity, but for a long period of time in its history the town was confined only to the harbor area and its immediate environs. Because of its strategic maritime location on the east coast of the Deccan, it became after independence an ideal place administratively for the Indian Navy to headquarter its control over the entire east coast of the country. Navy personnel living in Visakhapatnam come from all of the various cultural regions of India. In addition to the Navy and other government-controlled industries like shipping, heavy plates manufacturing, and petroleum production, several fertilizer companies have also hired employees to move to Visakhapatnam from different parts of India. Although the higher-ranking officials of these organizations and businesses live within their own enclosed colonies and have their own segregated social gatherings, the lower ranks of workers and service men in this now heavily industrialized city have mixed thoroughly with the local population, contributing significantly to its diversification.

In the early 1980s, the processes of industrialization and urbanization further galvanized when the central Indian government set up a massive steel plant in Visakhapatnam which, in turn, attracted many other subsidiary industries to the city. Not only did this result in an even more mixed population drawn from all the different parts of India, but it also made Visakhapatnam something of a magnet for many business headquarters. Executives in these corporations began to hire employees not only from other parts of India, but also from nearby Andhra towns and cities, including many villagers seeking to improve their fortune. As a large town has transformed into a burgeoning city through a remarkable business and population growth rate, many small villages have been absorbed into the sprawling metropolis. Distinctive features of these Andhra villages are slowly disappearing in the wake of these new settlers.

Visakhapatnam is in the process of becoming one of India's major cities with an increasingly ethnically diverse and socially stratified population. In looking at how the city is changing, I have been especially interested in transformations of religious practice and belief, particularly in the context of goddess veneration which, I maintain, remains the single most popular form of religious expression in India. Four of the eight goddess cults that I examine further in this essay are located in villages that have recently been absorbed into Visakhapatnam as the city has spread. Before becoming part of the city, they were typical of any South Indian village: their economies were based on agriculture, and worship of local goddesses was the predominant form of religious practice. The four remaining goddesses are also local, but their origins are urban; they, too, have been affected by the pace of social change.

It is essential to understand how the religious atmosphere of villages in India differs from that of urban areas in order to contextualize religious change in centers that are undergoing rapid urbanization. As mentioned above, a typical Indian village's economy is based mainly in agriculture, and most village agriculture still relies on manual labor with the help of domesticated animals. Hence, villagers feel the need for divine protection from disease and danger not only for themselves and their progeny, but also for their crops and cattle. In villages goddesses tend to function in this type of general protective capacity.[3] In urban areas, on the other hand, where people's occupations tend not to be based on agriculture, people often petition goddesses for wealth, success, and protection for themselves and their children. In many cases, rural and urban local goddesses share a number of common features, while the motivations for worship vary largely depending on the interests of a particular goddess's devotees.

General Changes in Folk Goddess Worship

Certain factors have brought about significant change in recent years with respect to the form and intensity of goddess worship for people in both urban and rural areas. The first is the discovery of vaccinations. Until recently goddesses were regarded as both the causes and the curers of smallpox and other illnesses, especially in villages. Angry goddesses were thought to vent displeasure through the spread of "hot season" diseases, and only a process of "cooling" was thought to appease their anger. This particular association with the Goddess is slowly disappearing as inoculations slow the advance of dreaded diseases like smallpox and cholera. Second, as villages have been absorbed into urban areas, they have lost their borders, and villagers' expectations that the village goddess will function strictly as a border guardian have consequently changed. In the current context of urbanization, the function of the Goddess as a symbol of the village and its most powerful protectress shifts focus from village to family, from crops and cattle to one's job, and from one's children's health to their economic future.

Folk goddesses in Visakhapatnam are quite numerous. Even in this now decidedly urban environment, they comprise the most prevalent form of Hindu deity. They may be enshrined in small humble shelters or in grand temples, depending on the number and wealth of devotees forming their constituencies. Shrines may be dedicated to the very same goddess in different streets and neighborhoods, or to goddesses who are unique to a particular locality. Village goddesses tend to be worshipped aniconically, although this is not always the case. In the urbanized contexts with which I am concerned, the recent trend is to prepare images of these goddesses with many hands holding Vaiṣṇava and Śaiva symbols. The myths of these goddesses are generally preserved orally and narrated by a traditional non-Brahmin priest or elder; they may also be preserved in the form of songs sung by traditional singers at the time of annual festivals. In a changing urban environment, however, I have found that it may be impossible to recover a myth from any traditional source. Rather, this type of story may now be told by a recently appointed Brahmin priest who has collected narrative elements and reworked them into a Sanskritized framework.

In India generally, urbanization tends to be associated with increased Sanskritization and greater assertion of elements of Brahmanic orthodoxy. But it is my contention that the primary function of the village goddess as a protectress or guardian remains central in importance despite Sanskritization in relevant instances. My findings in this regard are somewhat at variance with Obeyesekere and Gombrich's recent large-scale study of Buddhism and the effects of urbanization in Colombo, Sri Lanka, which finds that formerly established normative patterns of religion (the so-called great tradition) have given way to the creation and proliferation of new and somewhat radical cults (1988, 10–13). This is not the case in Visakhapatnam, where changes in religious culture have been more a matter of amalgamating two different yet ancient patterns of religious behavior in order to meet more devotees' needs than of the emergence of radically new patterns that supercede or challenge the old.

In each of the case studies discussed, I address iconographic, mythic, and ritual details that reflect my theses regarding how goddesses are being transformed in this context.

Transforming the Goddess

Erukamma

Our first case reveals a very long process of a goddess's transformation. The story of Erukamma is a well-known myth of ancient origins that is now narrated enthusiastically by a non-Brahmin priest of the small and rustic, but very busy, temple of Goddess Erukamma in Dondaparthy, a village that merged into Visakhapatnam city several decades ago. According to this priest's account, a woman named Erukamma was causing horror by stealing children from the village and devouring them in a secret place on the village outskirts. A man of the Erukala (basket weavers) caste happened upon her while she was devouring a recently kidnapped child and cut off her head. After her death, people feared the potential malevolent effects of her revenge. They worshiped her to placate her, and through their petitions they were able to redirect her powers for the purposes of village protection.

This rather crude story contains the basic outline of an extensive myth preserved in classical Chinese Mahayana Buddhist texts. This myth tells how the laity came to worship the goddess Hāriti as a boon-confering *bodhisattva* who not only symbolizes the well-being of the *saṇgha* (monastic community), but is also adept at providing young or barren couples with children. In those traditions, Hāriti was originally a child-devouring *yakṣi* who was converted by the Buddha when he kidnapped one of her own five-hundred sons, causing her to suffer loss so that she could understand the pain she had inflicted on others.[4] The Buddha was able to elicit Hāriti's compassion for those whom she had made suffer. Having quenched her insatiable appetite for devouring children, the Buddha promised that she would instead be fed rice by his monks for as long as his *saṇgha* prospered. Hence, she came to symbolize the general material well-being of the Buddhist community and was also venerated by laity seeking offspring. Her cult appears to have been popular in Andhra, as in other parts of the Buddhist world, and scores of sculpted images of Hāriti, usually seated with a child sitting on her lap, have been found outside the remains of refectories of Buddhist monastic complexes. The best preserved images in Andhra Pradesh are found at Shankaram (see photo 6.1) and Nagarjunakonda.

Photo 6.1 Hāriti

Many local goddesses were incorporated first into the Buddhist tradition and then later into Sanskritic Hinduism. In his *Myth and Reality*, D. D. Kosambi notes how the cults of many village goddesses in Maharashtra were influenced by Buddhism during the middle of the first millenium C.E. (82–109). Many of these goddesses have been portrayed in rock cut relief sculptures in various Buddhist cave complexes and continue to be venerated today in nearby villages. The incorporation of Hāriti and her continued veneration would seem to be an analogous case in Andhra. With the eclipse of the Buddhist tradition by the eighth or ninth century C.E., and the concomitant sweeping wave of Śaivism of the same period, many folk deities became identified with aspects of the Śaiva cult. This seems to be the case with Erukamma, whom devotees identify with Pārvatī, the consort of Śiva. The icon of Erukamma seems much older than the Śaiva affiliation of this tradition, however. The image of Erukamma (see photo 6.2) in her

Photo 6.2 Erukamma

shrine depicts her with the cutoff head lying in front of her and her right arm wrapped around the kidnapped child sitting on her lap (Hāriti images are usually seen portrayed with her own child in her lap). The origin of this icon, though evidently quite old, is not known to the local people or temple administrators. The image clearly represents the local myth about this goddess, and no iconographic elements can be linked to Pārvatī whatsoever.[5]

As a form of Pārvatī, Erukamma is now served liturgically by a Brahmin priest during the rituals constituting her annual festival. But on all other days, a non-Brahmin belonging to an agricultural caste acts as the ritual preceptor. Worship of Erukamma is usually done directly by the devotees themselves who offer fruits, coconuts, saris, and blouse pieces to the goddess after applying turmeric and vermilion. But on special annual occasions, the Brahmin priest conducts rites on behalf of all devotees for a price. Animal sacrifices are rare, and devotees still take pride in saying that this goddess does not like non-vegetarian food, a reflection of her Buddhist associations with her mythic past.

These details indicate a rich and varied amalgamation of practices and beliefs encompassing aspects of folk, pre-Buddhist, Buddhist, and Śaiva religious cults. Like Hāriti, Erukamma might have originated as a smallpox goddess, capable of devouring children through illness but with protective powers that could be invoked through appropriate propitiation. In the absence of smallpox her protective function has now come to be extended to familial well-being, especially in relation to her power to produce male offspring. This is probably why she is identified by devotees as a form of Pārvatī, who is considered an ideal wife and a mother of two sons. There is, however, evidence of amalgamation in narrative and ritual traditions associated with Erukamma, and it is precisely this amalgamation that contributes to her continuing appeal to a diverse congregation.

Pyḍamma

In another village that has been absorbed by Visakhapatnam, the origins of the worship of Pyḍamma—a goddess functioning quite clearly as a guardian deity—are preserved in oral traditions maintained by lay devotees. It is said that people of that village once participated in a neighboring region's celebration for the goddess, who was renowned for her powers. As the villagers were journeying home on bullock carts, they encountered a young woman clad in a white sari, who stopped the cart of the village headman and requested a ride. Having boarded the cart, she declared that, given the devotion they had expressed during her annual festival, they need not worry about the well-being of their own village in the future; she had decided to take care of it, as a mother cares for her children. When the group reached the outskirts of their village, the young woman got down from the cart saying that she wanted a temple constructed for her worship in that very place. If the villagers would construct it, she claimed, they would always have her blessings. After this, she disappeared.

As time passed, however, the villagers became preoccupied with their mundane activities and neglected to construct her temple. People soon began to suffer from strange and peculiar diseases. At this point, a village elder had a dream in which the goddess appeared and told him she was still with them but was waiting for their recognition before she would begin to take care of them. Realizing their mistake, the villagers immediately took up the task of temple construction with great care and devotion. As soon as the temple was built, they installed an image of Pyḍamma and started worshiping her regularly with oil lamps, incense, and food. The people's afflictions disappeared, and since that time the villagers have remained ardent believers in the protective power of the goddess.

I found it easy to collect many contemporary stories regarding Pyḍamma's protective powers. One story that was told to me with particular enthusiasm was about a railway employee who had come to convey to the villagers a plan for extending railway tracks through the temple's grounds, requiring the temple's demolition. He and his family members then began to face severe problems, leading him to have the plan withdrawn. He became a devotee of the goddess and an ardent supporter of the temple.

People believe that Pyḍamma guards their area from all sorts of evils and that the village is progressing rapidly with economic development through her mercy. The educated devotees refer to her affectionately as *bhukti mukti pradāyanī,* "bestower of comforts in this life and liberation after death." An annual festival is held for her on the full moon day in the month of Phalguna (February–March) during which the goddess is carried in procession with dazzling lights and decorations accompanied by many entertaining troupes of dancers, musicians and singers, as well as fireworks. Clay images of the goddess are carried on women's heads to fulfill vows undertaken for the well-being of husbands and children.

Pyḍamma is now viewed by the people in the area as the incarnation of the goddess Durgā. The homologization of Pyḍamma with Durgā is expressed in different ways, most clearly in the contemporary iconography of the goddess, where Pyḍamma is made to resemble the goddess Durgā quite precisely. She is depicted with four arms, which hold a trident *(triśūla)*, sword *(khaḍga)*, kettle drum with a serpent wound around it *(nāga-ḍamaru)*, and a cup for drinking blood *(rudhira pātra)* (see photo 6.3). She sits on a throne, with her right leg folded up, and her left leg draping down to rest on the demon Mahiṣāsura's head. Given the weapons she holds and the head of the demon being crushed under her foot, she appears aggressive, although her face looks benevolent. In this way she represents a fiercely protective yet benign character. The image is painted every year at the time of her festival. She is clothed in a colorful sari and blouse adorned with ornaments; her face is neatly made up with collyrium on her eyes and a vermilion mark of auspiciousness (*kuṃkuma*) on her forehead.

Devotees of Pyḍamma are eager to identify their goddess and their form of worship as Brahmanic, yet they still observe animal sacrifices during the annual hot season ritual and on other special occasions. Educated devotees have introduced *yantra* meditation practices with the goddess as the object of meditation. This aspect of devotion emphasizes the goddess's ability to bestow *mokṣa*. The *dīkṣa* (vow) that is practiced by the devotees of the famous Kanaka Durgā in Vijayawada has also been introduced.[6] After being initiated by a Brahmin priest,

Photo 6.3 Pyḍamma

participants in the vow maintain a special vegetarian diet and undertake ascetic practices (including celibacy) for somewhere between nine and forty-one days. Devotees also wear only saffron-colored robes, sleep on the floor, observe restraint in speech, and spend leisure time only in praise of the Goddess.

Having lost its rural character many years ago, the village has ceased to view this goddess as a protectress of crops and cattle, and she is no longer associated with children's diseases. Village forms of ritual have also been thoroughly supplanted by more sophisticated urban and Brahmanic ritual forms, except for the annual festival. The contemporary cult of Pyḍamma is, therefore, a jumbled mixture of folk and Sanskritic forms of worship reflecting the sentiments of her wide variety of devotees.

Durgālamma

A similar example of Sanskritization is also evident in the cult of Durgālamma, a goddess from the former village of Durganagar, now also absorbed into Visakhapatnam city through urban expansion. The origin of Durgālamma is recounted in stories about a snake hole from which a very long serpent used to emerge and then suddenly disappear. The serpent was not known to have caused harm to anybody in the village. Villagers often witnessed smoke rising from the snake hole, followed by a sweet smell; devotees attributed these phenomena to Durgālamma, who was thought to be assuming the form of a snake to protect the village. Thus, they started worshipping the snake hole, and eventually a village elder built a temple over it. Following the temple's construction, no one reported any further appearances of the snake. A wooden image of the goddess was installed in an adjacent chamber, and a Brahmin priest was appointed to conduct *pūjā*s. In this instance, the origin of the goddess's worship took place completely within the context of folk belief and only gradually assumed a Brahmanic character. The worship of this goddess continues to be of mixed type; devotees not only offer prayers to the image with the help of priest, but also worship the snake hole directly.

The wooden image of this goddess (see photo 6.4) has four hands, with small bells in her upper hands and a vermilion box in the lower left. The lower right hand is in *abhaya mūdra*, a gesture of protection. Today the foremost function of Durgālamma is to provide longevity to the husbands of her female devotees, who often desire the boon that their husbands should outlive them. Although the myth associates the goddess with a snake, there are no snakes in her image. The iconography of the goddess reflects the enthusiasm for Brahmanic associations among her contemporary devotees who want to regard her not as a "mere village goddess," but as a form of Lakṣmī, the docile wife of Viṣṇu. The identification of Durgālamma with the goddess Lakṣmī but not with the great goddess Durgā, who, in fact, shares the same name, is intriguing. As in many contexts in Visakhapatnam, it may be that most contemporary devotees do not see the need for a warrior goddess, preferring a docile, wifely goddess like Lakṣmī, whose function is to protect husbands and provide wealth.

Photo 6.4 Durgālamma

Polamma

Yet another clear instance of Sanskritization of a village goddess is reflected in the following example from Peda Waltair, another village that has now become a part of Visakhapatnam. Although it managed to retain its village character until recently, Peda Waltair has changed dramatically during the last ten years with the addition of new colonies occupied by an educated, middle-class population from outside the city. Local devotees have been happy to present their goddess to these new arrivals, and Polamma now regularly attracts large crowds to her temple. What is especially interesting in this case is that there is no myth directly linking this goddess to the village where she is now worshipped. In Peda Waltair and similar villages, images of deities were simply imported from elsewhere, and people began to worship them based on others' claims about their protective powers. As for Polamma, stories about her protective powers spread quickly. She eventually became the guardian deity of fourteen other surrounding villages as well, all of which are now part of Visakhapatnam.

According to local oral traditions, in the sixteenth century a family from the fisherman caste went fishing and caught the image of the goddess in their nets. They brought the image home, claiming that it represented the goddess Polamma, and started worshipping her.[7] After a while, they began to feel that it was not appropriate to keep the image in their poor household, so they gave it to the landlord of the village.[8] He established the image in fields at the outskirts of the village (an appropriate place for a village deity who protects borders) and initiated the goddess's worship; since then a member of his (non-Brahmin) family cares for the image. The field where the image was established belonged to a rich man from a neighboring village. It is said that he became very angry that his land was being used, but the goddess came to him in a dream and ordered him to house her on his land. So he built a tiled house for the image and donated one-and-a half acres of land to the goddess. A Brahmin priest has recently replaced the traditional non-Brahmin one, and the image has been fully consecrated.

Elements of Sanskritization are clearly evident in contemporary worship of Polamma. Devotees, for example, now consider her to be the incarnation of the goddess Lakṣmī. *Pūjā* for the goddess is officiated by a Brahmin priest, and the second part of her name has been changed from *-amma*, the Telugu term for "mother," to *-amba*, the Sanskrit equivalent, so that she is now also called Polamāmba, especially among educated devotees. Generally, as a village goddess becomes increasingly well known, the suffix *-amma* tends to change into *-amba* to help legitimate the goddess's Brahmanic status.

The stone image of the goddess (see photo 6.5) stands with four hands. She holds an axe *(paraśu)* and sword *(khaḍga)* in her right hands, and a cup *(pātra)* and *nāga pāśa*, a snake in the form of noose, in the left. Two other goddesses, Nīlamma (also called Nīlamāmba) and Kunchamma (also called Kunchamāmba), now stand on either side of the image of Polamāmba in her shrine. The origins of these images are not currently known, although their names are those of popular vil-

Photo 6.5 Polamma

lage goddesses in the area. Nīlamma (see photo 6.6) is depicted in sitting posture with four hands. She is holding a trident and a sword in her right hands, and a cup and *nāga pāśa* in the left. Kunchamma (see photo 6.7) is shown seated on a pedestal with two hands holding a knife in her right hand and a cup in the left. All three images are benign in appearance despite the weapons they carry. These iconographic features conform to the iconographic texts where multiple forms of Devī are described (Gopinatha Rao 1985, 356–368).

Photo 6.6 Nīlamma

Photo 6.7 Kunchamma

Kanaka Durgā

In contrast with the goddesses discussed above, sometimes a goddess is borrowed from Brahmanic tradition to serve as the guardian deity of a village. This is true of the goddess Kanaka Durgā, who takes the form of Kanakamma in the village of China Waltair, which has undergone the same type of change as Peda Waltair. Hence, although the respective goddesses of these two villages have different origins, their cults have gone through the same kind of transition.

The image of the goddess Kanaka Durgā that resides in China Waltair is as old as the village itself. Some three hundred years ago, according to local oral traditions, the village head, whose name was Naidu, dreamed that the goddess Vijayawāḍa Kanaka Durgā told him she would take care of his village. The next morning he journeyed to Vijayawāda, where he procured an image of Durgā from the famous temple of the goddess Kanaka Durgā. He brought the image back to his village and assigned the task of its daily worship to his wife, who reluctantly agreed to the job. One night when the couple was sleeping, Naidu went into a trance in which the goddess led him to the sea and told him to take a dip. After bathing, he vowed that he and his future generations would worship the goddess with care and attention. Meanwhile, his wife awoke to find the house empty and the doors locked from the inside. There was a knock on the door, and she opened it to find her wet husband, who had returned from the sea, standing at the threshold. After learning what had happened she, too, for the first time, began to feel devotion toward the Goddess. Eventually she and the rest of the village became sincere devotees.

The transformation of a form of Durgā into the village goddess Kanakamma is, in effect, a type of "de-Sanskritization," meaning that a Brahmanical goddess has been turned into a local deity. This "de-Sanskritization," however, has been followed by a "re-Sanskritization" of the same goddess. Since the time of Naidu's dip in the sea until a few years ago, Naidu's (non-Brahmin) descendants served as the goddess's priests. Recently, however, the temple was rebuilt and the image reinstalled with consecration rites performed by a Brahmin pundit (scholar in brahmanical rituals), probably in response to an increasingly educated and professional congregation of devotees. A Brahmin has now replaced the traditional non-Brahmin priest, and this goddess has become "Brahminized" once again.

Whether this goddess is Śaiva or Vaiṣṇava has been an issue of dispute. The icon of Kanakamma came to be known as Kanaka Mahālakṣmī after the Department of Endowments identified it as Mahālakṣmī. But when it was reinstalled and consecrated, the pundits recognized its details and declared that it was Siṃhavāhinī (lion rider) and therefore Kanaka Durgā, an incarnation of Pārvatī, which corroborates local oral tradition. The image (see photo 6.8) stands on a pedestal made of a coiled serpent, depicting a goddess with four hands holding a noose (*pasa*) and spoon (*sruk*) in the right hands, and an *akṣaya patra*, a vessel that perennially supplies food, and kettle drum with a serpent wound around it (*nāga-ḍamaru*) in the left. This iconography conforms to the description of Tūlaja Bhavānī, a food-offering incarnation of Pārvatī, as recounted in normative iconographic texts. Tūlaja Bhavānī is said to hold a jewelled vessel containing food in one hand and a spoon in the other to distribute the food to her devotees, with her two additional hands holding a noose and a trident (Rajeswari 1989, 32).

In the cases of both Polamma and Kanakamma, it appears that even though Brahmanic, anthropomorphic images are installed as consecrated images and liturgically celebrated by a Brahmin, village characteristics remain predominant. Both are still considered to be earth mothers who are believed to assume the form of snakes to protect the village from all calamities. In both cases, devotees may sacrifice an animal to the goddess to show their gratitude on special occasions.

The annual rituals for Polamma and Kanakamma are almost identical in their details and reveal the agricultural base of their cults. The ceremonies start with an invitation for the goddess to attend the festival as an honored guest. This is done by offering food and water to a snake hole (usually an ant hill that is the abode of a snake) near the temple and bringing a sample of the soil from this hole to the

Photo 6.8 Kanaka Durgā

center of the village, which serves as a ritual stage. This soil is regarded as fertile, and the snake that lives in it is considered a symbol of fertility. The fertility of the goddess is equated with both the earth and the snake. The sample soil along with consecrated pots *(ghaṭas)* containing food and water are placed on the stage where all the festivities of the annual rite will take place over a fifteen to thirty day period. In one of the most important rites of the annual ceremony, *pāthana,* devotees bring samples of the crops they have reaped from their fields and offer them to the goddess. Today, devotees usually bring fruit rather than the traditional newly harvested grains. Another important rite associated with the goddess's festival, *toliyērlu,* also has strong agricultural overtones. In this rite, devotees plough the land around the stage with decorated ploughs to mark the beginning of agricultural year. On the final day of the annual festival, appointed low-caste individuals bring sacrificial animals and offer them to the goddess on behalf of the whole village. Because of legal bans imposed on various types of animal sacrifices, buffaloes are now excluded from sacrifice.

Mariḍamma

Mariḍamma is a goddess of the lowest caste community in Visakhapatnam. Although the present constitution of the government of India declares that caste should not be a barrier to individual progress, this caste remains economically disadvantaged. In Visakhapatnam, this community has constituted for many years a distinct, segregated community, although their colony is now surrounded by new settlements and is physically connected to the other parts of city.

The origin of the worship of the goddess, Mariḍamma, is simple but quite interesting in terms of the process of Sanskritization that it reflects. According to oral tradition, four generations ago a young married couple from the above-mentioned community were travelling to visit their relatives when they spotted a beautiful little Brahmin girl. This girl told the couple that if they would worship her, their lot in life would greatly improve. The couple agreed, and the next morning they saw a tiny Margosa or Neem tree—a tropical tree that has cooling shade and medicinal values—in front of their camp exactly where the Brahmin girl had stood the day before. They believed that the girl herself was transformed into a sapling, so they brought it home carefully, planted it, and initiated worship.

As the plant grew into a big tree, the number of worshippers increased, and a platform was built around the tree. Today devotees worship the tree whenever they wish by applying turmeric and vermilion to its trunk and offering fruits and coconuts. During annual festival days, both male and female descendants of the founding couple's family act as the goddess's priests. Since the goddess is believed to be a Brahmin herself, she does not take animal sacrifices. Village, caste, and Sanskritic elements all contribute to the identity of this goddess and her forms of worship, but in this case the Sanskritic elements appear to be pretty much ornamental and act primarily as factors of prestige.[9]

Ellamma

While many local goddesses in South India operate at the village level, others are more widely worshiped. Ellamma is one such goddess. In Andhra Pradesh, her worship has come to be even more prevalent in urban areas than in villages, although she is of village origin. This can be discerned from the Telugu meaning of the name "Ellamma" which, like the name "Polamma" (also Polimēramma), indicates that she is the mother or protectress of the (village) borders.

Elamma's cult originated in Tamilnadu, where it mixed with Brahmanic elements but also retained elements of its folk origins. Worship of Ellamma seems to have been present in the central part of Visakhapatnam since the town itself was constructed. At one time, a large grove of mango trees surrounded a modest shrine to Ellamma in the heart of the city. A modern urban landscape has now taken its place, and the goddess has to be content with a humble shrine at the roadside. She is worshipped in the shape of a small wooden image (see photo 6.9) accompanied by a smaller wooden image of Pōturāju (the common brother of all village goddesses, who acts as their assistant). Ellamma, like other typical village goddesses, is closely associated with serpent symbolism. Sometimes a snake hole is worshipped as the goddess Ellamma herself. Whenever she is portrayed iconographically, she is depicted with serpents all over her head or body (Ziegenbalg 1984, 137).

The myth of Ellamma is common throughout South India and is told with little variation in different regions (see Biardeau 1982, 131–133). In brief, Jamadagni, a famous Purāṇic sage, suspected his wife's virtue after she glanced at another man while drawing water at the river, so he ordered his son Paraśurāma to cut off her head. Paraśurāma did his father's bidding, and Ellama's severed head fell near Paṇchamas, who were then considered to be Untouchables. Paraśurāma approached his father to request a boon in exchange for having carried out his orders; ironically, the boon he requested was that his mother be restored to life. Jamadagni granted the boon,

Photo 6.9 Ellamma

decreeing that henceforth Ellamma would be worshipped by the Paṇchamas, since her head fell in the Paṇchama's colony. This myth is important in the sense that it links two castes that are hierarchically at opposite ends: Jamadagni is from a highly ranked Brahmin caste, but in the myth the worship of Ellamma becomes associated with a lowly Untouchable caste.

Although the priests of this goddess still come from the Paṇchama community, devotees come from all castes. Hence, there is some similarity here to processes discussed in relation to Mariḍamma, but Ellamma is not strictly associated with the Untouchable community. In some parts of Andhra Pradesh, she is usually identified with the goddess Ekavīra, the guardian deity of the Kākatiyas, the famous medieval dynasty that ruled over the Telugu area. Since goddesses are strongly associated with the protection of boundaries, it is not surprising that they should have figured prominantly in the cultic life of royal courts; boundaries of empires are simply an extension of village boundaries. It is in fact fairly common throughout Indian history that folk or village goddesses function as guardian deities for political rulers.

Kanaka Mahālakṣmī

The principal of protection is again evident in the cult of Kanaka Mahālakṣmī, who seems to have functioned as a guardian deity for the entire town of Visakhapatnam. According to a story preserved in the *Visakhapatnam Gazeteer*, at one time there was a king named Viśākha ruling over this region. His fort, which was located in the same place where this goddess's temple now stands, was surrounded by sea on all sides except the south. This south side was heavily guarded from possible invasions, and an image of the guardian goddess was also kept there and worshipped. In the seventeenth century, due to invasions by Marathas and Muslims, the fort was destroyed, and the image was mutilated and thrown into a well. Then in the early twentieth century, a Vaiṣṇava woman of this area dreamed of the goddess who told her from which well the image could be recovered. The image was found in its mutilated condition and was installed in 1917 as Kanaka Mahālakṣmī. A society was formed to take care of her daily worship.

The temple is wealthy owing to the goddess's popular patronage, but whenever there is an attempt to build a new temple to enshrine the image, the Goddess appears to a devotee in his or her dreams and orders that this not be done. When the society tried to build a new shrine for her several years ago, for example, a woman claiming to be possessed by the goddess said that she did not require any shelter, as she prefers to stay only in open places where she can be worshipped directly by devotees. In the cult of this goddess, again, we see clear compromises between priestly and popular beliefs and forms of worship. From the beginning of the cult, the society stipulated that there should not be any form of animal sacrifice to the goddess; hence, the goddess is offered only vegetarian food. Now the

Department of Endowments of the Andhra Pradesh state government, which has taken care of the temple since 1970, follows a similar policy of sponsoring Brahmanical rites. Brahmin priests conduct rites for the goddess at appropriate times. Nevertheless, non-Brahmanical elements also persist. Despite the presence of Brahmin priests, for example, devotees may also approach and worship the image without any mediation. Devotees fervently believe in the goddess's protective powers, and stories about her saving people from disease and danger are legion. People of this area often report that they have seen the goddess walking about the local environs incarnated as a teenage girl at all times of the day or night. She is venerated not only by Hindus, but by Muslims as well.

The mutilated image of the deity (see photo 6.10) reflects a peaceful and benign attitude. The one remaining hand holds a closed lotus. Her image conforms to the description of Sāmānya Lakṣmī, the simple portrayal of Lakṣmī with only two hands (Rajeswari 1989, 21).

Conclusion

My study of goddess traditions in Visakhapatnam suggests several points regarding how these traditions change in the context of rapid urbanization. Such change is often signaled in contemporary goddess iconography. First, goddesses now tend to be rendered anthropomorphically rather than aniconically even if they originated as village deities. Second, in the case of goddesses with village associations, such as Durgālamma and Polamma, there is a clear attempt to make them user-friendly to the urban population by disguising their village origins. In Visakhapatnam, despite the weapons they carry, almost all the goddesses appear gentle and benevolent. A shift in the use of symbols appears to be occurring, from those that designate the ferocity of goddesses (such as hands holding a skull full of blood, or serpents covering the entire bodies of goddesses) to symbols that are more benign. In addition to war weapons, for example, these goddesses tend to be depicted holding a cup. This cup acts as a container for the goddess to drink the blood offered to her. In some recent images, however, it has been replaced by a vermilion box (see photo 6.4). The disappearance of the blood drinking cup can be attributed to the disappearance of dangerous contagious diseases, which eliminates the need for devotees to offer blood sacrifice. The presence of the vermilion box in its stead indicates the growing number of women devotees who approach the goddess for the longevity of their married status. Traditionally, vermilion is offered either by a priest or by an

Photo 6.10 Kanaka Mahālakṣmī

elderly married woman to other married women as a way to bless their married status. At the same time, myth, iconography, and festival practices underscore the rural associations of these goddesses, with snakes symbolizing fertility and protective powers.[10]

There are numerous instances in which local goddesses are regarded as incarnations of "great tradition" goddesses, an extension of the notion articulated in the Devī-Mahātmya that all goddesses or *śakti*s are perceived to be different aspects of the one Śakti, the Great Goddess. Yet iconographic, mythic, and ritual elements that reflect the local origins of these goddesses are still evident in most cases. Sanskritization is evident, too, in the increased emphasis given to the performance of liturgies constituting regularized *pūjā*. Though there are still annual festivals held in honor of these goddesses, it is the daily *pūjā* that now has become the most important ritual occasion for many devotees. This shift from annual rite to daily *pūjā* seems clearly to reflect the transformation of goddesses from symbols of collective well-being and protection to their roles as boon-conferring deities benefiting the material and vocational aspirations of devotees. Accordingly, goddesses are seen as increasingly responsive to the needs of male devotees, since husbands are seen as the economic centerpiece of nuclear family livelihood. At the same time, many of these goddesses are accessible for direct worship to their devotees without a priest's mediation.

In the contexts explored in this essay, Sanskritization in general seems to be motivated by two factors. First, Brahmanic associations bring with them an element of prestige. This is most clearly evident in cults like Mariḍamma and Ellamma, where communities of the lowest order in the caste hierarchy appropriate Brahmanical associations. Second, and more to the point of this essay, Sanskritization of goddess cults in urban contexts, where the population is very diverse, provides a way for members of different classes, castes, and ethnic groups to relate to the goddess, since in India Sanskritic forms of worship transcend local barriers and include divergent groups. Adaptation of some forms of Sanskritic patterns of ritual, iconography, and myth seem to function as a religious lingua franca for many Hindus, making the cults of local goddesses accessible to all.

These case studies in Visakhapatnam also reflect other nuanced changes that are occurring in different locales. For example, the insistence of devotees that their goddess is a form of Lakṣmī represents a change in aspiration among contemporary folk living in Dondaparthy and Durganagar areas. The general expectations of Indian society about the roles of women as devoted wives and mothers are evidenced here by devotees through the attributed qualities of their goddesses. This does not mean, however, that the unmarried goddess Durgā is ignored in Visakhapatnam. There is extensive worship of Durgā images during the ten day India-wide festival of Dasahara in October, and in the case of local goddesses like Pyḍamma there is a deliberate attempt in the iconography and form of worship to show that the goddess is the form of Durgā. This attempt can be attributed to educated devotees, especially those retired from their jobs who are seeking *mokṣa* and who are thus active in transforming Pyḍamma into the form of Durgā through the introduction of meditation and penance. In the case of Polamma and Kanaka Durgā there is not much enthusiasm to identify them with one of the Sanskrit deities. There was a debate among Brahmin pundits about the identity of Kanaka Durgā's image, but devotees do not participate in it. Worshipped by many villages from the very beginning, these two goddesses are famous as they are for their protective powers. Finally in the case of the devotees of Kanaka Mahālakṣmī in the business center of Visakhapatnam, middle-class worshippers have pooled their efforts to retain a Brahmanic deity as their own deity without priestly mediation. Unlike the devotees of Mariḍamma, who until recently were not accepted into Brahmanic temples, the devotees of this area have many temples in which to offer prayers with priestly intervention. But like the devotees of Mariḍamma, they too found a need for a local vegetarian deity whom they can approach directly.

While my study reflects the fact that Sanskritization seems to be proliferating, it needs to be emphasized strongly that the basic power of these goddesses still has to do with their protective capacities. Although some older, educated devotees add *mokṣa* to the boons offered by their goddess, the primary function of these goddesses remains the fulfillment of this-worldly desires. It is this power that unites them all, supporting the perception that there is just one powerful Goddess with many forms. What is "great" about the Great Goddess is her perceived ability to care for her devotees in their worldly pursuits and desires. At the heart of her dispensation are the motherly qualities of compassion, love, fertility, and protection. In seeking Mahādevī in Visakhapatnam, therefore, what we find is not so much an elevated vision of what the goddess may symbolize in abstract philosophical discourse about her cosmic ultimacy, but rather a celebration of her consistent, fundamental association with the power to grant protection and material prosperity.

Notes

1. This is a free translation from the Telegu into English.

2. The fieldwork upon which this study is based was completed over many months in 1993 and 1994. I conducted interviews with priests and devotees at these goddess shrines throughout regions of Visakhapatnam by recording their personal experiences and documenting rituals performed for these goddesses.

3. I compared the information I drew from my personal observations and interviews during my fieldwork in many village and urban folk goddess temples in Andhra Pradesh with early works, such as Ziezenbalg 1984 and Whitehead 1980.

4. For a summary of the story and citations of the relevant Taisho texts, see Lamotte 1988, 688–689.

5. Another possible explanation regarding the origins of this goddess might be connected to the *mātṛkā* (mother goddess) figures, who are often portrayed with children in their laps. The *mātṛkās* are usually seven in number and are considered to fuse aboriginal and Vedic symbolism with literature and iconography associated with Skanda, who was absorbed into Śaivism as the son of Śiva. The seventh mother came to be seen as Pārvatī, wife of Śiva and Skanda's mother. This identification seems to be so popular that devotees of Erukamma could easily identify the goddess as the incarnation of Pārvatī, the seventh *mātṛkā*. See Harper 1989, 47–71, for a discussion of the cult of the *saptamātṛkā*.

6. Kanaka Durgā in Vijayawada was originally a village goddess independent of the Brahmanic tradition. A remnant feature of propitiating her as a village goddess is evident in the offering of animal sacrifices, which take place quickly and without much publicity once a year during the time of her annual festival. There is a tendency among most of the villagers of Andhra Pradesh to identify their village goddess with Kanaka Durgā of Vijayawada.

7. The name "Polamma" is a short form for Polimeramma, a Telugu word meaning "mother of borders." Since many goddesses act as border guardians, many village goddesses are called by such names.

8. The committee of the temple of Polamma maintains records from which we know that land was donated to Polamma during the sixteenth century by the village landlord, traditionally the wealthiest and powerful member of the village.

9. This case has parallels with the one described in Cohn 1955, 53–57.

10. Scholars acknowledge that many village goddesses were introduced into Brahmanical literature as *mātṛkās* (mothers), who were characterized as bloodthirsty and destructive but who later came to be identified as the benign consorts of male deities. Some of the *mātṛkās* are portrayed iconographically in fierce form with emaciated bodies, protruding tongue, rolling eyes, wearing a garland of human skulls, and carrying a skull filled with blood.

Chapter 7

Reconstructing the Split Goddess as Śakti in a Tamil Village

Elaine Craddock

It was another hot, sultry afternoon in July; the overcast sky seemed to press down on me along with the heavy air, and the grey light made the temple area feel even more desolate. There is a proverb in Tamil that declares that Māriyammaṉ, the smallpox goddess, should not reside where she can hear the sound of the grinding stone that women use to grind flour and spices; in other words, people should not build their houses too close to Māriyammaṉ's temples because it is too dangerous for people to live near her. Therefore, this famous pilgrimage temple in Periyapāḷaiyam, a small village near Madras, stands by itself on a desolate stretch of land at the edge of the village. The goddess of Periyapāḷaiyam is called Bavāṉiyammaṉ, but she is considered a form of Māriyammaṉ. Stories and praise songs about Māriyammaṉ are told about Bavāṉiyammaṉ as well, along with the stories that are specifically about Bavāṉiyammaṉ and the village of Periyapāḷaiyam. Devotees use Māriyammaṉ and Bavāṉiyammaṉ interchangeably.

I was sitting with my research associate, Mr. G. Stephen,[1] under a huge thatch canopy held up by bamboo poles talking to Selvam, an ardent devotee of Bavāṉiyammaṉ. Selvam is a member of the barber caste, and underneath this canopy is where he and his coworkers shave the heads of people who have given their hair as a vow to Bavāṉiyammaṉ. Devotees shave their heads in return for Bavāṉiyammaṉ's grace and blessings: for the birth of a child, recovery from illness, prosperity in business, even doing well on an exam. People bring other offerings to the goddess, but hair is a special symbol of personal sacrifice and devotion, particularly for women, who are expected to keep their hair long as a mark of beauty and traditional femininity. Selvam was telling us how Bavāṉiyammaṉ's grace had converted him from a life of petty crime to one of devotion to her, how he had crept into her temple one night to steal money from the offering box, but when he looked up at her face a divine light emanated from her eyes and penetrated his soul. He now lived near the temple and worked to support his family, doing much of his business during the busy annual festival that takes place from July through September.

By the time I met Selvam, I had visited more Māriyammaṉ temples in South India than I could remember. I had seen enough to know that the European missionaries' accounts of a cruel Māriyammaṉ, who demanded unspeakable atrocities of her devotees, were severely at odds with devotees' own fervent praise and love of Māriyammaṉ. But I was not expecting Selvam, the barber, to break spontaneously into a song he had written to Bavāṉiyammaṉ. As I listened to him sing passionately of his devotion to her, I saw that she was not just a fearful deity but the object of intense love. Selvam's description of seeing the light emanating from Bavāṉiyammaṉ's eyes connects the sacred experience of *darśan,* the exchange of vision between the deity and the devotee, with the contemporary world of Tamil goddess films, in which a favorite dramatic element is showing the beams of light emanating from the goddess's eyes to guide the hero or heroine back to the devotional fold. She may have many arms holding weapons, and sometimes fangs dripping blood, but she is also a loving mother to her devotees. After all, the "ammaṉ" in Bavāṉiyammaṉ means "mother" or "woman" in Tamil, as well as "goddess."

Māriyammaṉ is traditionally the goddess of smallpox; she has the power to afflict with pox, as well as to take it away. Smallpox is a sign of the goddess's favor, a manifestation of her dwelling in the body of the devotee. Pox is also a reminder not to stray from ever-mindful devotion to her. In the past, whenever an outbreak of smallpox would occur—usually at least once a year—a clay image of Māriyammaṉ would be made, or a clay pot would be used to call her down. Blood offerings would be made to her, she would be taken around the boundary of the village, and then her image would be thrown into the river. If she were satisfied with the devotions, she would take the pox away from the village. Since the eradication of smallpox Māriyammaṉ continues to function as both a destructive and healing force, a mother whose children are her devotees, whom she punishes and rewards as she sees fit. She is often pictured as a fierce, angry goddess with a voracious appetite for blood sacrifice and a capricious character, a vivid manifestation of ambivalent power. Originally a low-caste goddess, emerging from the agricultural milieu in which the majority of Indians still live, she now draws devotees from urban as well as rural areas and across caste lines. Some high-caste Hindus, however—influenced both by the British Raj and by indigenous forces of elite reform—denounce Māriyammaṉ and her ilk as pre-enlightened, irrational superstition.

Devotees consider Bavāṉiyammaṉ to be one of the Seven Sisters, a group of goddesses related to each other partly by their efficacious responses to human need. They are probably related to the Seven Mothers, the *saptamātṛkā* in Sanskritic mythology, and are widely represented iconographically (Erndl 1993, 11–12, 26–28, 37–38, passim). Many of the village temples in Tamilṅadu have seven stones that are frequently interpreted as the Seven Sisters or the Seven Mothers. The particular names of the seven goddesses differ widely; most of the goddesses named are responsible for disease and healing. Bavāṉiyammaṉ devotees most often named Ellamma and Gaṅgamma as her sister goddesses; several also named Kālī as a sister goddess. Some devotees told us that what differentiated Bavāṉiyammaṉ from Durgā or Kālī is that she is born in an anthill, but ultimately all three goddesses are really the same goddess. What seems important is that the goddesses are linked, and their identities and functions overlap and intersect.

In fact, devotees consider all of the many village goddesses to be one Goddess, one Śakti. *Śakti* is the female, primordial force that pervades the universe, that brings the universe into being. *Śakti* is anthropomorphized as the Supreme Goddess, the creator of the cosmos as well as the cosmos itself, and devotees use the epithets "Śakti" and "Ammaṉ" interchangeably to refer to this one divine female. Particular goddesses are recognized as distinct, yet they are also multiple forms of the same, unified Śakti.[2] To her devotees, Bavāṉiyammaṉ is the Goddess, Śakti, whom they perceive to be a protective mother. Bavāṉiyammaṉ is also connected to her devotees through other kinship roles, as is evident in the annual festival at Periyapāḷaiyam.

There is, however, another side to her identity, for this protective mother is also a bloodthirsty deity who traditionally requires blood sacrifices from her devotees. Both explicit and implicit themes of sacrifice, suffering, and death pervade the myths, songs, and ritual activities associated with Bavāṉiyammaṉ/Māriyammaṉ. These themes are closely tied to the Goddess's nature as Śakti, power. As Śakti, the Goddess embodies the power of life and death that pervades and sustains the created world *(saṃsāra)*. Such power is associated also with the act of sacrifice, especially blood sacrifice, along with the act of killing that it entails and the physical suffering that comes with sacrificial death. It is especially the transformative nature of this power that is emphasized in myths and rituals associated with the Goddess in this context.

From Sacrificial Victim to Śakti Incarnate: The Reṇukā Myth

The stories explaining how Māriyammaṉ got to be *who* she is vary from region to region. In the northern areas of Tamilnadu, especially in Chingleput and the Madras area, the story of how the Goddess became Māriyammaṉ or one of her sisters tends to be a version of the story of Reṇukā, found in the Mahābhārata (3.116.1–18). This is one common rendition:

The Story of Reṇukā

> In an *āśram* near the village live Jamadagni and his wife Reṇukā. Every day Reṇukā goes to the river to gather water for her husband's *pūjā*. She has the gift of bringing water without a vessel of any kind; through the power of her chastity, she forms the water into the shape of a pot and carries it home with her. One day as Reṇukā is bending over the river to collect some water, a Gandharva flies overhead, and she sees his reflection in the water. Admiring his beauty, she instantly loses her chastity, and with it her ability to collect water without a vessel. So she goes home empty-handed and despondent.
>
> Through his spiritual vision Jamadagni sees his wife returning without the water, so he knows she has lost her chastity, and in a rage he orders their son Paraśurāma to kill his mother. Paraśurāma assents on the condition that his father grant him a boon, which Jamadagni agrees to do. So Paraśurāma obediently picks up an ax and chases his mother to kill her. Reṇukā runs and hides in the house of a washerwoman. The washerwoman tries to protect her, but Paraśurāma finds them and chops off both of their heads. Paraśurāma goes back to his father, reports his deed, and asks for his boon. Jamadagni says, "I will grant you whatever you ask." Paraśurāma asks that his mother be brought back to life. Jamadagni gives Paraśurāma a vessel of water and tells him to attach his mother's head to her body and sprinkle her with water, and she will come back to life.

> Paraśurāma rushes to the washerwoman's house, attaches two heads to two bodies and sprinkles them with water, and they both spring back to life. But alas, in his haste Paraśurāma has attached the wrong heads to the wrong bodies! Jamadagni refuses to take his wife back, as she now has the body of an untouchable. So Reṇukā becomes the goddess Bavāṉiyammaṉ, and the washerwoman becomes Mātaṅkiyammaṉ [whose shrine is usually located near the main temple.][3]

In the version of this story found in the Mahābhārata and in many folk versions of this tale, the action of the male protagonists is played out on the body of the wife and mother. But the Mahābhārata episode is a story of filial piety, whereas the Periyapāḷaiyam version describes the making of a goddess, partly through the Untouchable woman who protects Reṇukā. The village tale is also about the construction of a community: Reṇukā's individual dismemberment and reconstruction lead to greater community integration. Some versions of the Reṇukā story we heard differed in the details, but an important point is that nearly everyone we met in Periyapāḷaiyam knew some version of this story. For them, Reṇukā *is* Bavāṉiyammaṉ.

Reṇukā's suffering and untimely death is in fact a common path to deification in village cults. Stuart Blackburn details how people who lived or were known in the village and who died violently may be worshiped as part of the most localized realm of the divine hierarchy (Blackburn 1985, 255–274). Although Bavāṉiyammaṉ is here identified with Reṇukā, a pan-Indian figure, the playing out of this mythic scenario is influenced by the ways village cults appropriate divine power from local beings. In this story Reṇukā is a local woman, living in "the village." Some renditions of this common tale specify that she and Jamadagni live in an āśram in Periyapāḷaiyam. When her son chases her with an ax, she runs to another local woman, identified by caste. Her grisly murder echoes the crucial element in the deification of local beings: the innocence of the victim is not what matters, it is suffering and violence that transforms a person into a deity. Blackburn reports that this point was driven home to him when he was discussing why a particular woman, rather than her evil sister-in-law, was deified. He assumed that the sister-in-law wasn't worshiped because she was evil, but the villagers replied, "No . . . the sister-in-law is not a goddess not because she is evil *(keṭṭa)* because she didn't suffer; Nalla Taṅkāḷ [the goddess] might be evil, too, but we worship her because she suffered and died" (260). A person who has suffered and died a violent and unnatural death has too much power and must be transferred to an acceptable category—a deity people can propitiate—rather than left to wander around tormenting people on Earth. By worshiping this deity, people can safely make contact with this force, and that power is made accessible. Although Māriyammaṉ, along with her northern sister Śītala, may be more widely known throughout India than some of the more narrowly localized goddesses, she embodies the inimitable and immediate power of violent death transformed that characterizes the most sought after local deities.[4]

Much of the scholarly discussion of the Reṇukā myth has centered on Reṇukā's sexual transgression and on male fear of dangerous female sexuality (Brubaker 1978; Harper 1969; Hart 1973). But Frederique Marglin argues persuasively against the notion that female sexuality is inherently dangerous and must be controlled by a male consort (Marglin 1985, 39–60). She shifts the focus instead to the dangers of celibacy for non-ascetic males and females in the world of birth, death, and rebirth—that is, the world of *saṃsāra*. Marglin then reinterprets female sexuality in the context of auspiciousness and inauspiciousness, which encompass but are not bound by notions of purity and pollution. Sexuality, menstruation, and birth are impure but auspicious processes.

Female sexuality is not only inherently auspicious, but it is also regenerative, for it is linked to childbirth and therefore to creation. Analogously, in religious ritual, it is sacrifice that makes (re-) generation possible. For example, in Ṛg Veda 10.90, the cosmic *puruṣa* is the sacrificial victim from whom is born the entire universe. And in many Tamil village festivals, a buffalo is sacrificed to Māriyammaṉ in order to feed her and regenerate her power, as well as to revitalize the connections between the goddess and her devotees.

In the myth Reṇukā is beheaded; when her head is placed on the Untouchable woman's body, she is restored as the goddess Bavāṉiyammaṉ. Reṇukā is like a sacrificial victim; her violent death catalyzes her regeneration in a more powerful form, as the Goddess who appears on Earth to support her devotees.[5] *Śakti,* female power, includes both inauspicious, fierce aspects as well as benevolent, auspicious aspects, and in this case *śakti* cuts both ways. The fierce power that Reṇukā gains through her suffering is transformed when Reṇukā becomes Bavāṉiyammaṉ, whose fierce power is viewed by her worshipers as a protective potency that demonstrates a mother's supreme love.

Devī as Śakti has cosmogonic/cosmological associations in many contexts, but in the worship of the Goddess in Periyapāḷaiyam, *śakti* also means action: *śakti* is the Goddess's ability to make things happen, to act on behalf of her devotees. Women devotees in particular worship Bavāṉiyammaṉ in order to maintain their families' welfare; they act so that the goddess will act in response. Women's ability to act on behalf of others is part of their *śakti,* which flows from the goddess. It is generally believed that women, by virtue of their femaleness, have more *śakti* than men. In conversations with Bavāṉiyammaṉ devotees, I was struck by the way they responded to questions about the goddess. When asked about Bavāṉiyammaṉ's *śakti,* devotees would answer with "action-oriented" language: "If *X* happens, then we worship Bavāṉiyammaṉ by doing *Y*. In our village when children get sick, we take them to Bavāṉiyammaṉ; in that village over there, if their children get sick, they take them to Chiṉṉamma." In each village, in each place, people are intimately connected to their goddess through ritual interactions; the *śakti* that flows from the goddess to her devotees and back to her is negotiated through the proper ritual actions. The goddess is *śakti* because of what she does in response to devotional rituals performed by her devotees. Hence, her identity as Śakti is to at least some extent "constructed" through ritual interaction.

Suffering and Sacrifice in the Worship of Bavāṉiyammaṉ

Bavāṉiyammaṉ is part of an extensive mythic tradition in Tamilnadu that is connected to pan-Indian narratives about the Great Goddess and *śakti.* In the opening invocation of the hymn below, Māriyammaṉ is explicitly referred to as Mahādevī:

> May my guru prosper, may he support me in this endeavor.
> May Ganeśa, who has golden feet and
> whose steady strength and powerful support are always with me,
> Help me to artfully sing this praise song to
> Māriyammaṉ,
> Mahādevī, who is the Goddess of Smallpox.

In the following lullaby, Māriyammaṉ is referred to as *śakti,* and as the Mother. The song also lists several rituals common to Māriyammaṉ temples in Tamilnadu, many of which are practiced in Periyapāḷaiyam as well.

> The Goddess is multiple, yet all of her forms are *śakti.*
> Ganapathi [Ganeśa] will protect us, as I sing with love

A lullaby to Māriyamman̲, Viṣṇu's little sister,
Whom everyone on earth praises every day
with feeling,
As the queen of all women.

O lady who appeared, swinging on the hook,
People don't know you are the supreme guru,
You who swing here and there on the heavy hook with side ropes.

You sit as Śakti;
You received the sacrifice of a single sheep.
You sat on the village boundary and received the sacrifice of a male buffalo.

O you who are the goddess of all occupations,
You are the great ruler of all the directions.
Please come, Digambari.

O Mother who stands in the triangular center *(cakra)* as the first, as Śakti,
Please come, Śankari, O Mother, One Who Has Responsibility,
O Beautiful One who is the First Cause,
Sitting in the center of the four-cornered sacrificial fire *(homa)* pit
In the golden hall of Chidambaram.

O Sister of Narāyaṇan̲, Beautiful One,
Goddess of the Cremation Ground who afflicts with pox,
The thorns that pierced the sides of the body have gone completely away.

You spread the knife-like neem leaves all over the world;
Now you have taken back the neem spears that you gave.

O supreme Mārimutu, whose form is like fire,
Goddess of Fire that does not yield,
Goddess of Fire that cannot be reached.
O Goddess of Kaṇṇan̲ūr!

. . . You are a pearl in the world, O Mother,
Chaste Lady.[6]

This lullaby has no date, but was probably written within the last century. It combines both classical and folk elements in praising Māriyammaṉ: she is the First Cause of the universe (Tamil *mutal,* Sanskrit *pradhāna*), yet she haunts the cremation ground, like Turmāri in Padavedu, and like Kālī. She spreads the neem leaves that both stab like knives and cool heated skin; she afflicts people with pox, and she takes it away. She is a pearl in the world: the pearl is a gem, something of beauty, as well as a euphemism for the pox pustule that Māriyammaṉ afflicts her devotees with as a sign of her grace. She is the great ruler of all the directions, but she also guards the boundaries of the village. She sits at the center of the Vedic fire sacrifice, yet she also accepts the sacrifice of sheep and male buffalos.

Rituals to Māriyammaṉ encompass the practice of blood sacrifice described in this song. In Tamil villages the buffalo is traditionally the favored sacrifice to the goddess, with a special role reserved for the head. Across from the main temple in Periyapāḷaiyam is the *śakti maṇṭapam,* a platform that was formerly used for animal sacrifices to Bavāṉiyammaṉ, especially of male buffaloes, although the priests told us that blood sacrifices are no longer performed. In 1912 Edgar Thurston recorded one of the rituals at Periyapāḷaiyam as "[t]hrowing a live fowl on to the top of the temple" (Thurston 1979, 150), which is exactly what is done today.

In both myth and ritual the buffalo is a symbol of power, which is transferred to the Goddess through sacrifice. In some village rituals, the buffalo's blood is drunk in order to ingest its strength.[7] Why the buffalo is sacrificed to the goddess is explained by this version of a widely disseminated myth:

> Once upon a time there lived a Ṛishi who had a fair daughter. A Chaṇḍāla, *i.e.,* an Outcaste, desired to marry her. He went to Kāsī (Benares) in the disguise of a Brāhman, where, under the tuition of a learned Brāhman, he became well versed in the *śāstras* . . . and learnt the Brāhman modes of life. On his return he passed himself off for a Brāhman, and after some time made offers to the Ṛishi lady, and somehow succeeded in prevailing upon her to marry him. She did so, her father also consenting to the match. They lived a married life for some time, and had children. One day it so happened that one of the children noticed the father stitch an old shoe previous to going out for a bath. This seemed curious, and the child drew the mother's attention to it. The mother, by virtue of her *tapas,* . . . came to know the base trick that had been played

> upon her by her husband, and cursed him and herself. The curse on herself was that she should be born a Mari, to be worshipped only by low-caste men. The curse on him was that he should be born a buffalo, fit to be sacrificed to her, and that her children should be born as sheep and chickens. Therefore, during the periodical Mari festivals, buffaloes, sheep and chickens are used as victims, and the right leg of the male buffalo is cut off and stuck in his mouth, in memory of his having stitched the shoes in his disguise as a Brāhman. (Whitehead 1988, 84–85. Cf. 117–119)

This folktale contains a rich combination of themes that underlie the study of Māriyammaṉ and her devotees. On the most practical level the story explains why animals, specifically buffaloes, sheep, and chickens, are sacrificed to Māriyammaṉ. But the mixing of castes, especially the mixing of Brahmins and Untouchables, is an ever-present and ever-explosive theme in Tamil folklore. When the Brahmin wife finds out that she and her children are defiled by her husband's untouchability, she curses the entire family, herself included, to reenact the blood sacrifice to the goddess again and again. Like the Reṇukā tale, this is a story about an ordinary housewife who is desecrated and transformed into a goddess. The story moves from the domestic *(akam)* sphere to a public *(puṟam)* sphere. The housewife who was previously concerned only with her husband and children becomes a goddess worshiped by the larger community with public rituals in public space.[8] In this sense this myth has parallels with the famous Tamil epic, *Cilappatikāram.* At the beginning of this story Kaṇṇaki is a good, simple wife, true to her husband even when he has an affair with another woman. But when she hears that her husband has been wrongly accused of a crime and executed, leaving her a widow, she becomes enraged, tears off her breast and flings it at the city of Madurai, burning it to the ground. She transforms herself through her anger into a public goddess worshiped by many people. This epic is often cited as a supreme South Indian example of the power of a woman's chastity, equated with the heat of *tapas,* but it is also the story of an ordinary woman's transformation into a goddess through rage. "It is," notes A. K. Ramanujan, "as much a theory of emotion as a theology; together they make a special recognizable genre, the folk myth of the village goddess" (Ramanujan 1986, 64).

In the praise song above Māriyammaṉ also appears "swinging on the hook." Although the origins of hookswinging have not been clearly established, it has long been a popular ritual at Māriyammaṉ temples in particular, and has explicit connections to blood sacrifice

(Oddie 1986, 93–106; Oddie 1995, 47–68; Thurston 1989, 487–501; Oppert 1986, 480–482). Gustav Oppert makes a distinction between a few Māriyammaṉ temples where only "bloodless oblations" are allowed, and the majority of her temples in which animals are sacrificed and hookswinging performed (Oppert 1986, 476–477). The earliest references to hookswinging are sixteenth-century European accounts, including one that was written by a Venetian traveller who witnessed a hookswinging ritual in Madras in 1582 (Oddie 1986, 94; Dubois 1906, 597–598). A devotee who has made a vow to perform this ritual is suspended in the air by means of hooks inserted into the flesh of his back; the hooks are tied to a rope, which is in turn connected to a horizontal beam balanced on a vertical pole. Although English language newspaper reports of hookswinging rites refer to the performer as a "victim", the evidence suggests otherwise (Dirks n.d., 1–22; Oddie 1986, 96–106; Oddie 1995, 5–7, passim; Dubois 1906, 597–598). Hookswinging enhanced a person's status in the village. Most of the swingers were men from low-caste communities, although sometimes women or members of higher castes participated or supported the tradition financially (Elmore 1915, 33; Oddie 1986, 95–101; 1995, 30–41). The swinger undertook the vow in response to illness, danger, childlessness, or other personal distress; he also performed the ritual for the good of the village, for the health and welfare of everyone (Thurston 1989, 492–493; Dirks n.d., 1, passim).

In the nineteenth century the practice of hookswinging began to decline in the Madras Presidency. Prior to 1853 there was little official discouragement in general, but police interfered in hookswinging rituals in and around the city of Madras (Oddie 1986, 103–106; Oddie 1995, 82–107). After 1853 pressure from missionaries, government officials, and some educated Indians to abolish hookswinging increased. In 1893 Oppert reports that during the last few years sheepswinging had been substituted for human hookswinging in Periyapāḷaiyam (Oppert 1986, 477). In 1906 Thurston notes that the hookswinging apparatus still lay outside the Periyapāḷaiyam temple (Thurston 1989, 489). None of the devotees we talked to in Periyapāḷaiyam mentioned anything about hookswinging, and we saw no evidence of any hookswinging rituals.[9]

Hookswinging is a kind of blood sacrifice, but it is also a dramatic enactment of an individual's devotion to Māriyammaṉ, a self-sacrifice that the entire community can participate in and derive benefit from. The fact that Māriyammaṉ is praised as "swinging on a hook" points to the notion that she herself models the kind of self-sacrifice that characterizes profound devotion. When a true devotee enacts the sacrifice by swinging on the hook, Māriyammaṉ herself appears, drawn by the devotion of her worshiper. Hookswinging enacts ritually the experience of smallpox: the disease is painful, but it is also the sign of the goddess's grace, for she has in effect chosen her devotees by afflicting them with pox. The goddess directs attention to herself through the disease: devotees need Māriyammaṉ, but she also needs to be fed, to be sustained by her devotees. Her concern that she get enough food is one of the reasons she gives people pox. Paṭṭamma, a sixty-five-year old woman vendor at the Periyapāḷaiyam festival, told us this story, similar to other stories we heard from devotees:

How Mutumāriyammaṉ Got the Boon of Smallpox

Mutumāri is Yama's younger sister. One day she came to Yama and said, "Older brother! I was born after you, but you alone receive all the *pūjā*. Your name is spreading like anything. You should give me half of the *pūjā* as my share."

Yama replied, "You were born a woman, so nothing comes to you as your share."

"Are you going to give me something?" Mutumāri asked again. "Half for you and half for me. Tell me whether you'll give it to me or not."

"I'm not going to divide up anything to give to you," Yama replied.

"Okay, we'll see what happens. If you don't give me anything, if you take it all, Yama, what will I eat?" Mutumāri asked.

Mutumāri threw seven pox seeds on Yama. By the third day there were so many pox on his body, he was unable to swallow. Not even saliva could go down his throat, so Yama's eyes were bulging in pain. His tongue was hanging out.

"Little sister! Where are you?" Yama cried out. "I will give you part of my share!"

"Oh, Big Brother, what will you do for me?"

"Ammā! You are Māriyattā, the Goddess of the Anthill. All those whom you afflict with smallpox will come to you as your share of the *pūjā*."

"Okay," said Mutumāri. Yama's tongue fit inside his mouth again, and he could swallow.

"Little sister, you were going to kill me with smallpox!" Yama shouted.

"Don't scold me," Mutumāri said. "Who else do I get?"

"Those who are bitten by snakes, or scorpions, and those afflicted with dysentery, let them all come to you as your

> share. I will take the rest. But Mutumāri, Mother! Have you already taken my son? So be it. Take him as part of your share. Now go!" Yama said.
>
> And that's how Mutumāri got the boon of smallpox from Yama.

Yama is the god of death, who in this story is taking more than his share of people on Earth. But by standing up to her chauvinistic older brother, Mutumāri gets to mark her devotees with smallpox, insuring that she will get enough to eat. Smallpox is a boon for Mutumāri, setting apart her community of people on Earth who will serve her, and it is a boon for her devotees, who are thus favored by the goddess with her grace.

The praise song quoted above alludes to the "knife-like neem leaves" that Māriyammaṉ spreads all over the world and then takes away. Neem leaves are pointed and sharp on the end, and can symbolize the pain of pox; neem leaves are also cooling, and are used to cool the person afflicted with pox. For these reasons the neem tree is especially sacred to Māriyammaṉ. The most popular ritual at the Periyapāḷaiyam temple is the *vēppañcelai,* or "neem sari" ritual, for which devotees remove their clothes, put on garments made of neem leaves strung together, and circumambulate the temple. A few yards from the Periyapāḷaiyam temple is an area where the neem garments are sold, and where men, women, and children put them on; during the festival this area was a flurry of activity. Sometimes devotees wearing neem garments will circumambulate the temple three times while performing *aṭittaṇṭam,* the ritual of rolling a coconut and prostrating at every step. These rituals have been practiced at Periyapāḷaiyam for some time. Thurston describes the activity at the temple around 1912:

> The leaf-wearing vow is resorted to by the large majority of the devotees, and performed by men, women and children. Those belonging to the more respectable classes go through it in the early morning, before the crowd has collected in its tens of thousands. The leafy garments are purchased from hawkers, who do a brisk trade in the sale thereof. The devotees have to pay a modest fee for admission to the temple precincts, and go round the shrine three or more times. . . . To impress on devotees the imperative obligation imposed on them to wear the leaf garment in worshipping the goddess, it is said that a young married woman, being without children, made the vow to the goddess that, on obtaining a son, she

> would go on a pilgrimage to Periyapāḷayam, and worship her in accordance with the ancient rite. Her prayer having been answered, she gave birth to a son, and went to Periyapāḷaiyam to fulfill her vow. When, however, it was time to undress and put on the vēpansilai, her modesty revolted. Unobserved by her party, she secretly tied a cloth round her waist before putting on the vēpansilai. So attired, she went to the temple to worship. On seeing her coming, the goddess detected her deceit, and, waxing wroth, set the woman's dress all ablaze, and burnt her so severely that she died. (Thurston 1979, 150–151)

This story highlights the notion that one's ego can obstruct the fulfillment of a vow to the goddess only with serious consequences. The proper performance of a vow requires the devotees to concentrate more fully on the goddess, thereby diminishing egocentric delusions. Although devotees may ask her for mundane, even egocentric gifts, they believe that their goals will be accomplished only through the goddess, and that she will respond only to their sincere devotion to her. Surrendering the ego through love and devotion for the goddess is therefore not separate from the fulfillment of earthly desires.[10]

Another popular ritual at Periyapāḷaiyam, as at many goddess temples, is head shaving. At the beginning of this article, I describe sitting among piles of hair under the pandal where the barbers shave the heads of devotees who have made a vow to Bavāṉiyammaṉ. Head shaving is done in fulfillment of a vow. For example, parents may make a vow to return to the temple to offer their hair if the goddess will grant them a child, or if a sick child recovers. A child's first head shaving, the *muṇḍan,* one of the *saṃskāras* or life-cycle rites, will be performed at the temple when the child (especially a boy) reaches the age of two or three. Head shaving is a thanks offering in response to a range of personal situations. It is especially popular during the annual festival, when you can see mounds of hair growing under the barbers' busy hands. The cut-off hair, a polluting substance, is usually disposed of by burning it or throwing it in the nearest river.

Head shaving is also performed at the temples of male deities, but it is especially connected to goddess shrines. Erndl notes that the connection between head shaving and the Goddess has not been fully investigated, but I think her suggestion that shaving the head is a type of symbolic head offering is sound (Erndl 1993, 70). Reṇukā's head was cut off, transforming her into a goddess for her devotees; she then appeared in an anthill, a symbolic head, which I discuss later. The myth of Dhyānū Bhagat, the devotee who cut off his own head and offered it to the Goddess, explains why coconuts are offered at temples: when the Goddess joined his head back to his body he asked that in the future, devotees not be asked to prove their devotion through such dramatic offerings (46). Head sacrifice is integral to many streams of the Goddess tradition, so it seems logical that head shaving is a devotee's symbolic head offering.

The Head in the Anthill

Bavāṉiyammaṉ has been transformed through suffering and rage from a woman into Mahādevī, but Bavāṉiyammaṉ is also very much a local goddess. In hymns to Māriyammaṉ written on palm-leaf manuscripts a century or so ago, Periyapāḷaiyam is hailed as one of the places where she attained fame. Pilgrims still throng to her temple, especially during her annual festival. The village of Periyapāḷaiyam traces its history back to the time when the local landowner discovered Bavāṉiyammaṉ inside an anthill. Many of the priests and devotees in Periyapāḷaiyam told a remarkably consistent story about how Bavāṉiyammaṉ arrived in the village. The story shows how the anthill, along with the temple tree and the snakes that dwell in the anthill, form a nexus of sacrifice, fertility, and rebirth. The version one of the Naidu priests told us goes like this:

> Although the area surrounding the village of Periyapāḷaiyam is now dry and barren, many years ago it was covered by a dense forest. Veṅkala Zamindar lived in the village then. He was a rich man who owned more than fifty cows. Every day a young cowherd took the cows up to a hill near the forest to graze. One day, one of the cows did not give any milk. For three days after that the cow was dry, so Veṅkala Zamindar suspected the cowherd of stealing milk. He beat the boy and shouted at him to confess his crime. But the cowherd insisted he had not stolen the milk, telling the zamindar that every evening the cow wandered off by itself into the forest.
>
> The next evening, Veṅkala Zamindar hid at the edge of the forest and waited. When the cow wandered into the trees, he followed it and watched. Deeper in the forest, next to a river, was an anthill. The cow went up to the anthill and poured milk over it, then wandered back out of the forest to join the other cows. Wanting to know why the cow was pouring milk over the anthill, Veṅkala Zamindar walked up to it and broke it open with his ax. Inside was a stone head, in the shape of

a *liṅga*; blood was trickling down from the forehead where the ax had struck it. Veṅkala Zamindar ran home in terror.

By the time he reached his house, he was feverish and his body was covered with pox. That night, the goddess appeared to him in a dream. "I am Bavāṉiyammaṉ," she told Veṅkala Zamindar. "I've come to reside in this place. If you want to be cured, build me a temple in the auspicious place near the anthill. You must build it in the time it takes to boil a pot of millet. If you do this, you will be cured, and the people of this village will prosper."

Veṅkala Zamindar called the men of the village and they rushed to the forest and built a temple for Bavāṉiyammaṉ near the anthill. As soon as the temple was completed, Veṅkala Zamindar entered and offered turmeric, flowers, fruit, and a coconut to the goddess. Immediately, he was cured. Ever since then, Bavāṉiyammaṉ has protected the village.[11]

The concept of a rooted deity inhering in a particular place seems to come from the earliest recorded period of Tamil history (Hart 1975, 21–27). Often the divinity reveals him or herself, as in this myth, in a *svayambhūliṅga,* a *liṅga* that appears spontaneously, that "chooses its own place on earth." Once the divinity is revealed, the sacred place is fixed by the power of the devotees' devotion. In this myth the goddess emerges from an anthill, out of the earth; the goddess is identified with the soil, the earth, and in this manner is associated with the concept of *pratiṣṭhā,* the stable foundation on which all life rests (Shulman 1980, 51, 139). In agricultural societies, the soil is the locus of both life and death; the violence that accompanies ploughing and reaping is what allows new life to grow. Tamil caṅkam poems often draw an explicit analogy between the harvesting of grain and the shedding of blood in war (Hart 1975, 31–40). The Tamil goddess is identified with the soil, and therefore with fertility and death.

The anthill as a locus of divinity is a common element in the South Indian folk tradition, as well as a common sight in villages (Elmore 1915, 79, 94; Meyer 1986, 58–59). The anthill also has a long history of symbolic links to the sacrifice, specifically to the "head of the sacrifice." J. C. Heesterman has elucidated these links in the Vedas and Brāhmaṇas, in which "standard elements and acts of the ritual are referred to as the head of the sacrifice, their installation or performance signifying the severing and/or restoration of the head. The sacrificial cake is called the head, the potsherds on which it is baked representing the skull bones . . ." (Heesterman 1967, 23). In the Ṛg Veda the head contains the essence of the universe. Vedic cosmology posits a universe cyclically moving between disintegration and reintegration, death and rebirth, which finds ritual expression in the fire altar that restores the disintegrated cosmic *puruṣa.*[12] The early Vedic myths describe the head of the sacrifice being obtained through a competition between the *devas* and the *asuras* that echoes real battles on Earth. In the *sūtras* of the Black Yajur Veda, Heesterman sees evidence of the preclassical culture wherein real battles took place for cattle and land (Heesterman 1967, 35ff). The head referred to in the sacrifice is here the head of an enemy conquered in battle. After the enemy's head is cut off, according to the ritual described in the Black Yajur Veda, the head is replaced with an anthill containing seven holes. The anthill is thus linked to the sacrificial beheading of a buffalo in rituals to village goddesses, and to the beheading of Reṇukā.

In the Periyapāḷaiyam myth, a *liṅga* appears when the zamindar breaks the anthill open with an ax. The *liṅga* as the *axis mundi*, the center of the universe that connects the three worlds, is shown vividly in this version of a very well-known myth from Tiruvaṇṇāmalai (southwest of Kāñcipuram) in which the *liṅga* appears as a pillar of fire:

> Brahmā and Viṣṇu quarreled over who was superior. Śiva appeared to them in a *liṅga* of fire. Viṣṇu tried to find its base by digging in the form of a boar, while Brahmā became a goose and flew toward the top. Neither could find any limit to the *liṅga*. They recognized it as a form of Śiva, who made the fiery *liṅga* into the mountain Tiruvaṇṇāmalai. (Shulman 1980, 42)

The *liṅga* links the shrine to heaven as well as to the nether world, the abode of serpents, the realm of chaos and death out of which new life and order are created. The *liṅga* rising out of the anthill is also related to the traditional inhabitant of the anthill, the serpent, who has an extensive mythology. For instance, the goddess Mātaṅki, who is considered the deified washerwoman in the Reṇukā myth, is said to have revealed herself when a king struck an anthill with his spear, piercing the head of the goddess. Mātaṅki emerged from the anthill holding the heavens in her left hand and the cosmic serpent Ādiśeṣa in her right hand (Elmore 1915, 94–95). Snakes are identified with the great cosmic serpent and are treated as divinities.[13] The serpent is also associated with sacrifice and rebirth, for which it is a natural symbol, as it emerges in a new skin from its own old skin. The earth is itself fixed on the cosmic Ādiśeṣa, eternally reborn out of the act of aging (Shulman 1980, 120). Ādiśeṣa marks boundaries. He encircles the universe of time: when Viṣṇu lies down on him, it is the end of an age, or *kalpa*, and the beginning of a night of Brahmā; when Viṣṇu wakes up, it is the beginning of a new *kalpa*, or day of Brahmā. He also encircles the universe of space, moving around the zodiac in the course of a year (Hiltebeitel 1991, 310).

The Periyapāḷaiyam temple embodies the sacrificial themes in the myths. About one hundred meters away from the main temple is a small structure housing a giant anthill, with a large picture of Bavāṉiyammaṉ behind it and a stone head in front; there is a sacred neem tree here as well, and several smaller anthills scattered around. Devotees offer raw eggs and milk to the snakes who live inside the anthill. Serpent-stones, *nākakkal*, are set up around the tree in the temple compound, where people come to pray for fertility. The tree, along with the *liṅga*, represents the *axis mundi*, with roots in the netherworld and branches that reach up towards heaven. This anthill temple is attended by its own scheduled caste priest.[14] Outside of the temple grounds but in the village of Periyapāḷaiyam is a middle-aged woman named Gaṅgamma who is a devotee of the goddess Gaṅgamma, considered locally to be one of the Seven Sisters along with Bavāṉiyammaṉ. Gaṅgamma has a large anthill growing on one of the inside walls of her house which she worships. When I saw it, the anthill was anointed with kumkum, turmeric, and had a decorated pot, a symbol of the goddess, on top of it. Through the power of the goddess, Gaṅgamma has been a healer in the village for twenty years.

In the main temple, the central image is only Bavāṉiyammaṉ's head (next to a small *liṅga*). In a small shrine next to the main temple is the washerwoman who was killed along with Reṇukā, called Mātaṅkiyammaṉ. Five traditional priests from the Naidu caste perform functions in the temple, as well as two brahmin priests who were appointed to serve largely in the shrines for Vināyakar (Gaṇeśa) and Veṅkaṭacalapati (the god at Tirupati), at the front of the main temple. So Bavāṉiyammaṉ's body seems to have disappeared, possibly absorbed by the earth from which she emerged, leaving only her head exposed (see Masilamani-Meyer 1989, 90–91; Sax 1991, 18ff; Doniger 1995, 19). Paraśurāma, her son, is her first devotee: he stands vigilantly in front of her image in the temple, in perpetual worship of the goddess he has helped to create. By murdering his mother and giving her the body of an Untouchable, he has taken her away from her husband, who as a Brahmin refuses to take back a wife with such a defiled body. Interestingly, although devotees in Periyapāḷaiyam insist that Bavāṉiyammaṉ is married to Śiva, he plays virtually no role in her worship in this village. The striking contrast between the focus on Reṇukā's wifely conduct in her marriage to Jamadagni and her subsequent transformation into an independent, though motherly, goddess is partly illuminated, I think, by Bavāṉiyammaṉ's annual festival.

The Festival: Bavāṉiyammaṉ and the Mother's House

The annual festival at Periyapāḷaiyam reveals that while Bavāṉiyammaṉ is a protective mother to her devotees, she is connected to her geographical place and her devotional community through other kinship ties as well. During Bavāṉiyammaṉ's thirteen-week festival in the months of Āṭi, Āvaṇi, and Puraṭṭāci (July to October), the third Sunday is reserved for the local villagers. After 4:00 P.M., tickets for temple *pūjā* that day are no longer sold and everyone enters free. At about 6:00 P.M., the four surrounding "sub-villages" of Periyapāḷaiyam come in procession to the temple. Each village has dancers who perform *kaṭakam,* or "pot dance," and *kutirai pommai,* or "horse puppet dance." These dancers stop at the houses of richer people who can give monetary offerings, then dance for a long time in front of the temple where Bavāṉiyammaṉ can see them. The order in which the four sub-villages come to the temple is the order of their familial relationships to Bavāṉiyammaṉ: the first village in the procession is Ambēdkarnagar, whose people were the first to see Bavāṉiyammaṉ when she appeared in Periyapāḷaiyam; this village's deity is considered Bavāṉiyammaṉ's mother. The people of this first village told the residents of the second village to come and see the goddess; the deity of the second village, Taṇṭamānagar, is Bavāṉiyammaṉ's *māmaṉ,* or mother's brother/uncle. Third in line is Rāllapāṭi, whose deity is Bavāṉiyammaṉ's *akkā,* or older sister; and the fourth village is Aṟipakkam, whose deity is Bavāṉiyammaṉ's *aṇṇaṉ,* or older brother. So Bavāṉiyammaṉ has come back to her natal home; customarily when a married daughter comes to her natal home on a visit, she comes without her husband, as a daughter. This kinship situation in Periyapāḷaiyam helps explain why Bavāṉiyammaṉ's husband plays such an insignificant role.

As far as I know there are no songs welcoming Bavāṉiyammaṉ home from her husband's house, as there are for Durgā *pūjā* in Bengal, for example. Part of the reason may be the practice of cross-cousin marriage in Tamil society, which means (at least in theory if not always in practice) that a daughter does not go far from her natal home when she marries, staying at least in the village if not in a large family compound. Natal and marital ties overlap with such relatives as the mother's brother, who plays a significant role in the daughter's life as an uncle but who is also a possible marriage partner, especially if he is the mother's younger brother. The term for mother's brother is *māmaṉ*, which also means father-in-law, since the ideal cross-cousin marriage would take place between the girl and the mother's brother's son, so the mother's brother would become the girl's father-in-law as well as her uncle. The term for the mother's brother's son is *maccāṉ*, which is also the general term for bridegroom. So in the ideal Tamil kinship and marriage pattern, a girl's natal and marital homes intersect. The closeness of the natal and marital homes can cause tensions between husband-wife and sister-brother bonds. And because a girl's potential marriage partners—her cross-cousins and uncles—may visit her natal home frequently, the control of sexuality can be a particularly charged issue in Tamil households.

And yet, although a Tamil girl's marriage may not take her as far away from her natal home as customarily happens in the North, her marriage represents a break from her natal home and her life with her mother. In Tamil a girl's natal home is referred to as *"tāy vīṭu,"* the mother's house. In Tamil *"ammāvai tēṭi"* (seeking mother) is a stock phrase that applies to all souls seeking the lap of the Great Goddess, but which is especially resonant for girls, who "seek their mother" whenever they visit their natal homes (Trawick 1990, 165–167). In India, and certainly in Tamil culture, love for the mother is cultivated extensively. This fierce love for the mother might be expected to produce intense rivalry among siblings to possess her, but in fact a central theme in Tamil culture is the strong bond between siblings, particularly between brother and sister. Tamil culture contains many isomorphous identifications between several related pairs: brother-sister, mother-child, and husband-wife. Local shrines that contain a larger stone and seven smaller stones are variously interpreted as

1. a mother and her children;
2. a brother and his younger sisters;
3. a sister and her older brothers;
4. a husband and his wives;
5. a wife and her husbands.

In Tamil myths and stories, cross-cousin marriage is represented as a continuation of the sibling tie (Trawick 1990, 170–204; Shulman 1980, 243–258). Brenda Beck claims that the core of the kin system in Tamil culture is not the senior male but is rather a woman surrounded by her father, brother, husband, and sons (Beck 1974, 1–28).

The brother-sister pair of Viṣṇu and Pārvatī is very popular in Tamil tradition. Every year in Madurai the marriage of Mīnākṣī (Pārvatī) and Sundareśvara (Śiva) is celebrated; Aḻakar (Viṣṇu) makes a twelve-mile journey to attend his sister's wedding, but before he enters the city he finds out the wedding has already taken place, and in anger refuses to come any farther. He turns around and proceeds to a nearby village, where he spends the night with his Muslim consort before going back to his own temple (Hudson 1978). The tensions between brothers and husbands and sisters and wives, as well as women's power to protect the male members of their families, are core elements in the Tamil myths and stories about sibling and marital ties (Trawick 1990, 172ff; Wadley 1980; Reynolds 1980; Daniel 1980).

Margaret Trawick argues persuasively that girls feel more anxiety over the break than their mothers, because the daughters have more to lose. The mother stays in the same place and may have other children to occupy her; the daughter, however, has no other mother to turn to. Trawick posits that men seek continuance through their sons, who carry on the family and to whom the father can bestow property. Mothers, on the other hand, do not seek continuance through their daughters to the same degree that fathers do through sons. For one thing, women generally do not pass land on to daughters. Second, a woman's status is enhanced with the birth of sons, not daughters. And if a mother has only daughters, who marry out of the household, then there is a possibility she will be alone in her old age. So although a mother must see some of her own life experiences in her daughter's life, she may not see the daughter as continuous with herself, since the daughter will literally belong to another house eventually (Trawick 1990, 166–169). But the daughter may desire to maintain the continuity with her mother, with the life she has known. Trawick suggests the girl may feel shattered by her marriage, by her break with her mother, which is reflected in the myths of goddesses like Māriyammaṉ who are dismembered by males (167). Consequently, the daughter feels reintegrated with herself upon returning to her mother's house.

Reṇukā is literally shattered by her marriage, by the allied action of males: Jamadagni orders their son to kill his mother. Paraśurāma dismembers his mother; when he attaches his mother's head to an Untouchable body, he remakes her into the goddess Māriyammaṉ, so that she is not only his own mother, but everyone's mother. Reṇukā is cast out of her husband's house and returns to her mother's home in Periyapāḷaiyam; the shattered daughter is reunited with her mother and her mother's household. The four villages who hold a privileged place in Bavāṉiyammaṉ's worship represent her mother, sister, brother, and uncle, who is a potential marital link in the ideal pattern of cross-cousin marriage; thus, the Goddess's return unites her natal and marital homes, as women on earth are considered the power that holds families together. She returns as a daughter and as a mother as well; the villagers come to her as her children, seeking refuge. Reṇukā's son both beheads and reconstructs his mother; he is her first devotee, perpetually standing in front of her shrine, representing the devotee who comes to the Goddess as a child to the mother. The devotee thus "constructs" the Goddess not by beheading her, but by worshipping her as a mother, by fixing her power in this place. Several devotees told us stories about Māriyammaṉ appearing to them as a protective mother, in response to their need. I include here one of the most vivid of these stories, told during the festival by an approximately forty-year-old coconut seller named Śāntiyamma, who was insistent that we tell this story to others "because it is true and shows Māriyammaṉ's nature":

> Last year when I had set up shop during the festival, in the seventh week, the big pandal caught fire, everyone was running around, so the vendors had to pack up. So I closed shop, not having received anything before the fire. I was very hungry but decided to go back home. As I was walking through the fields I saw a small hut with a woman in the doorway, wearing a yellow sari and with untied hair that was so long it touched the ground; she had turmeric on her face, and a big kumkum *poṭṭu* [dot] on her forehead. This woman calls to me, "Where are you going?" I tell her about the fire at the temple, and that there's no business now. I ask the woman in the hut if she's there with her family; the woman replies that she's alone. The woman then says to come inside and eat, but I refuse. The woman insists, "No, you're hungry, eat well."
>
> I go into the house, then the woman says, "I don't have a banana leaf to serve you on." I tell her all the leaves got burned. The woman asks me to wait, she will come back soon. She leaves and comes back with a banana leaf and serves me fish curry. I told her, "I can't eat this much!" but the woman replies, "You will, you're hungry." I eat all the curry, then start to leave. I think, I must thank this lady, and go back inside, but there's no one there. Only then did I realize it was Māriyammaṉ who had fed me.

Conclusion

Devotees consider Bavāṉiyammaṉ to be Mahādevī, the unity of all goddesses. As Śakti she is all-powerful, but she is not removed from the human realm: she is transformed from the woman Reṇukā into a powerful goddess through suffering and violence. Suffering is an experiential link between goddess and devotee, for through smallpox and related diseases, she causes her devotees to suffer. Yet devotees also experience her directly and are given the chance to surrender themselves to her devotion. This self-surrender is not necessarily undertaken in order to reach a lofty spiritual state; rather, Bavāṉiyammaṉ's devotees know that if their devotion is sincere, the goddess will grant them and their families worldly desires.

Since the Goddess embodies powers of both new life as well as death, she is identified with the sacrifice, which brings both life and death. The myth of Reṇukā/Bavāṉiyammaṉ is about the making of a goddess: when Paraśurāma cuts off Reṇukā's head and puts it on the Untouchable woman's body, he sacrifices his mother and reconstructs her as the Goddess; she is now not only his mother but becomes everyone's divine mother. The head is considered the locus of the ego, of self-pride; when her head is chopped off, Reṇukā becomes the Goddess, showing her devotees that by sacrificing their pride, their ego, they, too, can become infused with her grace.[15] Vedic and Purāṇic themes, reworked in myths and local stories about the Goddess, link Bavāṉiyammaṉ to the Vedic "head of the sacrifice" through the anthill in which she appears on Earth. Through their worship and devotional rituals, devotees of the Goddess make personal sacrifices that reaffirm their connection to her and her connection to the place and the devotional community. Thus, the Goddess and her devotees mutually construct each other.

As Śakti Māriyammaṉ is Mahādevī, but she is simultaneously the most immanent of deities, who has chosen to come to Earth to be close to her devotees. Devotees move effortlessly between Bavāṉiyammaṉ as local goddess with a particular history and as Mahādevī; the goddesses are particularized, yet unified. Mythically, Bavāṉiyammaṉ is linked to Vedic themes of sacrifice; but she is special to Periyapāḷaiyam, where she appeared in an anthill to be closer to her devotees. As Bavāṉiyammaṉ, Mahādevī's *śakti* is understood experientially, as the grace of pox, a child's good health, a successful business enterprise. Ritual interactions with the goddess carried out in a truly devotional mode result in concrete benefits for the devotee. Bavāṉiyammaṉ is therefore the Divine Mother, punishing recalcitrant children but responding powerfully to their needs and devotion, never being too distant from them. Paraśurāma literally put his dismembered mother together to become the goddess of all; her devotees continue to construct her as Śakti, the Divine Mother, through their own concrete experiences of her.

Notes

1. I realize the usual term is "research assistant," but Stephen, who has a Ph.D. in folklore, did much more than assist me. Without his linguistic skills and his ability to engage people in our project, I would not have been able to conduct nearly as much research as we did together. That is why I usually use "we" when referring to my activities during field research.

2. Reflecting the perception of goddesses as both distinct and One Goddess, I switch between "goddess" and "Goddess" depending on whether I am emphasizing a distinct, localized identity or a unified identity. Neither term excludes the other.

3. We collected this version, or a version very close to this, from many devotees between April and August 1990. Some versions substitute a Cakkiliyār woman for the washerwoman. Cakkiliyārs are Untouchable leather workers. See Doniger 1995 for a provocative analysis of the Reṇukā story and other Māriyammaṉ myths dealt with here.

4. Hart 1980 argues that worshiping the dead influenced the evolution of devotional Hinduism in South India.

5. See Biardeau 1989, 26 for a discussion of Reṇukā as the victim of the sacrifice in the context of a Māriyammaṉ ritual in Periyar District, Tamilnadu.

6. These two songs are portions of my translations of D–306: Māriyammaṉ Kaliveṇpā, and D–171: Māriyammaṉ Tālāṭṭu, transcriptions of palm-leaf manuscripts collected from the Government Library in Madras in March, 1990. Many of the palm-leaf manuscripts I found mention Periyapāḷaiyam as one of the seven most important pilgrimage sites for Māriyammaṉ. Kaṇṇaṉūr is another famous pilgrimage temple. I am grateful to William Harman for bringing my attention to these manuscripts.

7. See especially Beck 1981 for an insightful discussion of a Māriyammaṉ festival in Kaṉṉapuram, Tamilnadu, in which buffalo sacrifice is integral and in which Śiva plays a central role as Māriyammaṉ's husband. Myths from this area link Māriyammaṉ with Durgā and her killing of Mahiṣa, the buffalo demon. In Periyapāḷaiyam Śiva plays virtually no role, nor have I found any myths explicitly linking Bavāṉiyammaṉ to Durgā.

8. See Ramanujan 1986, 41–75 for an application of the classical Tamil poetic divisions *akam* and *puṟam* to folk material. He also gives a longer, more elaborate version of the Brahmin/Untouchable marriage story which he collected from a woman in Mysore. See also Hart 1975, 81–158; 1988, 467–491.

9. At Periyapāḷaiyam and at many other goddess temples, especially during festival times, there are at least a couple of devotees with small spears or tridents piercing their cheeks or lips. A few devotees wear limes (a cooling food) suspended from hooks inserted through the skin on their chests. At other Māriyammaṉ temples in the central and southern regions of Tamilnadu, I witnessed devotees pulling small temple cars by means of ropes attached to hooks inserted in their backs.

10. See Erndl 1993, 158–161, for a provocative discussion of the coexistence of spiritual and material concerns in the "this-worldly *bhakti*" of the Goddess.

11. We collected many versions of this story in Periyapāḷaiyam during 1990; most of them were very close to this version. A couple of people used "pāḷaiyakar," the Tamil word the English spelled "poligār," to denote the zamindar. One of the temple priests told the story with a slightly different ending: at the same time as a particular cow was going every day to pour milk on the anthill, one of the village forefathers was returning from the fields with food parcels, which he put near the anthill while he slept for awhile. When he woke up and tried to pick up the parcels, they were stuck to the anthill. He went to the village to tell everyone. When they came back to the spot they tried to break the anthill with an ax, but the Ammaṉ's head appeared, with blood trickling down the forehead. They applied turmeric to the wound, then worshiped her. In this version the Ammaṉ's need for food offerings is more clearly articulated.

12. In the first layer of the fire altar, "five real skulls must be placed; a human skull in the middle; west, east, south, and north of it skulls of respectively a horse, a bull, a ram, and a he-goat" (30). Concerning the intimations of actual human sacrifice in the ritual, Heesterman states that "Even apart from the question of human sacrifice, a sacrifice at which the heads of the victims are severed is perfectly irregular and cannot very well be made to fit the classical system. Obviously the system breaks here" (30–31). He then continues to detail the evolution of the ritual and its abstraction of real death. He neither denies the possible fact of human sacrifice nor dwells on what is obviously difficult to prove. See also Hiltebeitel 1988, 328, 372ff. for a discussion of the "head of the sacrifice" in the Draupadī cult.

13. Shulman 1980, 119. Some priests at shrines to Śiva or the Goddess claim that the snakes live in a passageway between the anthill and a tree near the shrine, or between the anthill and another shrine. The snakes can thus receive their offerings of milk and eggs at the anthill, then receive more offerings at the other shrine! Several priests we talked to at temples in and around Madras with anthills and pipal trees or *liṅgas* told us that the snakes move through this passageway regularly. Pipal trees are usually in Śiva temples, some people say because they exude a milky sap that resembles semen.

14. This priest told us that there are Māriyammaṉ temples everywhere because Pārvatī was dancing in the sky, when suddenly her body broke apart and her bones scattered all over; a Māriyammaṉ grew from each piece of bone. This story echoes the tale of the *śakti pīṭhas*, in which pieces of Sati's dead body fall throughout India and become seats of the goddess's power. See Sircar 1973, 5–7. Also quoted in Erndl 1993, 32–36.

15. Cf. Kinsley 1986, 172–177; 1997, 144–166 for a discussion of the goddess Chinnamastā, who carries her own severed head in her left hand, cut off by the sword in her right hand.

Chapter 8

Perfecting the Mother's Silence

Dream, Devotion, and Family in the Deification of Sharada Devi

Jeffrey J. Kripal

> One day . . . when a certain young monk told the revered Sarat Maharaj, "Mother said such-and-such," in order to support his own view on a particular topic, [Maharaj] said in a serious tone, "Look, many times even I cannot be certain whether it was Mā or I who said something." . . . Truly, when [the young monk] shared with Mā the intentions of his heart for his own purposes, Mā only consented to this out of love for this son; in fact, he has passed his own words for Mā's own.
>
> —Śrī Śrī Māyer Smṛtikathā

Introduction: Toward a Hermeneutics of Hiddenness

Sharada Devi (1853–1920), the wife of Ramakrishna Paramahaṁsa (1836–1886), is known to her many devotees as "the Holy Mother."[1] But she is much more than a mother. She is Sharada the Devī, the Great Goddess of the Ramakrishna tradition, variously identified as a form of Kālī,[2] Durgā (MK 59, 71), Ādyaśakti (MK 99) Annapūrṇā (MK 369), Sarasvatī (MK 54), or simply, as her honorific title suggests, "the Goddess" *(devī)*. Sharada herself, or at least that textual form of her that we have in print, seemed to share such a Great Goddess mythology, for she could speak confidently of all these goddess-figures as "my parts" (MK 350). The later iconic tradition, moreover, has more than supported such a claim with numerous god-posters, such as the

All translations from the Bengali are my own; I am grateful to Narasingha Sil for help with difficult passages.

one I purchased in Calcutta in 1990 depicting the "three forms" *(tina rūpa)* of Kālī, Durgā, and Tārā descending "into the one body" *(eka aṅge)* of Sharada Devi—a perfect poster representation of the Great Goddess figure in Hindu mythology.

Poster perfect or not, however, such grand mythological claims and brightly painted visions appear extreme from a strictly historical perspective. Sharada, after all, was as ordinary and delightfully human a woman as one is likely to find in religious literature—or in real life. Consider, for example, the following humorous scene. A female devotee enters the room and sees two women sitting before her: Sharada and her attendant, Golap-Ma. The devotee knows that one of them is "the Holy Mother," but she cannot tell which one. Realizing this, Sharada and Golap-Ma decide to have some fun. Each insists that she is "the Mother." This confuses the poor woman to the point of exasperation, until Golap-Ma ends the game by castigating the visitor for not being able to recognize the real Holy Mother and her obvious display of divinity (MK 233).

But what really was there to see? Certainly this devotee was not the only one to mistake Sharada for an ordinary woman. Even Sharada's own family claimed to see nothing. And Yogin-Ma, another of her female attendants, often complained about Sharada behaving like an ordinary, worldly minded woman, spending all her time taking care of Radhu, her mentally retarded[3] adopted niece, and her always bickering family members. Sharada herself was critical of her family and often voiced a common-sense skepticism in regards to her own divinity. When a disciple, for example, made a comment about how people in the future would perform *sādhana* to attain her, she replied, "What are you saying? Everyone will say, 'My Mā had such a bad case of rheumatism, and she used to limp so" (MK 187). It was thus all more than a little puzzling to Sharada why so many people, even doctors and lawyers (MK 279), would come and visit this limping village woman with aching knees and a mentally handicapped "monkey" (MK 328) for a daughter: "Look, I often think to myself, 'I am just the daughter of Ram Mukherjee, and there are many women of my age at Jayrambati [her village]. How am I different from them?. . . . And why are these people coming like this?'" (MK 279). The texts generally approach such disarmingly honest questions with what we might call a "hermeneutics of hiddenness." This interpretive strategy works by accepting Sharada's ordinariness as a divine illusion and her self-confessed confusion as an intentional act: "You know nothing! From her words it seems as if Radhu is indeed everything to her. [Thus] Mā keeps herself so hidden" (MK 364; cf. MK 15). In short, she isn't ordinary, we're just blind and unseeing.

Once this hiddenness is posited and the hermeneutics is in place, any doubts can be read as forms of ignorance and the tradition can then safely proceed, in the face of seemingly insurmountable odds, to read out of Sharada's simple village wisdom, household chores, and undeniable charm the mythological truths it knows are there. Eventually, of course, Sharada herself begins to believe and responds accordingly with symbolic visions and cryptic statements. But more often than not, she responds by saying little or even nothing, that is, *she remains silent*. By remaining silent, either through a quiet acceptance of other people's interpretations or through an actual voiceless presence, a kind of religious *tabula rasa* is created upon which the devotees can paint practically anything. And paint they did.

Perhaps she enjoyed the attention. Perhaps she saw no reason to refuse those who came to her with their numerous physical ailments, emotional sufferings, and religious needs; they, after all, very much needed a mother's love. Whatever internal motivations Sharada may have had, her silence, coupled with the devotees' verbosity, was extremely effective, for only here, in a submissive compassionate presence that raised no objections and offered only an occasional humorous "but," could the ritual, mythological, textual, and technological means of the tradition transform her into the Great Goddess it needed. Hence, as we shall soon see—through a dream at night, a bunch of flowers, a kiss of those feet, a simple bow, the exchange of food, a photograph, a publication, the construction of a building, a title of respect, a lock of hair—Sharada's silence is filled in, seen, interpreted, acted out, worshiped, created in speech and social etiquette, treasured, even photographed, until it is given a voice that can speak to the anxious conditions of British Bengal.

In the next few pages, I will sketch out some of the textual traces of this silence and what I will call its "perfecting." After a synopsis of Sharada's life and a discussion of what we might call the "narrative construction" of her divine identity through the selective interpretive memory (*smṛti*) of the hagiographical tradition (section 1), I will then turn to Sharada's two questions: "How am I different from them?" and "Why do these people come?" In addressing the former question, I will sketch in some detail the various psychological and social techniques by which Sharada was indeed "made different," especially as these pertain to the dynamics of the dream (*svapna*) and its "perfecting" (*siddha*) in ritual, initiation, and devotion (section 2); and in addressing the latter question, I will advance a thesis about the traditional familial nature of the Mother's charisma and the powerful emotional-devotional responses it so effortlessly elicited from her many visiting children (section 3). By addressing these two questions, I hope to develop a dialectical vision of the deification process that respects both the power of what the disciples *brought* to the deification process and the reality of what the they actually *found* in this being whom they so affectionately called "the Holy Mother."

Sharada's Life: Constructing the Goddess Through Narrative

Because Sharada's life has been—and continues to be—the focus of a daunting body of devotional literature in both English and Bengali that is now well into the thousands of pages, it is impossible in the context of an essay such as this to deal in any exhaustive way with this corpus and its historical, textual, and religious complexities. Fortunately, however, the task is made considerably easier by the fact that the texts, in their constant attempt to create a stable and relatively simple hagiographical identity from the confusion of conflicted sources, tales, and memories, return again and again to certain key moments in Sharada's life; not surprisingly, it is precisely these stable stories that end up playing the central roles in her eventual deification. Among these, we might isolate the following: her birth in 1853; her marriage to Ramakrishna in 1858; Ramakrishna's worship of her as "the sixteen-year-old goddess" (*ṣoḍaśī-pūjā*) in 1872; her childless widow status after Ramakrishna's death in 1886, and its resolution in the bracelet vision; her adoption of Radhu in 1900; her move into the newly built Calcutta Udbodhan house in 1909; and her death in 1920.

Sharadamani was born on 22 December 1853 into the family of Ramachandra Mukherjee and his wife Shyamasundari Devi in the village of Jayrambati, just a few miles down the road from Ramakrishna's natal village of Kamarpukur. Four more children would follow little Sharada, all boys: Prasanna, Barada, Kali, and Abhay. When Sharada was just five years old, she was married to Ramakrishna. It was not an auspicious start for the little girl. Ramakrishna's family was arranging the marriage with the specific intention of curing Ramakrishna of his recurring states of madness. Not surprisingly, they had considerable difficulty finding a willing family. For some reason—I am aware of no text that tells us why—the Mukherjee family agreed to offer their five-year-old girl to the madman from Kamarpukur. When, however, they learned that the wedding jewelry had in fact been borrowed and had already been returned (Ramakrishna had to sneak the ornaments off the child while she slept), Sharada's uncle arrived to take her back home in protest. Tellingly, Ramakrishna's mother worried that the marriage might be annulled.

The little girl would see her "crazy husband" only rarely and sporadically for the next thirteen years, until, having turned eighteen, she finally decided to see for herself if the rumors of his madness were true and, accompanied by her father, walked the sixty miles to Dakshineshwar sometime in March of 1872. What happened shortly after this would become one of the most important elements in the narrative construction of Sharada's divinity: Ramakrishna's worship of her as the goddess in the Śrī Vidyā Tantric rite of *ṣoḍaśī-pūjā* or "worship of the sixteen-year-old." The texts are confused about both the time[4] and the place of this ritual, but the textual consensus seems to place the event at Dakshineshwar during Phalahāriṇī Kālī-*pūjā* in June of 1872 (MK 227), in other words, just a few months after Sharada's arrival. On this summer night, Ramakrishna invited Sharada to a *pūjā* in his room around 9:00 P.M. The young wife arrived to discover all the items in place and no image on the ritual seat; she, it turns out, was to be the image. Ramakrishna sat her on the ritual seat and proceeded with the three-hour rite, worshiping her as a sixteen-year-old goddess. The ritual ended after midnight, with both Ramakrishna and Sharada in semiconscious states.[5]

The traditional biographers make much of this ritual; indeed, it is astonishing to see just how overdetermined the event becomes in the later tradition. The biographers suggest, for example, that the event signified: Ramakrishna's final triumph over sexuality; the successful conclusion of Ramakrishna's spiritual practices; the awakening of Sharada's consciousness of her own divinity (HM[G] 48); the establishment of a new model for married couples (HM[G] 47); and the unique situation of a prophet or saint giving special status to his wife.[6] Perhaps even more important for the tradition is the texts' insistence that, by reason of this rite, Sharada came to share in the fruits and powers of Ramakrishna's spiritual practices (a necessary move, since she seemed to have practiced none in her own life) and took her place as the eventual spiritual head of what would become an important religious movement (the texts leave no doubt that "his mantle fell on her" [GHM xviii–xix]). With a single ritual, the tradition could thus deify Sharada (for had Ramakrishna not worshiped her as the goddess?), explain why this goddess had performed no *sādhana*, and legitimate her already established role as the Master's successor.

After falling ill a year after the *pūjā*, Sharada left the temple compounds altogether: "Realizing that then at Dakshineshwar, she could be of no use to others and that on the contrary she would be adding to their anxiety, she left for Jayrambati" (HM[G] 53). The texts say nothing about Ramakrishna trying to stop her.

She would, however, eventually return to spend her days in a tiny octogonal cubicle in the temple music tower, sleeping, praying, and, most of all, cooking for her famous husband and his numerous male guests. Careful about keeping purdah, she was up at 4 A.M. to bathe and back in the tower before anyone could see her. Such a strict routine led to constipation (*vegadhārana*), which in turn gave her stomach problems (MK 304). Imprisoned within such a schedule and her tiny walls, Sharada would sometimes spend up to two months without even seeing Ramakrishna, despite the fact that he lived just a few yards away in the same temple complex and she was cooking all of his meals (MK 193).

Given all of this, it should not surprise us that Sharada once compared her marriage to Ramakrishna to that of Umā to the "hemp-addict" Śiva (HM[N] 134). It may have been divine, but it was hardly ideal. Things only got worse when the saint died in 1886. Now a widow, she was virtually ignored by the disciples, who had never considered her anything but the "guru's wife," and was abandoned by her legal guardian, who stopped her monthly temple pension, gave her Ramakrishna's village hut, and effectively left her to her own meagre means. There in Kamarpukur she suffered in obscurity and poverty (SK 138–139) until, through the campaigns of two persistent women, her mother and Golap-Ma, she was brought back to Calcutta in April of 1888. Significantly, even then there was considerable hesitation about a widow living among the men, for "men at large had not yet come to recognize her spiritual status" (GHM xxv). This judgment from an utter absence of religious experience was not reversed, or even challenged, until Sharada's attendants began to talk about extraordinary states of consciousness that they had allegedly witnessed on a pilgrimage with her at Vrindaban. The deification process had begun through unusual states of consciousness reported and defined exclusively by others (and by women, I might add). Here, as elsewhere, Sharada was strangely silent.

Sharada did not help matters much by refusing to give up her bangles and red-bordered saris, something every widow was supposed to do to mark her now permanent state of mourning and asceticism. Such a refusal produced its predictable result: the villagers criticized her for being a "merry widow." Torn between her own desires for the ornaments and the social demands of her culture, Sharada had a vision of Ramakrishna, who told her that he was not really dead but had simply moved, "as if from this room to that one" (MK 135). Sharada could keep her bracelets, since as a divine being Ramakrishna was not really dead. With a single blow, the vision thus resolved Sharada's personal crisis—even if it did not answer the villagers' criticisms—and hinted, even if by indirection, at her own essentially divine nature. Sharada, it turns out, as the nonwidow of the ever-living God, had to be recognized as the Goddess. The bracelets, once a social scandal and the mark of Sharada's attachment to the world, had become a powerful, if contested, sign of her husband's (and now her own) divinity.[7]

Alive or not, however, Sharada was clearly depressed about her physically absent husband, her own controversial widow status, and her utter lack of children (MK 383). Sharada went on a number of pilgrimages at this time, no doubt in an attempt to deal with her pain and suffering,[8] but these, it seems, ultimately resolved little. She was still a widow, and there were precious few social paths out of such a situation. From scattered but telling textual evidence, we might conclude that her condition continued to deteriorate. We are told, for example, that she had no connection at all with the household at this time, and that "nobody would dare approach her"; why, we are not told (SK 139). Another striking passage in the Smṛtikathā describes a Sharada who had to be carried from place to place, "like a statue," by Golap-Ma and Yogin-Ma (SK 11). Saradeshananda, of course, reads such a condition as a product and sign of her advanced meditation, but given what we know about Sharada's state at this time after her husband's death and before any new social identity had had a chance to form, we might see these statue scenes as psychophysiological responses to what, by any measure, was a desperate and, in many cases, hopeless situation.

At some point, however, Sharada had a vision that would at last pull her out from this statue-like existence. Ramakrishna appeared to her, showed her a young girl dressed in red, and said, "Take refuge in this one and remain [here]. Now many, many children[9] will come to you." Some time after the vision, her sister-in-law, then completely mad, walked by. Behind her crawled her crying little girl, Radhu. Sharada's heart was broken by this pathetic scene, and she decided then and there to adopt the child as her own. As she took the child in her lap, Ramakrishna appeared again and said, "This is the girl. Take her as your refuge and live. This is *yoga-māyā*"(MK 268–269). Sharada finally had her child, and a reason to live.

The texts suggest through their religious language and use of vision that this adoption of a girl who embodied the power of *māyā* effectively held Sharada "down" from *mokṣa*, but clearly other psychological forces were also at work; indeed, it seems just as likely that the adoption of Radhu held Sharada "up" from a rather severe state of depression. Whether we read the event as a hook to pull her up from the depths or a prop to her hold her down from the heights, one thing is beyond question: Sharada did, in fact, adopt a little girl whom she would keep by her side for the rest of her life. Sharada was finally a mother. But things were hardly what she expected. Radhu, it turns out, was as mentally deficient as her biological mother. Radhu's mother, moreover, became jealous of Sharada and often abused her. Radhu only made things worse, spitting food on Sharada (MK 321), beating her with a comb (MK 343), making scenes in front of the devotees, and going mad during her own confinement and pregnancy. Nothing was easy for poor Sharada.

Radhu was born in 1900. Sharada raised the girl, staying mostly at Jayrambati until 1909, when a house was built for her in Calcutta. Since the Udbodhan Press was located in its ground floor, the structure came to be know as the Udbodhan House. Here, protected by "the Mother's gatekeeper," the regal Swami Saradananda (who conceived of the building in the first place), Sharada would receive her many Calcutta devotees. It is significant that virtually all of the scenes recorded in the Māyer Kathā take place within this carefully guarded, minutely controlled devotional space. It could even be said, I think, that the construction of the Udbodhan House eventually resulted in the construction of Sharada as the Great Goddess of the Ramakrishna tradition. Here Sharada's movements could be regulated and her visitors could be controlled, even chosen, all within the official space of a growing, prospering, publishing religious movement.

It is clear that Sharada resented, if in her typically gentle fashion, the control both the city customs and the male monks held over her at Udbodhan and much preferred to stay in the more relaxing atmosphere of the village, where things were not run by the ticking of a clock. The texts often contrast the two locations, probably faithfully reflecting Sharada's own shared feelings. Saradeshananda, for example, describes Jayrambati as a malaria-infested place where Sharada had to work hard but could live "like the daughter," that is, freely, and Udbodhan as the place where Sharada did not have to work but where she did have to live "like the daughter-in-law" under the watchful, loving eye of Swami Saradananda (SK 13, 236–237).

Sharada would move back and forth between Udbodhan, where her Calcutta devotees could meet her, and her natal village of Jayrambati, where she could take care of her family, until her death on 20 July 1920 at Udbodhan. The bangles she had fought so hard to keep after Ramakrishna's death and which had become a powerful, if ever controversial, symbol of her nonwidow status stayed with her until the very end, even if they had to be tied to her wrists with strings to keep them from falling off her bony frame (SK 197).

Perfecting the Mother's Silence: What the Devotees Brought

It is now a truism of Western sociological and psychological thought that human beings are relational beings. We define ourselves in relation to one another. In some deep sense, we *are* these others. This is another way of saying that human identity, for whatever else it might be, is social identity, constructed anew in the ever-changing flux of human relationships. To answer Sharada's first question ("How am I different from them?"), then, we might say: "You are different from them because you are surrounded by different people whose specific needs, intentions, and acts bestow on you a different identity." Her biography certainly bears this out. Surrounded by temple authorities and the needs of her husband, Sharada lived in what amounted to a glorified closet and spent her days cooking in hiding, "as if she were [Sītā] in exile," as one perceptive visitor put it (MK 38). She was no more than this. Later, when Ramakrishna died and the disciples scattered, she became a widow (a pseudo-identity at best in nineteenth-century Bengal), for she had lost her single most important relational model, her husband. What was worse, she was childless; she was thus in the most precarious of social situations, a virtual nonperson. But as the movement took root and the women and disciples brought her back to Calcutta, when she (or her vision) declared that her husband was not really dead, and *especially* when Swami Saradananda built her a house and became "the Mother's gatekeeper," Sharada became someone else. She became what those around her "knew" her to be—a living goddess (MK 179). Sharada implicitly acknowledges such a social construction when she justifies her belief in the Master's power behind the new movement by pointing to the impressive numbers of people who now come to see her (MK 258).[10] Social success and public prominence thus became the measure of what was true and real.

Granted, it was not that "the Holy Mother" was created completely by her children, for Sharada herself certainly played a crucial and willing role in this genesis. But it is almost certainly true that, without the circumstance of a dead divinized husband, a piece of simple mythological logic that demanded that every god must have a goddess (MK 331),[11] the needs of a fledgling religious movement, and the difficult socioeconomic circumstances of British Bengal, Sharada the abandoned widow would have never become "the Holy Mother." But how precisely was this transformation effected? What mechanisms were at work in the construction of this Great Goddess who could speak confidently of the various goddesses of Hindu mythology as "my parts"?

"Perfected in a Dream": The Role of Dream, Vision and Initiation in Sharada's Deification

Although I recognize their heuristic value and central place in Western sociological thought,[12] I am uncomfortable with terms like "mechanism" and "construction." They give the impression that we are talking about clocks or skyscrapers instead of thinking, feeling human beings. Accordingly, I would like to adopt a vocabulary here that I think is much closer to the texts and their symbolic worlds. Specifically, I would like to turn to one of Ramakrishna's teachings that is especially well represented in the texts about Sharada, namely, his teaching that it is possible for a certain type of aspirant to be initiated or "perfected" in a dream (Datta 1935, 137). The compound *"svapna-siddha"* or "dream-perfected" is significant for our purposes, for, when coupled with a close examination of the texts and their descriptions of the dream-lives of the devotees, the concept can throw considerable light on some of the psychological and social processes involved in the deification of a human being such as Sharada.

If we look at a text like the Māyer Kathā for dreams, for example, we very quickly find them, and practically everywhere. Specifically, devotees are constantly dreaming of Sharada and of being initiated by her. But, interestingly enough, however auspicious or "perfect" the initiatory dream is seen to be, it is never enough for the devotee. Inevitably, the devotee feels compelled to act on it, to live it out. Specifially, she feels driven to seek out in her waking life the living presence she has seen in her dream. In short, she must make the psychological dream-experience "perfect" (*siddha*) in social reality and public space. Freud's notion that every dream is a wish-fulfillment is here given its distinctly Indian flavor: the dream-wish, already fulfilled or "perfected" in the dream, must nevertheless be perfected again through the ritual of initiation, the giving of a *mantra*, and the perfecting "practice" (*sādhana*) that both the initiation and the *mantra* imply. What began as a wish in the night is now an integral part of social reality, human identity, and religious institution. What is more—and this is the key—the dream affects not just the dreamer but the dreamt. After all, it is no small thing to appear in someone else's dream, especially when the dream is marked by an idealizing devotion (*bhakti*). The dream's perfecting (*svapna-siddha*), then, works in at least two directions, for it constructs both the dreamer and the dreamt.

Consider, for example, the case of Sarayabula Devi, a devotee whose lengthy conversations with Sharada make up a major part of the Māyer Kathā. In the course of these initial conversations, Sarayabula comes to Udbodhan and relates to Sharada one of her dreams. In it she saw Ramakrishna telling her to follow a certain lane, which she understood would lead her to Sharada seated on the porch of a thatched house. The Mother gets quite excited about the dream, for Sarayabula has seen things exactly as they are. Sarayabula, however, is not so sure, for she believes that Sharada's Jayrambati home is actually made of brick (the text never tells us whether the dream-straw or the brick-conviction is correct). The dream, she concludes, was a "mental deception" (MK 35).

But only if we read it literally. Such a dream, after all, can be read as a symbolic expression, never quite exact in its thatch or brick confusion, of where the movement that had originated with Ramakrishna was now heading: away from Ramakrishna and down the lane to Sharada. Such a walk is certainly born out in the Māyer Kathā. Ramakrishna's physical absence and the devotional necessity of having someone then and there to love is a common theme: "But we've never seen the Master; we know you," the devotees say (MK 301; cf. 95).

The technological feat of photography was of immense help here, as it could both fill in for these non-memories and preserve fading memories. Sharada benefited from such technology as much as any of the devotees. Since attaining a very bad blackened copy of Ramakrishna's photo from a temple cook while the saint was still alive, Sharada had been worshiping it. With Ramakrishna's death this "photographic memory" became Sharada's religious focus, since the reigning folk wisdom held the shadow/picture of the body to be identical with the body itself (MK 194). Accordingly, she worshiped the photograph daily. She fed it (MK 195). She asked visitors to salute it (MK 352). She took it on pilgrimage. She counselled a devotee to use it in an operating room as a lucky charm (MK 362). She used a bundle of divining sticks (and a verbal threat) with it to divine whether a lost son would return home (MK 302). She even believed that it could move to escape the peril of some ghee-hungry ants (MK 194). Such seriousness is only occasionally broken by Sharada's refreshing lightheartedness and down-to-earth sarcasm as she explains why it is no longer so difficult to serve the Master: "If you sit the Master down, he really sits. If you lay him down, he really lies down. After all, he's a picture!" (MK 192–193). She no doubt remembered plenty of times when it was not so easy "to serve the Master."

Despite such stable shadows, however, it seems that with the passage of time people were beginning to have some rather serious doubts about the historical Ramakrishna and his compassion and found real encouragement in Sharada's physical presence (MK 116). At least one disciple, the mad Nag, who knew both the Master and the Mother, was clear about his preference: "Mother is more compassionate than Father!" (MK 102) More common than Nag's starkly honest judgment was the more subtle attempt to bridge the past to the present by simply equating the Master and the Mother (MK 27, 78, 172), a tactic Sharada herself sometimes employed (MK 23). Even this realization, however, often functioned as a kind of cutting down of Ramakrishna.

Consider, for example, the unspoken thoughts of Sarayubula as she stood before Sharada one day: "Even if to you the Master is greater, to us you two are one" (MK 27).

Given this pattern of the receding, distant Father and the present, more compassionate Mother, it is not surprising to discover that the Māyer Kathā is replete with two types of disciples: those complaining about their futile efforts to attain a vision of the dead Master (MK 17, 181, 215, 257, 259), and those who dream vivid dreams of being intitiated by the living Sharada.[13] Numerous devotees—no doubt influenced by the photos of Sharada that were circulating in Mahendranath Gupta's Kathāmṛta and the movement's various publications—dream about Sharada granting them initiation, usually through a *mantra*. Such visions then lead them to seek her out for the very things they have seen in their night visions (MK 112, 300–301). Sharada usually responds to such stories by either asking the devotee about the *mantra* he received in the dream (Sharada herself seems ignorant of the dream's content), by not addressing the dream directly (MK 204–205), or by granting the dream-wish the devotee relates to her.

Consider, for example, the following scene. A woman enters the room and tells Sharada that she had seen her in a dream: "It was as if you were telling me, 'Eat my *prasād* and you will get well.' I said, 'The Master has forbidden me to eat anyone's left-overs.'" The dream, occuring from within the crisis of a disease, imagines a wish fulfilled, but only after, almost perversely, setting up a conflict between Sharada and Ramakrishna, both of whom are implicitly divinized from within the dream (*prasād*, after all, is food first offered to a deity and then shared by the devotees as sacred). The woman then asks for what the dream Sharada had promised her—Sharada's own *prasād*. Sharada's response is predictable: "Do you want to do what the Master has forbidden?" But the woman insists that such words were authoritative only as long as she made a distinction between the Master and the Mother.[14] "Now give," she asks again. Significantly, Sharada, in another form of her silence, yields to both the woman's dream interpretation and her gentle command (MK 24). A shift away from the divinized Ramakrishna and towards the equally divine Sharada is thus accomplished by a dream, a dream interpretation, the insistence of a desperate sick woman, and, perhaps most importantly, Sharada's silence. Such scenes could be easily multiplied, with Sharada's identity, purpose, and "inner nature" discerned from within dreams and then recreated in devotionally aggressive conversation. But, of course, the "perfecting" of the silence does not stop there, for these conversations are then recorded (or perhaps better, refashioned, for the tradition is explicit about its pedagogical editing principles [SK 240–242]) by authors in the stable form of texts, which are then read, reread, and used to fashion other texts and, no doubt, other dreams.

Related to these dreams that become social reality (initiation, new identity, institution, text) and then once again dreams are a series of visions that function in various ways to perfect Sharada's silence. These visions can be read as actual subjective "states"[15] or standardized literary creations. We have seen them at work in Sharada's own life, especially in times of crisis or doubt. Although not nearly as numerous as dream scenes (for dreams, although akin to visions, seem to be held in lower esteem and so are more appropriate for the devotees), these visions are also at work in the doubts and struggles of a few of the more prominent devotees and monks. Consider, for example, the following scene. A swami, in what seems to be a not uncommon mind set, is doubting the Holy Mother's renunciation and questioning her constant worldly concern with Radhu. Here again the extraordinary lack of the extraordinary in the life of Sharada becomes an issue. Sharada's reply to such criticisms was honest, if utterly ordinary: "We're women, and we're like this" (MK 295). Such an answer, however, was not enough for a tradition that was trying to divinize her. Something more, something out of the ordinary had to be created.

Hence, in the end, for the tradition if not for Sharada, the issue had to be resolved again by the extraordinary. One day while meditating on the bank of the Ganges, Yogin-Ma has a vision of Ramakrishna, who points to a new-born baby wrapped in intestines floating by. The Master asks Yogin-Ma the rhetorical question about whether the Ganges can be polluted by such a thing (the answer, of course, is "No"), and then declares: "Know that she's like that. Don't doubt her. Know that that one and this one (pointing to himself) are no different (*abheda*)." Corrected by the vision, Yogin-Ma goes to Sharada and apologizes for her lack of faith. Interestingly enough, in the very next paragraph, Sharada uses Yogin-Ma's vision to defend herself against the monks, who were unhappy with her spending time with a woman whose character they found questionable (MK 318–319). Visions, it turns out, can be very useful, even if they originally belonged to someone else.

In this vision of the floating dead baby, we see many of the motifs I have analyzed previously: a vision or dream that occurs in a crisis situation; a symbolic identification of Sharada and Ramakrishna; a form of Sharada's silence (she sees nothing and accepts Yogin-Ma's vision as legitimate); and a tendency for the dream or vision to take on social forms, in this case Yogin-Ma's verbal confession, Sharada's later use of the vision as a defense, and the textual account itself.

Ritual, Relic and Text: Other Means of Perfecting Sharada's Silence

The dream and the vision, however, were not the only "lanes" to Sharada's porch and her eventual deification. There were many means of perfecting the Mother's silence. Among them, a group of techniques that we might order under the categories of psychological projection, ritual act, textual record, and hermeneutics play especially prominent roles.

Projection was common in the divinization process. "I saw," a devotee comments, "that, to me, Mā was seated on the seat in the form of the Mother of the Universe like a queen" (MK 353; Cf. 355). The significant expression here, of course, is the phrase "to me," for it signals the possibility, indeed the probability, that Sharada's sanctity, far from being some objective reality that anyone with two eyes could see (for many saw nothing), was in fact a relational, dialectical experience created as much by what we might call "the devotional gaze" as by anything Sharada did or was. The identity of "the Holy Mother," in other words, was at least partially created, fashioned, and perfected by the *bhakti* of the devotees. Sharada became what others perceived and needed her to be.

This projecting *bhakti*, however, is not enough, for it needs physical cues and recognizable signals to know how and when to project itself. Ritual is crucial here. Indeed, without ritual, Sharada is just another unnoticed woman. As an anonymous female devotee confessed, she realized who the Holy Mother was only when she saw some devotees making salutations to her (MK 110). Sometimes the ritual acts were more dramatic and pronounced, making this ever-present possibility of unseeing virtually impossible: for example, a new cloth was layed on the road and a conch shell was blown (MK 298). With such a "red-carpet treatment," *no one* could miss "the Holy Mother" now.

Ramakrishna, Sharada, and the disciples were clearly all aware of this constructive potential of ritual. Ramakrishna had used the *ṣoḍaśī-pūjā* to divinize Sharada. Later, Sharada would commonly enforce simple ritual acts on visiting devotees in an attempt to divinize her dead husband. And the devotees just as commonly pushed each other into similar ritual gestures to deify Sharada. One devotee, for example, remembers how the Mother sat her down on a ritual seat and had her worship Ramakrishna (MK 297). Another devotee hints at the role of authority in such seemingly simple acts when she relates how Gauri-Mā told her to offer flowers at Sharada's feet (MK 297). Again, the ritual act, backed up by the power of social authority, defines, even creates the identity of the worshiped as divine.

Very much related to this ritual deification was the use of relics to stabilize and preserve the sacred person in a set of what I would call "physical meanings." Hence, when Sharada gives an old sari to a devotee and asks her to wash it before wearing it, the devotee (not unlike an adoring teenager in possession of a rock idol's shirt) immediately sees other possibilites and swears never to wash such a treasure (MK 102). In other scenes, strands of hair are given away (MK 70, 105), devotees quarrel over who stole Sharada's footprint, never thinking to simply ask her for more of the same (MK 328), and Sharada jokes about the devotees worshiping even a cat from Jayrambati for her sake (HM[G] 52). Thus, seemingly insignificant acts and objects—a salutation, a conch shell, a simple quick *pūjā*, a bunch of flowers, an old sari, a strand of hair, a footprint, even a pet—become the social signs that can both signal and create the perceived reality of divinity. The silence is thus "perfected," always by others, through meanings "made real" in physical objects and ritualized acts.

Texts also create. The Māyer Kathā, for example, is filled with references to Mahendranath Gupta's Kathāmṛta and the writings of Swami Saradananda. "Read the Kathāmṛta of the Master" is a common command of the Mother's (MK 110, 354), for by that act the Master is kept alive, renewed, and divinized: "I have read in the books of the Master," as one devotee puts it (MK 37). Sharada, too, was being created in this textual fashion, for there were many books already being written about her (MK 363). Such texts, along with the interpretations of the devout, become authoritative forms of knowledge, which are then used to criticize the dumb and unseeing (MK 363).

Although she wrote nothing that has come down to us (yet another form of her silence), Sharada was not naive about the new possibilities that the technologies of the printing press and the photograph offered, commenting at one point on the shrewdness of those who had taken photographs of Ramakrishna: "Which *avatāra* has been photographed . . . ?" she asks (MK 213). Nor was she innocent of the implicit marketing strategies that were being employed, sometimes at her own expense, to push these spiritual commodities onto the public; indeed, in one place, she even suggests her discomfort with Mahendranath Gupta's Kathāmṛta, which "filled their heads with ideas" (MK 210). Sharada was clearly not entirely happy with Gupta and his best-selling books. There were other times when she seems almost upset by what others have written about her. In one scene, for example, a devotee is reading from Akshay Kumar Sen's Rāmakṛṣṇa-Puṅthi, a highly devotional verse portrayal of Ramakrishna's life. When the reader gets to Ramakrishna's marriage to Sharada and the text begins to praise her as the Mother of the Universe, Sharada expresses herself through yet another form of silence: she gets up and leaves (MK 175). Some textual constructions were apparently just too much for her. Perhaps Sharada's reaction to Sen's flowery prose arose from the same feelings that produced her criticism of Ram Chandra Datta's *ṣoḍaśī-pūjā* account: "Everything that one reads in the books isn't correct" (MK 39). Yes, but after time and innumerable editions, that which is "correct" must give way to that which is "edifying" (SK 241). The object, after all, is not to reconstruct the life of an historical human being but to reveal the hidden presence of a god or a goddess.

Related to these advertised textual constructions that were at once powerful means of production and yet problematic for Sharada herself is what we might call Sharada's "rhetorical perfecting." Sometimes this is a fairly subtle process, as when Sharada's honorific title, "Devī" or "the Goddess," is taken as a literal truth, or when a devotee limits his claim by the use of the phrase "to me" ("*To me* Mā is the living Goddess"), or when a speaker employs simile when speaking about Sharada's divine nature ("It was *as if* the Goddess herself was standing before me"), or when a devotee watches Sharada scold Radhu for wanting to braid her hair and identifies Sharada as *muktakeśī* (she [the goddess] with dishevelled hair [MK 367]): here the tradition seems to preserve a sense that its claims are of a poetic, rhetorical, or even playfully punning nature. Sometimes, however, the rhetoric is heavier and becomes more literal. The title of the English translation of the Māyer Kathā is a good example of this rhetorical heaviness: *The Gospel of the Holy Mother* is not a title that is meant to be misunderstood. Mimicking Gupta's own English title (*The Gospel of Ramakrishna*), which employed a Christian category to relativize the colonial Christian challenge, the translators of the Māyer Kathā employed a Christian title (and more than a little King James English) to implicitly divinize and universalize their own subject, the Holy Mother. The implicit message of the title and the text is undeniable: Ramakrishna is as good as Jesus, and the Holy Mother is as good as either one of them.

Similar rhetorical forces are at work in what I call "listing." This is an extremely common rhetorical technique among Hindu, and now New Age, writers. A string of famous saints or incarnations are listed, with the "new kid on the block" tacked on at the end in an attempt to legitimate his or her status through the associations that a simple list sets up in the mind of the reader: "the Buddha, Caitanya, Jesus, and Ramakrishna." Despite its historical and intellectual vacuity (for these lists casually conflate, for example, the numerous christologies of the history of Christianity into a single, deceptively simple "*avatāra*" and advance no developed argument), this technique seems to work quite well. Hence, today we can find these same lists in India with

Ramakrishna's name in the beginning and the new contender—Swami Sivananada, for example—tacked on at the end (McKean 1996, 247). Sharada enters such lists usually through her spousal relationship to Ramakrishna, or occasionally, through superficial comparisons with other goddess-like figures, "the Madonna ideal," for example (HM[G] jacket cover). By this means, a kind of two-item list is generated (there are, after all, very few female incarnations), and Sharada shares in the established divinity of the other named figure.

This same textual perfection of Sharada's silence is extended further by means of various hermeneutical strategies. Here Sharada is created in the in-between of human dialogue and, more specifically, in the interpretations that the devotees carry away from these exchanges. Two things are striking about such exchanges: how silent Sharada is, and how elaborate the interpretations become. Indeed, the silence of Sharada and the grandeur of the devotees' readings seem to be correlated in some positive fashion: the more silent Sharada becomes, the grander the interpretations become. Consider, for example, the following scene. Sharada is instructing a certain Vaikuntha: "Vaikuntha, call on me." Realizing what she has just said, Sharada then immediately corrects herself, "Call on the Master." A devout Lakshmi immediately breaks in and like a good psychoanalyst catches Sharada's "divine slip," pointing out that she has never said such a thing before. Lakshmi then instructs Vaikuntha: "Call on Mā." The scene ends with Sharada signalling her acceptance by—what else?—remaining silent (MK 92). Note that Sharada does little here, except suggest to Vaikuntha that he direct his devotion to her and rely on her (as his guru?), not an outrageous suggestion given the late date (1909) and spatial context of the discussion (the Udbodhan house). Lakshmi takes it from there and transforms Sharada's slip into a new exclusivistic practice: "Call on Mā." Sharada certainly said nothing of the sorts, but that is in fact what the scene comes to mean, for Sharada, in her typical fashion, refuses to deny Lakshmi her devotional interpretation.

Sometimes the writers are even more aggressive and Sharada is even more silent. In one such scene, Sharada tells a story about her being chased around the village by her crazed cousin, Harish, who had gone mad by taking drugs that his wife had allegedly slipped him to deter him from renouncing the world (GHM 78).[16] Sharada relates how her "own form" finally came out when she got tired of running around buildings. Turning on a very surprised Harish, she jumped on his chest, pulled out his tongue, and began to slap Harish until her fingers turned red. It worked. Sharada, no doubt proud of her accomplishment, leaves it at that (MK 173–174). An editorial footnote in the English edition, however, interpets the story's "mystical meaning":

Sharada's "true nature," the note tells us, is her identification with the violent goddess Bagala, one of the ten Mahāvidyās of the Great Goddess tradition (GHM 78). What began as a slightly humorous, slightly tragic family embarrassment ends as a grand mythological claim. Sharada, of course, knew nothing about the footnote. She only knew that she had defended herself by beating up her abusive cousin.

Or, again, consider the depressed devotee who goes to Mahendranath Gupta to complain about how he went to Sharada with his troubles and received no help from her: depressingly, she said absolutely nothing and just stared at him. Gupta asks if she looked at him. Yes, indeed she had, and for some time. Something then clicks inside: "It seemed to me," the devotee confesses, "that Mā had sent me to M [Gupta] to make me understand the meaning of her glance of grace" (MK 104). Finally, in yet another silent scene, some devotees arrive after a long trip and relate how all of them were convinced that it was "Mā's blessing" that protected them from a violent storm on the journey (MK 334). In these last two scenes, we are in the realm of pure projection. Sharada has become an absent blank slate upon which virtually anything can be (and is) written.

Any doubt that arises within such a symbolic system can be answered by one of a number of hermeneutical strategies developed by the tradition. There was a ready answer for any question or seeming contradiction. We have already seen how Sharada's worldliness was interpreted away by Golap-Ma's vision of the floating dead baby. The contradictions by no means ended there, nor did the hermeneutical resources of the tradition. If a man, for example, was horrified for letting himself be initiated by a woman, Sharada was quick to point out that it was really the Master who initiated him through her (MK 347). Or if a devotee came complaining about having no visions, Sharada was ready to point out that "all those are lower things" (MK 299), despite the tradition's clear reliance on them as a marker of divinity and spiritual progress. When no answer is immediately available, Sharada often resorts to flagrant ad hominem attacks. When, for example, she is criticized by her sister-in-law for making monks of good boys and ruining families, Sharada responds by accusing her of living "like a mere pig" and practicing animality (MK 283), and when the villagers criticize a swami for his frequent visits to Sharada, Sharada predicts that they will have to be born again and again, and, unless the grace of God intervenes, that they will "rot in the world" (MK 349).

Two problems, however, were particularly difficult for the tradition to explain away: Sharada's "nonexperiences," that is, her extraordinary lack of what the tradition would normally recognize as religious experiences (vision, trance, ecstasy, etc.), and her physical suffering. Sharada's nonexperiences are particularly interesting, as they are perhaps the most striking feature of Sharada's personality and presence. The texts, of course, invoke all sorts of interpretive means to explain this lack. Foremost among them is the textual creation of a number of extraordinary visionary and ecstatic experiences. The texts are insistent that Sharada *did* indeed have this or that extraordinary experience, but such claims are countered *from within the texts* by a number of contradictory moves and personalities. For example, the theology of substitution that was invoked to explain the *ṣoḍaśī-pūjā*—which argued that Sharada shared, by reason of the ritual, in Ramakrishna's *sādhana*s and so did not have to perform any herself—would not have been necessary at all had the tradition recognized that Sharada did in fact practice *sādhana* and have her own experiences. And the criticisms of very close attendants, like Yogin-Ma, who was clearly disgusted with what she called Sharada's "worldliness," and her own family members, who were quite blunt about her lack of anything approaching the religiously profound, only make sense in the context of these same nonexperiences. Moreover, it is essential that we recognize that virtually *all* of the extraordinary experiences of Sharada reported in the texts are reported and defended *by others*, and even when they are reported or described by Sharada, it is *a Sharada of the texts* who "speaks." And the historical Sharada, we must remember, had absolutely no control over the production, editing, or publication of these central texts, all of which appear after her death. It cannot be repeated enough—*Sharada was silent* on such matters. The tradition, of course, interprets this silence as a mark of her humility, but it just as easily could have been a sign of her reluctance to engage in a construction that she did not recognize as legitimate, at least for herself.

Sharada's numerous physical ailments (gout, malaria, etc.) are at least as problematic as her nonexperiences. The texts, after all, assume that suffering is a product of impurity. This sets up a simple logical problem for the writers: if Sharada is absolutely pure, then why did she suffer so? The answer, although not terribly original (it was used before with Ramakrishna, the *avatāra* with throat cancer), was at least simple: she suffered because she was absorbing the sins of others (MK 26). This symbolic move was no doubt rooted in traditional notions of caste and purity[17] and the vicarious capabilities of the holy man or woman, but it was also designed to homologize Sharada to Ramakrishna. In a roundabout way, it was also no doubt designed to answer the Christian exclusivistic claims about Christ's once-and-for-all atonement. It is no accident that Sharada, like Ramakrishna, is described in the texts in terms that could easily be transposed into a nineteenth-century missionary's sermon. Thus, with a single move the tradition can explain away a seeming contradiction (the Goddess has gout) and implicitly advance, once again, the deification of its object, all the while advancing the claims of its other divine being, Ramakrishna, and implicitly relativizing the exclusivistic claims of colonial Christianity.

Finally, it is necessary to discuss, however briefly, the hermeneutical uses of that most ultimate form of silence—death. "Look," Sharada says in one scene, "as long as I'm alive, none of these [her family members] will be able to know me. Afterwards all will understand" (MK 322). An identical if differently symbolized claim was made in regards to Ramakrishna, who was often compared to the hidden king who examines his city in disguise only to disappear again as soon as he is found out (MK 348–349). It is significant in both of these cases that the event of physical death and the discovery of divinity are coterminous (this, no doubt, is the "afterwards" of Sharada's comment). I would suggest that this is an accurate historical perception couched in mythological language. Psychologically speaking, it is virtually impossible to deify a human being when he or she is literally standing in front of you, or, much worse, when he or she is your sister or cousin. It should not surprise us, then, that families of prophets and saints are notoriously difficult to convince.

Joining the Mother's Family: What the People Found

I began this essay with Sharada's two questions: "How am I different from them?" and "Why do these people come?" I have answered, if incompletely, the first question. But what about the second? It seems just as important, for although there are clearly scenes in which Sharada does in fact function as the proverbial blank state by reason of her multivalent silence, it would be a serious mistake to imagine that Sharada was nothing but this blank state. People certainly also *found* something here, as they flocked to her, like a "row of ants" (MK 349) as she once put it in one of her many moments of exhaustion. Why? What was it that these pestering ants found in this patient woman? In Sharada's terms, "Why do these people come?"

To answer this second question, it is important that we first realize the historical situation of the people who came to Sharada and, more specifically, the nature of the sufferings that they were enduring at the hands of both the colonial powers and their own indigenous socioreligious system. Here indeed there is ample evidence for the mythological understanding of the tradition's "social malaise theory": when the *dharma* has declined and seems on the brink of dissolution,

God descends to rescue it from disaster. The *avatāra*, in other words, is by definition *a figure of crisis*, a presence invoked by extreme conditions and potential social breakdown.

Sharada herself is clear that Ramakrishna descended so that those who have been "burned" by the sufferings of the world might obtain peace and solace (MK 298). Although there is always the danger of exaggeration, it is astonishing to see how often such texts as the Māyer Kathā and the Smṛtikathā return to these "burning sufferings" and the battered, destitute nature of the devotees' worlds. The texts give ample space to that scapegoat for everything considered wrong about India, British colonialism, but, as if possessing a certain balanced wisdom, they often refuse to lay all the blame at the foreigners' feet. Yes, there are descriptions of police surveillance and harrassment (MK 125; SK 169–173), mail censorship (SK 96), and imprisonments (MK 94). And there are numerous references to social sufferings—dead babies and children (MK 111, 122, 271, 318), famine, grueling poverty (MK 35), and clothing-less women committing suicide out of shame (SK 165)—that could be traced to the socioeconomic consequences of colonialism. Sharada, moreover, does indeed sometimes see the colonial origins of a particular social problem; she is convinced, for example, that the lack of clothes in the country is a direct result of the people giving up their spinning wheels and depending on the Company for their cloth (SK 166). But Sharada, although obviously disgusted with the British and the perfume of the "women in boots" (MK 322), is nevertheless relatively uninterested in political matters (MK 262–263, 330) and sees the British as her children as well, living with her Indian children in "one house" (MK 263). Not surprisingly, she sometimes flagrantly ignores the demands of the swadeshi movement for the desires of her devotee-children; in one scene, for example, she ignores the ban on imported cloth to dress them in what they actually want instead of what is politically correct (MK 263).

She is, on the other hand, cutting and precise in her attacks on a whole array of Hindu social practices. She seems bent, for example, on criticizing the utter lack of sexual discipline among some of her devotees and—this seems to be the real point—the debilitating number of children such a lack of control inevitably produces (MK 46, 61, 325). Utterly disgusted with those who have twenty-five children and then weep because ten have died, Sharada exclaims: "They're all animals—animals!" (MK 46). She is also very critical of the excesses of caste and its purity codes (MK 256, 268), mourns the lack of education and skills among Bengali women (MK 131, 221–222), attacks the practice of child-marriage (MK 131), and complains about the miserable state of abandoned widows in Benares, who, often deprived of any support from their families, live out their days in dark dank rooms eating rice soaked in water (MK 126). Moreover, when Sharada is silent about other social matters, the Māyer Kathā is not: its pages are filled with explicit, if casual, almost innocent descriptions of Indian racism (MK 191–192, 304), Hindu-Muslim communal violence (MK 251), cheating, fake beggar-monks (SK 129), street beggars (MK 34–35), beaten, escaping, abandoned and suicidal wives (MK 31, 53–54, 176; SK 52), child widows (SK 52), beaten laborers and servants (MK 148), and stunting child marriages (MK 131). Again, the same list could have been pulled out from any number of nineteenth-century Hindu reform speeches or Christian missionary sermons.

Sharada lived in a religious world in which monks threatened and physically beat their servants (MK 148, 327–328; SK 224–228), women had to bow to men (MK 275), and purity codes rendered whole classes of human beings unworthy of human dignity. So powerful and omnipresent was this social system that even Sharada was susceptible to its harsh judgments. Hence, she was not above cruelly criticizing the daughter of a woman whose husband had abandoned them for renunciation: "What poverty! And so much greed!" Sharada complained, "The girl ate and ate until she almost vomited!" (MK 314). Sharada seemed incapable of seeing what the social reformer—Hindu or Christian—could have pointed out to her, namely, that the girl was slowly starving because her father had abandoned her for a religious practice. This was no moral fault of the girl's; it was the product of a cruel social system and an even crueler socioeconomic situation. A similar lack of perspective is evident in her inability to separate her by all accounts horrible experience with the adopted Radhu from other situations where adoption might render a positive social good: adoption, Sharada seemed to teach, was a nightmare to be avoided at all costs.

Despite such troubling moments, what Sharada generally offered her visitors was a welcome respite from these cruel colonial, social, and religious worlds. If her husband dug a foot down to rid himself of the dirt where an evil man had sat (MK 207) and threw away whole beds to clean his room of the atheist's defiling presence (Mitra 1897, 96–97), Sharada could refuse no one who addressed her as "Mother." If Ramakrishna screamed for Ganges water when a woman touched his toes (Gupta 1987, 2.53–54), Sharada visited effortlessly and naturally with a former prostitute who came to her, despite Ramakrishna forbidding her to do so (MK 207).[18] (Nag, it seems, was right about Mother being kinder than Father.) If the monks beat and threatened their servants into submission, Sharada yelled at the monks for their inhumanity and their gall for asking her to participate in such tactics

(MK 327–328; SK 205–206). If women ran from their husbands (MK 80) and threatened suicide for the treatment they received from their mothers-in-law (MK 54), Sharada usually offered them a listening ear and a warm heart. In short, whereas the world of the culture was structured around the harsh hierarchical systems of caste and purity, Sharada's world generally operated with considerably more compassion and love: in effect, she supplanted the social codes of *dharma*, caste, and purity with the simplicity and unconditional love of a family and a mother. Hence, she can consistently describe her devotee-children as "one family" that shares a single caste (MK 341, 357) and measure her love out equally to the coolie, the hawker, and the brahmin (SK 49). Such a familial context no doubt explains why texts like the Māyer Kathā and the Smṛtikathā often read like elaborate descriptions of petty family quarrels and homey household scenes: an argument over how to roll bread and a description of Sharada fumbling to fill a hurricane lamp are by no means unusual and in fact take up hundreds of pages in the literature on Sharada. For all its idealizing tendencies, this was a very real family.

This attempt to create an ideal family was no doubt partially driven by Sharada's painfully disappointing experiences with her own family, which was hardly ideal. Indeed, Sharada often expressed frustration, even disgust, with the pettiness, worldliness, greed and outright insanity of her own family. Radhu and her mad mother were particularly difficult to deal with. And the biographers are insistent that none of Sharada's brothers, except the last (who died while in medical school), had any talent or spiritual tendencies, and that they competed incessantly for Sharada's patronage (GHM xxix). Perhaps this is why Sharada actively encouraged her devotee-children to avoid them (SK 235). In a cry of frustration that perhaps tells us much about the psychology of *mokṣa* and its relationship to the tightly knit bonds of the Indian extended family, Sharada minced no words in her desire never to be born again among them: "In your house again? No way" (MK 242). Such a conflicted family situation no doubt played a large role in the creation of Sharada's ideal devotion family.

To put it differently, we might say that Sharada's devotional family was everything that her public culture and her own family experiences were not. Or more accurately, Sharada's devotional family embodied the positive, nurturing, loving aspects of her culture and family experience, recreated anew within the boundaries of a religious context. Dream, devotion, ritual, and text had effectively replaced, at least for a time, the pestering brothers, insane nieces, dead children, arranged marriages, and abusive husbands of the devotees' actual historical families. What is more, these same processes had deified a man and his wife—"the Master" and "the Mother"—and set them up against the humiliating conditions of colonialism. The Indian family was restored in its ideal devotional state. God and now the Goddess were on their side against the British and the Christians. Things could not get much better. This, no doubt, was why the people came, like "a row of ants" to Sharada, "the Holy Mother."

Conclusion: Recognizing a Muddy Diamond

The textual tradition contains numerous *ukti* or "sayings" about the divine-human, the *avatāra*, and the difficulty of recognizing his or her hidden presence in the world. The *avātara*, for example, is compared to the lantern that casts a bright light all around itself, except up close around its own base (ie, near the prophet's or *avatāra*'s family) (Mitra 1897, 181). We are also continually reminded that even Rāma and Kṛṣṇa were not recognized by their family and friends. And then there is the parable about the uncut diamond at the bathing ghat that is used to rub off the soles of bathers' feet until a jeweler comes by and recognizes its true hidden worth (MK 350).

This last saying presumes that divinity is something objective, a thing "out there" only waiting to be discovered. In Sharada's case, at least, this is patently wrong. There was nothing objectively, obviously divine about Sharada. Otherwise, visitors would not have mistaken her for an ordinary woman, devotees would not have complained about her utter ordinariness, family members would not have abused her so, and the tradition would not have needed to develop its hermeneutics of hiddenness to explain away the banal nature of her life. Far from being something obvious "out there," this particular goddess could only be detected in an "in here," in the heart of the devotee who, through text, photo, and ritual, had been told what to feel, what to see, and what to say. Sharada Devī, in other words, was a hermeneutical creation interpreted into being out of a distance, out of an absence, out of a provocative silence. Divinity, it seems, is nothing like the proverbial diamond.

Or is it? After all, there *was* something there, even if it had to be cut, smoothed, and shaped by psychological processes, social contexts, and specific types of people before it could be sold to the public; and even for the devout few who had already "bought" this divinity, it still had to be shaped just so and polished more than a little by dream, projection, ritual, text, rhetoric, and, ultimately, the silence of death. Moreover, even a "real" diamond's worth is finally a social construction, a kind of interpretation that a specific community of social actors agree to share; chemically speaking, a diamond is just another kind of rock; its value is not at all inherent in the chemical structure of the crystal. Perhaps Sharada is like the diamond after all, if not in the sense that the proverb intended. Possessing an undeniable grace, cut and polished in the dreams, rituals, texts, and interpretations of others, she became, almost despite herself, something eminently valuable for the culture, something to prize, cherish, even worship as divine. She became Sharada Devi, Sharada the Great Goddess.[19]

Abbreviations

GHM	The Gospel of the Holy Mother
HM[G]	Holy Mother: Sri Sarada Devi
HM[N]	Holy Mother: Being the Life of Sri Sarada Devi Wife of Sri Ramakrishna and Helpmate in His Mission
MK	Śrī Srī Māyer Kathā
SK	Śrī Śrī Māyer Smṛtikathā

Notes

1. The Bengali expression is *Śrī Śrī Mā* or "the twice-blessed Mother," which is usually shortened to simply Mā, an emotionally rich and affectionate term that can mean "mother," "mom," or "little mother" (i.e., daughter). I have opted to retain the intimate and familial "Mā" in my translations.

2. Śrī Śrī Māyer Kathā, 353, 99; Cf. 226; hereafter MK.

3. The editors of the English translation of the Māyer Kathā describe her as "physically weak, and mentally a moron" (*The Gospel of the Holy Mother*, xxx; hereafter GHM).

4. Despite the tradition's insistence that "the Mother was not likely to forget" such an important event (*Holy Mother: Śrī Sarada Devī*, 41, n. 1; hereafter HM[G]), she does seem to have forgotten many of the details, including how old she was at the time. In a number of humorous textual moments, Sharada relates that she was sixteen—not an illogical choice, given the name of the ritual—and then the editors immediately jump in, usually in footnotes, to state that she was actually eighteen or even nineteen (HM[G] 48, n. 1, 50; MK 227).

5. For two psychological readings of this ritual, see Sil 1991, 147–148; Kripal 1998, 133–136.

6. *Holy Mother: Being the Life of Śrī Sarada Devī Wife of Śrī Ramakrishna and Helpmate in His Mission*, 43; hereafter HM(N).

7. Sharada's bracelet-theology finds at least one intriguing echo in the devotional literature of the time. For example, in Satyacharan Mitra's biography

of Ramakrishna, Ramakrishna tells the story of a queen who worshiped her husband while he was alive and refused to wear any of her expensive jewelry, opting instead for a simple wrist-bangle. When her king-husband died, she broke this simple bangle and replaced it with a shimmering gold one, a sign for her that her divine husband was now one with God and her marriage to him now eternal (Mitra 1897, 175–178). Two points are important to keep in mind here: the story was published in 1897 and so could have been influenced by Sharada's own bangle-theology; and Ramakrishna tells the story to defend the traditional prohibition against widow-remarriage ("No one becomes a widow, therefore what is the use of widow remarriage?" [Mitra 1897, 178]).

8. The Smṛtikathā describes the Vrindavan pilgrimage thus: "There her tortured heart became very peaceful, and she immersed herself in difficult religious practices and the singing of devotional songs" (Śrī Śrī Māyer Smṛtikathā, 136; hereafter SK).

9. The promise hints at the source of Sharada's depresssion: her lack of children.

10. What we might call "psychological synchronicity" also played a role in Sharada's growing sense of divinity; hence, she confesses that she was led to accept the title of "goddess" because of the strange manner in which her thoughts so often found expression in subsequent external events (MK 64).

11. This logic, essentially Tantric in its structure, seems to have been particularly powerful in Bengal, where earlier mystical movements, such as the Kartābhajās, engaged in virtually identical divinizations and theologies of dual incarnation. Ramsaran Pal and his wife Sarasvati Devi, for example, became the first Kartā (lit. "Master") and Kartā-Mā in the early nineteenth century: "Rāmśaraṇ proclaimed himself the Kartā, the Master or Lord, of this new religion and as the incarnation of God . . . in human form. In the eyes of their devotees, Rāmśaraṇ Pāl and his wife Sarasvatī thus came to be regarded as far more than mere mortals, but rather as the eternal Male and Female principles of the universe—the *Ādi-Puruṣa* and *Ādyā-Śakti* incarnate" (Urban 1998, 85).

12. Consider, for example, Berger and Luckman 1966.

13. Ramakrishna does appear in dreams but less often and usually either to a boy or male disciple (MK 230) or, most significantly, alongside Sharada (MK 112).

14. The woman's comment implicitly recognizes the dream's conflict as the illegitimate product of an anachronistic understanding: Ramakrishna's *past* prohibition against eating left-overs would have been ignorant of Sharada's *present* divine status. Sharada's present divinity, in other words, has effectively transformed any of her polluted "left-overs" into pure *prasād*. The dream thus sets up a conflict between the past and the present (and, I might add, between Ramakrishna and Sharada) and opts decidedly for the present.

15. The expression is Sharada's, who, in answer to a question about whether visions are seen within subjective states (*bhāve*) or with the physical eyes (*sādā cokhe*), replied matter-of-factly: "in subjective states" (MK 238). Sharada demonstrates a similar common-sense psychological view of visions

when she suggests that a child who claimed to have seen the Master in fact only imagined him "with his eyes closed" and then mistook this interior state for exterior reality (MK 201). She does, however, claim that she had at least one rare vision "with open eyes" of an eleven to twelve-year-old girl resembling Radhu (no doubt, the key element) with dry hair, rudraksha beads, and ochre clothes. This girl followed her everywhere until Sharada performed the ascetic feat of the five fires to "exorcise" the haunting presence (MK 238).

16. The Bengali text records simply that his wife made him mad (MK 174).

17. Related to this model of suffering are all of the scenes describing Sharada "stung" by the touch of various devotees: although traditional readings take these scenes as proofs of Sharada's psychic abilitites to see the inner nature of the devotees, they are more likely embodied expressions of Indian purity codes and their implicit caste structure.

18. It should be pointed out that Sharada, although liberal in many ways, did not entirely reject her culture's purity codes. She assumed, for example, the dangers of eating together, lying on the same bed, and using someone else's towel (MK 360), and often complained about the pain she experienced from too many or the wrong kind of people touching her.

19. While this essay was in press, I was re-reading June McDaniel's *The Madness of the Saints: Ecstatic Religion in Bengal* (Chicago: University of Chicago Press, 1989) and discovered that McDaniel had approached Sharada Devi in a way very similar to my approach here, through what she calls the "attribution of *bhāva*," that is, the manner in which others attributed to Sharada's most mundane activities (falling asleep, walking, resting, laughter, etc.) psychological states that she herself seldom expressed having. I was delighted to discover our shared conclusions but bothered that, given the late date, I could not properly acknowledge McDaniel's work in the body of the essay. I nevertheless would like to do so here.

Chapter 9

Goddesses and the Goddess in Hinduism

Constructing the Goddess through Religious Experience

Kathleen M. Erndl

Prologue: A Question to Ponder

Is there one Goddess or are there many goddesses? On one level, it is possible to speak of the Hindu Goddess as a single omnipotent being, Mahādevī or the Great Goddess. On another level, it is possible to speak of various manifestations of this Great Goddess such as the three cosmic goddesses, Mahālakṣmī, Mahāsarasvatī, and Mahākālī who are manifestations of the one Mahādevī. On still another level, it is possible to speak of numerous individual goddesses as distinct entities with their own distinctive personalities, iconographies, stories, and cult practices. And there are many other levels in between. However one speaks of the Goddess, singularly, or goddesses, plurally, she is connected with *śakti*, the dynamic creative power or energy pervading and sustaining the universe. *Śakti* is such a fluid concept that it seems to transcend distinctions of singular and plural. Even having understood this about *śakti*, it is difficult for me, a European-American interpreter of Hindu Goddess traditions, writing in the English language, to find a way to speak about the Mahādevī which evokes her both unity and multiplicity *at the same time*. As John S. Hawley points out in his introduction to *Devī: Goddesses of India*, problems with capital and lower-case G/g and with whether or not to use the definite article "the" are problems in the English language, not in Indian languages.[1] Similarly, I wonder whether the strong monotheistic bias in European culture has made the use of singular and plural more problematic in English than they are in Indian languages.

Introduction

Scholars—and I refer here to Western or Western-trained Indian scholars—have proposed various models to account for the seeming contradiction between the unity and multiplicity of Hindu female deities. One such model could be called a "diachronic" or "historical model" which posits that over time various local and tribal goddesses became incorporated into Hinduism through identification with Sanskritic goddesses or with a Great Goddess. Such a process could work from the "top down" as in the Devī Māhātmya, whose Brahmin author, writing in Sanskrit, explicitly identified the tribal goddess Cāmuṇḍā as the "killer of the demons Caṇḍa and Muṇḍa," that is, Kālī, who in turn was identified as an emanation of Candikā/Ambikā who is also referred to in the text by such names as Durgā and Mahādevī. The work of such scholars as Thomas Coburn and C. MacKenzie Brown has familiarized us with this process (e.g., Coburn 1991, 1995; Brown 1974, 1990). The process can also work from the "bottom up" in which the devotees of a local goddess identify her in oral tradition or vernacular pamphlets with goddesses or the Great Goddess of the Sanskritic tradition. I have used this approach in my own work to show how such local goddesses as Nainā Devī, Vaiṣṇo Devī, and Jvālā Mukhī have been identified over time with the Goddess of the Devī Māhātmya or with the story of Dakṣa's fire sacrifice, Satī, and the *śakti pīṭhas* (Erndl 1993). Historical approaches also emphasize the chronological multilayered nature of portrayals of goddesses in narrative contexts, with texts picking up themes from other, earlier, contexts and transforming them into a new vision of the Devī. For example, C. Mackenzie Brown, in his chapter for this volume, discusses how the Devī-Gītā picks up and synthesizes earlier Devī-related themes with newer Tantric themes.[2]

A second model could be called a "synchronic" or "psychological/structural model." This model, of which there are numerous variants, appeals to certain abiding categories of Hindu psychology or social structure to account for the coexistence of multiplicity and unity of goddesses. Models that hinge on "ambivalence" or "benevolence and malevolence" or "tooth mothers" and "breast mothers" are of this type.[3] A more recent model has been proposed by Stanley N. Kurtz, in his book *All the Mothers Are One* (1992). Kurtz argues that the Hindu theological propensity for lumping all goddesses together is linked to the presence of multiple mother figures in Hindu households who in the Hindu (male) psyche become one great Mother. Similarly—but in a more sociological than psychological vein—William S. Sax has proposed that the multiplicity of goddesses is not contradictory but rather that the goddesses are embodiments of different points in the female life-cycle. The tendency to conflate multiple goddesses into a single goddess, Sax argues, is part of a male-dominated gender politic which homogenizes the richness and variety of female experience into a single category, that of woman (Sax 1994, 172–210).

Both of these types of models are useful, depending upon what kind of interpretation one is trying to elucidate. In no way do I intend to criticize the excellent work done by the scholars, many of whom are contributors to this volume, using these models. In this essay, I attempt to complement these models with an alternative model. Or, to be more precise, it should not be called a model at all, since the term model implies some kind of regular pattern of predictability. Rather I will call it an approach, an *experiential* approach.[4] It could also be called a personal or contextual approach. In my work on Hindu Goddess traditions, I have become aware of how utterly irrelevant scholarly debates on goddesses and the Goddess are not only to the religious experience, but also to the understandings of ordinary Hindu devotees, who move with apparent ease between universality and particularity in their ritual and devotional lives, speaking of the Goddess (singular) in some contexts and of particular goddesses (plural) in other contexts and often even within the same sentence.

Devotees are not usually concerned with a general explanatory model, but rather with the specifics of their experience in a particular context. I cannot imagine a Hindu devotee saying, for example, "I worship Jvālā Mukhī as the Mahādevī, because she was originally a tribal fire goddess who through a process of Sanskritization became identified with the pan-Indian Durgā." Nor could I imagine my hypothetical devotee saying, "I consider Lakṣmī, Sarasvatī, and Kālī to be the same Goddess, because my three mothers, that is my mother and my two aunties who raised me, were respectively rich, wise, and frightening."

Of course, I am gratuitously presenting these models in the crudest possible way. My point is that the historical model is trying to say something about change on a broad scale, over time, something that no one would have personally experienced, while the psychological/structural model reflects very much an outsider's "take" on what the insiders themselves are experiencing. In this experiential approach (which is also an experimental approach), I attempt to say something about religious experience, about how certain Hindu devotees construct the identity of the Great Goddess and their relationship to her. The identity of the Great Goddess, as understood and interpreted by individuals and communities, is fluid and context-specific. It is fluid in the sense that the "meaning" of the Goddess is multivalent and capable of multiple understandings and interpretations which may be extremely idiosyncratic. This fluidity is often cited as one of the attractive features of Hinduism, though I am also reminded of an observation made to me by a charismatic Mother/Guru: "One of the problems with our *sanātan dharm* is that people can make up anything they want and get away with it."[5] The identity of the Great Goddess is context-specific in the sense that it is dependent not only on personal experience, but on personal experience as conditioned by the particular situation, geographic, social, theological, political, in which the person resides. Ordinary devotees see no contradiction between the universal Great Goddess who is the supreme being of the universe and her manifestation as a particular rock, plant, or human being, for these are mediated through their own experience.

I would not have attempted to say anything about so slippery a subject as personal religious experience, except for two instigating events. The first was a chance conversation I had with Tārā Devī, a Kangra village woman, in the fall of 1991. That conversation forms the centerpiece of this essay. The second was the invitation from Tracy Pintchman to contribute to a panel on "Constructing the Identity of the Great Goddess" in the fall of 1994. In talking with Pintchman, I remembered my conversation with Tārā Devī and thought that my reflections on it might be a relevant contribution. Before proceeding further, I wish to reiterate the tentative and experimental nature of both the approach and the content of this essay. It is, despite much thought, still *kaccā* (Hindi; unripe, uncooked). Also, I do not claim to represent Tārā Devī's "true" feelings or experiences; whatever these may be are, of course, framed through her memory and interpretive categories and further filtered through our interactions with each other and through my questions and interpretative categories.

A Conversation with Tārā Devī

I am not sure whether or not it is accepted ethnographic etiquette to discuss informants with each other, but in this case the discussion not only happened naturally but also yielded fascinating questions. Tārā Devī, at the time I met her in Kangra in the fall of 1991, was a thirty-four-year-old married Rajput woman with four children. Elsewhere I have related Tārā Devī's account of how the Goddess possessed her and gradually revealed her "orders" to her, and of Tārā Devī's discovery of images that emerged from the ground. I have also written of her transformation from a near invalid into a Mātā,[6] a Goddess-possessed healer with a home temple and large clientele (Erndl 1997). In that article, I suggested that Tārā Devī's identification with the Goddess was empowering for her and for other women in her village. Here I attempt to deal with the question of how she constructs the identity of the Great Goddess. The question of the relationship between goddesses and the Goddess came up unexpectedly in the course of a conversation we had one day.

For the several months that I spent with Tārā Devī, I was in the habit of coming to her house on the three days of the week that she received visitors (clients or "pilgrims", as she called them). With her permission, I would observe and tape record her consultations with the pilgrims, photograph the rituals she performed, and participate in impromptu devotional singing from time to time. During lulls between all these activities, there would sometimes be an opportunity for me to converse with Tārā Devī or ask her any questions that were on my mind. On one such morning, when I had arrived at her home, she was busy running back and forth between her kitchen and her temple. Her husband, who was usually at work in another village all week, was home because of a toothache. She served me tea and bananas. At first we were the only ones there, and she asked me what I had been doing for the past few days. I had just returned from a day-long trip to both Simsā Mātā and Sagūr Mātā, so I told her about them.

Sagūr Mātā is the shrine in the nearby village of Sagur where a young Kumhār (Potter caste) man is regularly possessed by the Goddess and sees a clientele much in the same way Tārā Devī does. Simsā Mātā, located in village Simsa east of the Kangra area towards Mandi, is an old established temple to the goddess Śāradā Devī where women undertake a special form of asceticism and pray to the Goddess for the gift of a child. Tārā Devī had grown up near Simsā Mātā, so she had been there and was familiar with the practices of the place. But our conversation focused on Sagūr Mātā, her human vehicle, and her nature as a goddess.

> T[ārā] D[evī]: He was forbidden to marry. She was a very good Mātā. What can I say about the gods? He probably had gotten the order that he was not to enter into married life. Mātā got a bit angry. Just like that with drum and cymbals, he went off to marry that girl. Then he got married. But he does a lot of service for people.

K[athleen] E[rndl]: So Mātā forbid him to get married?

TD: At first she forbid him to get married, then later she ordered him to get married. But even so, it wasn't a complete order from Mātā. People come to him from far, far away. Then Mātā set aside Friday, Sunday, and Tuesday. Otherwise at first (just like here) he would play day and night. She was also a very good Mātā, "Four-Armed Mātā." They say that he gives very good advice. If I go into his affairs, it won't be right. She will get angry. It's like that.

Here, I was puzzled by the fact that she referred to the Mātā at Sagur as "a very good Mātā," as though she were a different Mātā than the one at her place. The Four-Armed Mātā (Caturbhujā Mātā) is an iconographic depiction of the Goddess, usually standing, with four arms. Going back over my notes later, I realized that I had once recorded a conversation between Tārā Devī's husband and a pilgrim about Sagūr Mātā in which Tārā Devī's husband said that the goddess there was called Cāmuṇḍā Mātā. A sign outside the Sagūr Mātā temple identifies it as Chaturbhujā (Four-Armed) Cāmuṇḍā Mātā. The main temple in the area to Cāmuṇḍā Mātā, also called Cāmuṇḍā Devī, located in Jadrangal village on the banks of the Ban Ganga, is one of the major Goddess temples in the Kangra Valley. The spot is identified locally as the place where Kālī, as recorded in the Devī-Māhātmya, killed the demons Caṇḍa and Muṇḍa, thus receiving the name Cāmuṇḍā.

Jvālājī, on the other hand, is Tārā Devī's *iṣṭa-devī* or chosen goddess, but it would be more accurate to say that it was Jvālājī who chose Tārā Devī rather than the other way around. Jvālājī is another name of Jvālā Mukhī, the Goddess of the "Flame Mouth" who is enshrined in her famous Kangra temple in the form of eternal self-born flames. According to Kangra tradition and some Sanskrit sources, the flame emerging from the rocks at this site is the "flame-tongue" of the goddess Satī which fell there when Śiva dismembered her body after she immolated herself in her father Dakṣa's sacrifical fire. It is this Goddess who regularly possesses and gives "orders" to Tārā Devī and who is enshrined in Tārā Devī's home temple in the form of a flame. Tārā Devī had once told me that she would also become possessed by other deities and that she often had the *darśan* of all three-hundred-thirty million gods. I had not previously asked her how the various goddesses (and gods) were related to each other, nor had I asked her whether, when she used the name Mātā, she meant the Mātā, any Mātā, or her Mātā (Jvālājī), mainly because I had relegated such inquiries to the category of "stupid questions" after trying unsuccessfully with numerous other informants to get a coherent answers to them. Nevertheless, her comments gave me an opening, so I plunged ahead.

> KE: O.K. Please tell me this; the Mātā at Sagur is "Four-Armed Mātā," and here she is "Jvālājī." What is the difference?
>
> TD: The difference is this: Look over there at the flame. [She gestures toward the *jot* or flame which she keeps burning all the time in her shrine.] He [the young man at Sagūr Mātā] does not burn it day and night, but *here* whether people come or not I have to keep that flame burning day and night. *That's why they call her Jvālā Mā.* Even if I have to go out somewhere, I pour ghee into it and go out. And my heart isn't in it [when I go out]. My heart keeps on getting nervous. When the flame goes out, I think, "What has happened?" When I go to sleep at night, I pour a lot of ghee into it, so that it will keep on burning. But *there* [at Sagūr] only at the time of *ārati* (the devotional waving of lamps to worship the deity), there is just a tiny flame. He pours ghee into it and lights incense for five or ten minutes. That's why there she is "Four Armed Mātā," and here she is "Jvālā Mātā." Actually, all the goddesses come here.
>
> When I got home that day, I typed the following into my laptop computer:
>
> This is very interesting conceptually. The difference between the two goddesses is not ontological, but functional. What makes the two goddesses different is not any inherent difference in the goddesses as entities, but *in how they are worshiped*. Or rather it is how they are worshiped that makes them different. Is Tārā Devī a nominalist? You don't worship this goddess with a flame because she is Jvālājī, but rather she is Jvālājī because you worship her with a flame! Fascinating. That's like saying the there is a country called the U.S.A. because it has a flag with fifty stars, because if it didn't have fifty stars, it wouldn't be the U.S.A.! Wonderful! There seems to be a different system of logic operating here. Maybe this is the key to understanding the whole conceptual and symbolic framework underlying spirit possession.

Reading this again now, I am not quite sure what I meant. If I thought I had the key then, I have lost it now. Now I doubt she was stating a general rule, along the lines of "ritual prescriptions define the identity of the Goddess," but rather was recounting her own *experience* of the Goddess as Flame and her own experience of the Goddess's order to burn the flame continually. Her concept of who the Goddess is, that is, of the Goddess's identity, is inseparable from her own interactions with the Goddess. To continue with the conversation:

> TD: You ought to go to Sagur sometime to see. There when the *khel* ("play," possession) comes, he makes a sound like "si si." He must have called you for Monday.
>
> KE: Yes, on Monday I'll have an opportunity to meet and talk with him, because not so many people come on that day. . . . So [I try again], are these goddesses one or are they different?
>
> TD: Devī is one, but she has different names. Some call her Kālī Mā, some Durgā; they have all been made from Pārvatī. The names are different, but they are in fact one. Wherever you go, her *līlā* [divine play] is unique.

Here, she seems to be making a more general theological statement, that the Goddess is one, but that different forms have all come from one (Pārvatī) and have different names. At the same time, while asserting this unity, she immediately stresses the uniqueness of the Goddess's manifestations and activities *(līlā)* in various places.

> KE: And what about Viṣṇu, Śiva [male deities], and so forth?
>
> TD: At the time when I do *ārati,* they all give me *darśan.* All three-hundred-thirty million gods come to me. A to Z they all give me very good *darśan.* Even at this moment, if I want to, I can have *darśan.* . . . Śivjī's, Pārvatī's, whoever's *darśan* I want, it will happen. Even if the pilgrims don't come, still I get enjoyment. I keep muttering with my rosary, and I keep getting their *darśan.* A boy once came here . . . [In the meantime, a woman came in, and Tārā Devī gestured to her and said] Her son has become my brother. Therefore there is a very good connection between us. And I have told her about you.

She introduced me to this woman, and our conversation on the topic of goddesses and the Goddess ended. It is noteworthy that here, too, Tārā Devī has shifted without missing a beat from an abstract, general philosophical discussion of the nature of the Goddess to her own concrete, personal *experience,* which from her viewpoint is far more immediate and relevant. What she seems to imply is that all the goddesses (and gods, too) are one not only for a philosophical reason, but also for an experiential one. Because all three-hundred-thirty million deities give her their *darśan*—that is, because she is capable of experiencing them all—they all exist, and they are all one.

A Conversation with Sagūr Mātā

To round out my discussion of Tārā Devī's construction of the Great Goddess and to provide some contrasts, I will provide an abridged version of a conversation I had with Suresh Kumār, a twenty-seven-year old married Kumhār (Potter caste) man with one child who lives in Sagūr village. He and his Goddess are usually referred to as Sagūr Mātā. It was a discussion about Sagūr Mātā and the identity and difference between that goddess and Jvālājī, Tārā Devī's goddess, which led me to the issues discussed in this chapter.

> S[uresh] K[umār]: When I was studying in school, while I was studying during school time, the Goddess entered me. At that time I was in tenth class. Then for five days I practiced devotion to Mātā and [gesturing toward the image], this image of Mātā came out by itself.
>
> KE: From the ground?
>
> SK: From the ground. When it came out, I started worshiping it. . . . When I started worshiping it, Mātā said, "Now you have to drive away the sorrows of the suffering. So whatever devotees come here, give them holy water, ash, and foot nectar." When the suffering people started to come—maybe Mā herself had called them—Mā's power (influence) also started to increase. Then Mātā built this temple herself. After the temple was built, the inn was built. After that Mātā also built our house. Then through Mātā's grace, this marble (tiling), and so forth, was installed. Subsequently, on Tuesdays and Sundays there is a large crowd. Out of their own faith, they offer gifts, and so forth. And they keep making supplications *(ardās)*. . . .
>
> When Mātā comes, my body becomes a bit heavy. After that weight on the body, a vision of Mātā's little arm comes, and after that I hear a sound in my ears, like an airplane. When I become afraid of the sound, then sparks come out of my hands and those sparks fall on my eyes. When the sparks

fall on my eyes, then the body becomes unconscious. Then the voice that comes out is Mātā's voice. Then I don't know where I am, and it seems to me as if I am in a dream and am roaming around in the jungle and mountains. Mātā enters completely and whatever is said, it is Mātā herself saying it.

KE: Do you remember anything that Mātā says?

SK: No, at that time it is Mātā herself who is speaking, and I am unconscious. I have to ask the devotees what it was that she said. Then they themselves tell me [that she had said] what method to use; do this, do that.

KE: What is your opinion about this? Why does this happen?

SK: Look, at that time [when the possession first began], I was in my childhood. I was fourteen years old at that time. What do we village children know, what is Mātā, what is playing, what is "asking" [consulting a medium], but she alone told me the path of worship and devotion. She gave me knowledge, and then the whole Rāmāyaṇ, and so forth came to me. If I hadn't had Mātā's support, then how could I remember so much so fast? Without a guru there is no knowledge, but my guru is Mātā alone. I ask her everything, and she alone tells me everything. When someone comes from outside and sits here, Mātā tells everything. If she says to do this, I do it just like that. I go only according to what she says, and I have faith in her.

KE: How did you learn the method of worship?

SK: She alone told me everything. Previously I learned things just by seeing them done. The flame and incense are in every home. Then as Mātā went on giving me light, the work went on increasing, and I also started doing recitation. Then however much light Mātā went on giving, that much power came into my body, for giving devotion to Mātā. Then I got some books, and now through Mātā's grace, I have learned much. Everything has happened through her grace. No one told me anything. I didn't start anything. Whatever she tells me, that is the way it is. . . .

These three images have come out. [He shows me.] One small Mātā and along with it a *piṇḍī* [aniconic stone] also came out. And this big image came out by itself. And this came out afterwards. [Then he shows it to us and asks what we think it looks like. He tells us that one can see in it:] a conch, Gaṇeśa's trunk, Gaṇeśa's ears, and Śesnāg (the cosmic serpent) too—Śesnāg's head and tail. The third thing is Hanumān, and the fourth is Mātā. This is Mātā's forehead and eyes. In this there are five forms: Conch, Gaṇeśa, Śesnāg, Hanumān, and Mātā. And it is very heavy.

KE: Please tell me about your marriage. Did Mātā give you permission or what?

SK: First my Mummy and Daddy got all my sisters married, and then Mātā gave me permission that first I should build a temple and afterward get married. Then Mātā built this temple herself. It was built through her *śakti*. How could I have built it? Then I asked Mātā and Mātājī said, "If you renounce, then you go outside the house and do so, and if you live here as a householder with me, then you will have to get married, because otherwise the evil eye falls on other's daughters and daughters-in-law. Therefore, marriage is necessary. If you don't want to live as a householder, go outside. Go into the forest and practice devotion. Don't stay in the house like this." Then I said, "Where will I go in the forest? I am not like a sadhu or faqir. I am still in my childhood." Then Mātā said, "Get married. There is nothing wrong in that. The life of a householder is true; the life of a householder is devotion." Mātā gave permission and I got married.

KE: When Mātājī speaks, what language does she speak?

SK: She speaks Hindi, Mandiyali, Kangri, Panjabi. She speaks all the languages. I don't know about English [laughs], but if an American comes sometime, she will converse with that person in English. But it's like this, that if I say, Mātā keep talking with me, it doesn't happen like that. Many times the congregation is sitting here and Mātā says, "I am leaving." And she leaves. And the people keep sitting there. Many times the people have to go back home and they don't get their questions answered. In that situation, if we were to do it ourselves, to speak on our own, how much money we would make! But Mātā would go away. We wouldn't be that greedy. I don't say anything on my own. When Mātā herself doesn't speak, what am I to say? When Mātā says something, when she answers the question, only then do I speak. If I say something on my own, then what kind of temple is this? Then why would people come here? Like that, everyone can speak. You

> can speak. I can also speak. . . .You should come on Tuesday or Sunday in the morning at *ārati* time. Devotional singing is also going on, and you can also tape Mātā's *satsang*.

I returned a few weeks later and was able to witness him in trance. People, mostly women (though a few men and a boy showed up later), were seated inside the temple with offerings and a personal item to present along with the question. He was seated inside the shrine enclosure on the right hand side, as one faces the Devī image. As I sat down, he was just preparing to go into trance. A red curtain was drawn across his sitting area. I noticed that his head was covered with a large orange scarf *(cunnī)*, such as a woman would wear. As he went into trance, he emitted some hissing, gurgling, and heavy breathing sounds. Then, gradually, a falsetto, feminine sounding voice broke through with phrases like "Jay Mātā dī" (Victory to the Mother). One by one, each questioner would enter and sit down across from him inside the enclosed shrine. He would ask if the person had been there before, give a diagnosis and cure, then ask for the next question. While in the possession trance, he would speak as the Goddess herself, taking on a female persona and speaking in Hindi using feminine verb endings as a woman would.

Conclusion

While both Tārā Devī and Suresh Kumār grew up in rural Kangra, in the shadow of major Goddess temples, where worship of the Goddess in various forms is an important part of daily life, neither before their possession by the Goddess had been well versed in Goddess rituals, nor had either given much thought to theological subtleties concerning the nature and identity of the Goddess. After their possessions, however, both have gone through a process of gradual initiation into ritual practices through a series of "orders" from the Goddess. During this process, both have also become recognized as mediums of the Goddess and as healers to whom people come for advice and assistance. Despite age, caste, and gender differences, both have been accommodated into the culturally recognized niche of the Mātā, the possessed person who participates in the divinity of the Goddess. There are, however, idiosyncratic differences in the experiences, ritual practices, and ways in which the two understand the identity of the Goddess. Tārā Devī hints that her own Mātā is different from Sagūr Mātā, because the two possess different people; the physical manifestation and appearance are different. I have often heard pilgrims make statements such as, "I believe in this Mātā" or "this is a good Mātā," leaving it ambiguous whether they are referring to the Goddess or the human vehicle as Mātā. If Goddess possession transforms a human being so that she (or he) actually *becomes* the Goddess (even temporarily), or if the identity of the Goddess and the human vehicle are intermingled, then the construction of the Goddess would also be the construction or reconstruction of the Self. Tārā Devī's imagery focuses on the flame as a transformative agent; she calls it the "Goddess's power" (*khudarat* or *śakti*). She speaks of herself before the Goddess entered as a different person, who through the power of fame was transformed from an invalid into a skilled healer. Her language is often visual; she speaks of the experience of *darśan* frequently.

Like that of Tārā Devī, Suresh Kumār's construction of the Goddess is based on his own experience. The actual content of that experience, however, varies somewhat, with more emphasis on auditory and bodily sensations than on visual imagery. Although he does see a vision of Mātā's arm, he is also overwhelmed by hissing sounds and feels the sensation of wandering through the jungle. Though he was not ill before Mātā came to him, as Tārā Devī was, he was poor and uneducated. Now he provides his family with a regular source of income and has also acquired considerable religious knowledge and expertise.

Both Tārā Devī and Suresh Kumār have been recipients of a series of "orders" from the Goddess that have gradually transformed their lives and identities, while at the same time serving to reveal the presence of the Goddess to others. That is, in both cases the Goddess "ordered" her human vehicles to build temples, display her images, and serve the pilgrims who came with their problems. In one respect, Suresh Kumār's identification with the Goddess involves a more thorough-going transformation than it did for Tārā Devī, that of gender. When he becomes possessed by the Goddess, part of "becoming the Goddess" is to become a woman. That did not prevent him from getting married and fathering a child, however, all at the Goddess' instigation. Tārā Devī was already married and had children at the time of her initial possession, while Suresh Kumār was an unmarried boy. It is a common pattern in Kangra (and elsewhere) for unmarried women and girls who become possessed by the Goddess to remain unmarried and lead a life of celibate service, while those women who are already married work out varying degrees of accommodation between their duties to family and Goddess. Suresh Kumār's marriage, then, is somewhat unusual under the circumstances (a fact to which Tārā Devī alludes), but, according to Suresh Kumār, the Goddess ordered him to marry unless he planned to leave home and become a renunciant. The fact that he is an only son and that his parents would have wanted him to stay home and marry must surely have played a role in the "negotiations" with the Goddess. The lack of any formal institution for Mātās allows for this kind of flexibility and fluidity of life-styles and practices.

While Tārā Devī's Goddess is named Jvālājī and Suresh Kumār's is named Four-Armed Mātā or Cāmuṇḍā with the differences in mythology and iconography which those names denote, they are also on another level identical with the Mahādevī, the Great Goddess who both includes and transcends all manifested forms. But from another viewpoint, even goddesses who bear the same name are not identical. Tārā Devī's Goddess Jvālājī is in practice not identical with the Goddess of the famous temple with the same name, for she is mediated through the person and experience of Tārā Devī in a particular time and place. Through the experiences of devotees like Tārā Devī and Suresh Kumār, the identity of the Goddess is constructed and reconstructed on a daily basis.

Notes

1. Hawley 1996. Note that Hawley uses the singular in the prologue title and the plural in the book title.

2. This type of historical development is also a key methodological assumption in Coburn 1985, 1991 and in Pintchman 1994.

3. See, for example, Babb 1975, O'Flaherty 1980, Gatwood 1985, Obeyesekere 1984, Ramanujan 1986, 41–75. The terms "Breast Mother" and "Tooth Mother" first appeared in Jung 1938, 75–110.

4. An interesting essay that takes an approach similar to mine is Sarah Caldwell, "Surrender, Transformation, and Cognitive Love: Approaches to the Anthropological Study of Religious Experience." Paper presented at the American Academy of Religion Annual Meeting, Chicago, 1994.

5. For more on Usā Bahn, see Erndl 1993, 123–28 and Rohe 1994.

6. Mātā, both a common and proper noun, means "mother" and is used also for goddesses (and the Goddess), goddess-possessed women, female ascetics, and other holy or respected women.

Chapter 10

What Is a "Goddess" and What Does It Mean to "Construct" One?

Thomas B. Coburn

As Tracy Pintchman notes in her introduction to this volume, for many centuries religious life in the Indian subcontinent has known a "Great Goddess" tradition, with historical roots that go back much further. She also notes that for the past two decades scholarly interest in Hindu goddesses has flourished, vastly enriching our understanding of the relevant phenomena. The essays gathered in this volume take that process a good deal further, and the first impression one might have here is of the diversity of *what* is being studied and of *how* it is being studied. The geography ranges from the Punjab and Bengal to Kerala and Tamilnadu. The languages drawn upon include Sanskrit, Bengali, Hindi, Oriya, Telugu, Malayalam, and Tamil. The evidence includes ancient texts and contemporary interviews, male-authored documents and possession-experiences of women, myth and ritual, both old and new. Some of the evidence is subjected to scrupulous philosophical dissection, while other evidence is presented in thick ethnographic detail. Essays vary in their interest in methodological issues. In Tracy Pintchman's introduction and Kathleen M. Erndl's essay, we are introduced to four different models for ordering this richly diverse material, and the intervening essays invite their application. The historical (one versus many) model, the psychological/structural model, the experiential approach, and the emphasis on narrative are clearly complementary to one another, and the careful reader will surely have found resonance with each of them at different points in specific chapters.

What I would like to present here at the end are two ruminations on both the evidence and the models used to understand it. I offer them heuristically, as an invitation to further reflection on the material in these essays and elsewhere. I will refer selectively to some of the issues raised in earlier chapters, but space does not permit exhaustive retrospective analysis.

What prompts me to undertake this line of reflection is the realization that while some of the essays in this volume address the question of what it means to *construct* the Great Goddess, none of them reflects explicitly on what it means to call something a *goddess* in the first place. I should like to explore both of these in what follows.

The specific observations in earlier essays that open up this line of thinking are these. Tracy Pintchman suggests that "the identity of the Great Goddess . . . has more to do with *what* she is than with *who* she is . . ." (90). The very subtitle of her essay is suggestive, for *negotiation* is a dialectical phenomenon, involving give-and-take, in this case between an overarching Mahādevī and particular goddesses. C. Mackenzie Brown suggests that the construction of deity is not just projection, but a reciprocal process, when he speaks of the meditator *installing* Bhuvaneśvarī within his/her own body in the letters of the *mantra* Hrīṃ (33). Mark Rohe captures the paradox of great specificity regarding the place of Vaiṣṇo Devī and great ambiguity about her identity, an ambiguity that he judges to be "an asset that permits the individual devotee to enter into a meaningful relationship with her regardless of that devotee's own devotional preferences" (57). Later he writes that "pilgrims are able to create (*sic*) a meaningful relationship with her no matter what their devotional traditions or personal beliefs may be," (72) but his conclusion reaffirms that this is a *reciprocal* relationship: "Through her blessings, Vaiṣṇo Devī recreates the lives of her devotees, and they continually recreate her according to their own beliefs. Hence, the construction of Vaiṣṇo Devī as Mahādevī remains an ongoing process" (74). Usha Menon's interpretation parallels Pintchman's, for she finds that Oriya devotees both recognize the reality of Mahādevī-*śakti*, who "transcends the embodied universe . . . beyond all moral and social norms," and "they make sense of her by domesticating her, by socializing her, by defining her in terms of a particular role, that of mother. When they acknowledge her immanence, it is as Mā, Mother" (53). Jeffrey Kripal is most suggestive on these matters. He aspires "to develop a dialectical (*sic*) vision of the deification process that respects both the power of what the disciples *brought* to the deification process and the reality of what they actually *found* in this being whom they so affectionately called 'the Holy Mother' " (173–174). He takes deliberate issue with the mechanistic and reductionist understanding of human beings that pervades sociological discussion of "the social construction of reality" (179–180), and his provocative conclusion virtually forces the relational understanding of deity that I shall explore later. In a similar vein, Sree Padma observes that what is seen to make the Great Goddess "great" in urban Andhra Pradesh is her responsiveness to the "worldly pursuits and desires" of her devotees (142), and Elaine Craddock concludes that "the Goddess and her devotees mutually construct each other" (167).

What I find critical throughout these observations is the authors' consistent efforts to understand the practices and views and experiences of Goddess devotees on their own terms. This produces, on the one hand, a serious engagement with lives that are lived on the basis of relationship with the Goddess. The existence of such a relationship, one that is mutually transforming, is taken at face value by our authors—and sometimes with even greater seriousness, a matter to which we shall return. The authors' posture of sympathetic understanding, on the other hand, resists the reductionism about deities and religious matters in general that has characterized much so-called secular thought in recent centuries, but that has been a part of the Western heritage since classical Greece.[1] We are in the presence here of rich new evidence, thoughtfully analyzed, that invites further reflection.

Let me begin by introducing and developing some familiar history-of-religions terminology. "Goddess," like other basic terms in the field, such as "god," "deity," "sacred," "profane," or "scripture," is a *relational* concept. That is, it does not refer to the intrinsic qualities of an object, person, text, place, act, or other datum. Rather, it refers to that datum in relationship to and interaction with particular persons, either individually or collectively.

Religious life, of course, is not the only sphere of human life that is characterized by relational language. The most obvious instance is in the area of kinship terminology. Every woman and man is necessarily a daughter or a son, which relate any individual to his or her parents. But no one is necessarily a mother or father. Rather, one *becomes* one by having a child. Thus, "mother" and "father" are also relational terms, but they do not necessarily apply to each individual. Moreover, relational terms do not describe the intrinsic qualities of the individuals to whom they are applied, but refer to the network of extrinsic relationships in which they find themselves enmeshed. More subtle, but also more illustrative of what is meant by calling something a relational term, are the terms "aunt" and "uncle." One can go to bed one evening and wake up as an aunt the next morning without doing anything. One *becomes* an aunt by virtue of one's relationship to others. What is required is simply that one's sibling produce a child. The network of relationships around one is what makes (or fails to make) one an aunt, uncle, cousin, sister, brother, and so on.[2]

Other situations can also help us understand what it means to say that "deity," "goddess" and other terms in the study of religion are relational terms. For instance, goldenrod is a vivid yellow flower that blooms in late summer, and shellfish is a usually edible form of seafood. But goldenrod and shellfish are also allergens which induce in some people weeping and sneezing, runny eyes, hives or worse. Such people, we say, are *allergic* to goldenrod or shellfish, thereby characterizing the relationship between some people and some objects. A full phenomenology of the human experience of goldenrod and shellfish would have to include the special relationship that some people have with them.

Within the study of religion, recognizing the relational quality inherent in the subject matter has proven useful in a variety of contexts. For instance, if one seeks worldwide commonalities across the written documents of religious life, the effort soon founders because of the overwhelming variety. "Neither form nor content can serve to identify or distinguish scripture as a general phenomenon" (Graham 1986, 134). Nonetheless, the possibility of talking about "scripture" as a genus reemerges when one stops looking for essences and reconsiders the evidence in terms of its relationships, that is, when one recognizes that

> the sacrality or holiness of a book is not an *a priori* attribute but one that is realized historically in the life of communities who *respond* to it as something sacred and holy. A *text "becomes" scripture in* living, subjective *relationship* to persons and to historical tradition. No text, written, oral, or both, is sacred or authoritative in isolation from a community. . . . What is scripture for one group may be a meaningless, nonsensical, or even perversely false text for another. . . . This *relational,* contextual *quality* is [therefore] of paramount importance for the study of "scriptural" texts. (Graham 1986, 134, my italics)

What is at stake here might be diagramed as follows, where D represents a particular document, P1 represents a community (or individual) for whom D is a religiously significant document, whose relationship to the document is a religious one (Rr), and P2 represents a community (or individual) for whom the document is not religiously significant, whose relationship to the document is not religious (Rn) (see figure 10.1).

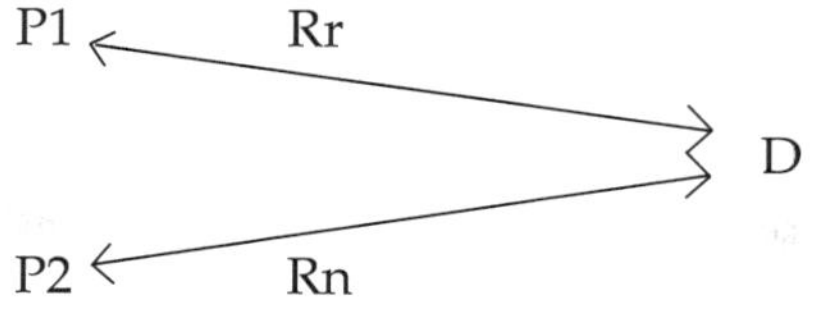

Figure 10.1 Diagram of the Relational Quality of Religious Life

The utility of such a diagram for comparative purposes becomes apparent in applying it to particular instances, such as letting D represent the Qur'an, P1 represent Muslims, and P2 represent Christians. One might subsequently wish to expand the diagram for broader comparative purposes, for instance, by having D represent the Jewish Bible, and developing multiple P postures, one for Jews, another for Christians, and another for Muslims, since the Jewish Bible has been religiously consequential for—has been in relationship with—each of these groups, but in very different ways. One might also, of course, want to acknowledge the varied relationships that Jews themselves have had with the Jewish Bible. The basic point is that relationships are primary, and the way they vary matters a great deal.

The applicability of this line of thinking to broader isssues in religious studies is readily apparent. If we think of D on the above diagram as any datum, we can think in fresh ways about why travel to Benares (D) is a religious pilgrimage for some, but not for others, or why some engage in ritual activity on Sunday (D), while others do not. It is also immediately applicable to thinking about deities, about gods and goddesses. Indeed, if we sustain the same degree of phenomenological dispassion as our authors do, allowing "the expression *gods* to represent a general type of religious experience" (Paden 1994, 121), then we can let D on the above diagram stand for Deity and begin to explore the implications. The rationale is simple:

> . . . a god is a form of religion that can have any content. . . . A god is not a bare object—like a statue in a museum—but part of a bilateral relationship. A god is a god *of* someone or *to* someone. Only in the eyes of a religious person can a god be a god as such. A god is a category of social, interactive, behavior, experienced in a way that is analogous to the experience

> of other selves. With gods one receives, gives, follows, loves, imitates, communes, negotiates, contests, entrusts. A god is a subject to us as objects and an object to us as subjects. We address it, or it can address us. (Paden 1994, 124)

In bringing such an analysis and our heuristic diagram to bear on the essays in this volume, five observations produce questions for subsequent reflection and investigation.

First, deity as initially schematized in our diagram is genderless. But the language in the citation above is already gendered, using the word *"god"* rather than *"deity"* or *"goddess."* This is not surprising, given the legacy of English-language usage regarding religious matters. But to be more precise, deity conceived of/experienced as gendered should be seen as one alternative among several. Insofar as intimacy characterizes the relationship between human beings and deities, and insofar as gender-marking is one possible vehicle of intimacy in any context, it is not surprising that deities in India and elsewhere are gendered. As Usha Menon notes in her essay, it is precisely the intimacy and great familiarity implied by the pronoun *tu* that prompts Oriya Hindus to apply it to Mahādevī understood as "Mother" (50). The Hindu tradition, of course, is replete with instances of deity conceived as neuter, or as beyond gender, or as androgynous, or as male. All of the instances of deity examined in this book are necessarily female, variously exploring Mahādevī, the Great Goddess. A question to bring to bear on these essays and other studies of goddesses in India might therefore be: are there commonalities in this conception of deity as female that are distinctive, that set the Goddess apart from other Hindu conceptions of deity? The essays in this book bring us a good deal closer to being able to answer such a question.

Second, if deity (D), located at the right-hand pole of the relationship schematized above is *sometimes* conceived of/experienced as gendered, so are the human participants (P), at the left-hand end of the pole, necessarily gendered in every instance. It is therefore worth revisiting each of our essays to look at the gender of those who are in relationship with the Goddess. Are there differences between the ways women and men relate to the Goddess in different settings? Sometimes the answer is not determinable on the basis of the evidence given us here, and sometimes the question may prove irrelevant. But the question is, in principle, an important one if religious life is indeed about relationships, and if gender-marking and gender-awareness are critical in most relationships in which we humans find ourselves.

Third, it will prove fruitful to ask what the *media* are that enliven and sustain the relationship between devotees and the Great Goddess.

This would be a question worth asking of any devotee-deity relationship, in any cultural context, but it is particularly appropriate in India, where there are such close parallels between relationships between humans and relationships between deities and humans. The essays in this volume provide rich, diverse evidence of what it is that mediates and invigorates humans' relationships with Mahādevī, varying by context and including possession, meditation, study, and very specific kinds of ritual action, both private and public. But there is another reason to attend to the question of what mediates devotees' relationships with the Great Goddess, beyond its intrinsic interest. For some years now, Jonathan Z. Smith has been urging the recognition that while religious history is as old as human history, "man, more precisely western man, has had only the last few centuries in which to imagine religion. It is this act of second order, reflective imagination which must be the central preoccupation of any student of religion. . . . For the self-conscious student of religion, no datum possesses intrinsic interest. It is of value only insofar as it can serve as exempli gratia of some fundamental issue in the imagination of religion. The student of religion must be able to articulate clearly why 'this' rather than 'that' was chosen as an exemplum" (1982, xi). As I appreciated earlier, the essays gathered in this volume are scrupulously concerned to understand the religious lives of Goddess devotees nonjudgmentally, on their own terms, and I have little doubt that those lives are, for the most part, portrayed faithfully. What is not clear to me is how much our authors deliberately *chose* to analyze specific media of religious life and why, in each case, they chose *a particular medium* for analysis. This is not to question the accuracy of their reports and analyses. It is to suggest that there is a great essay waiting to be written that examines each chapter in this book with an eye both on the medium of relationship between devotee and Goddess and on the self-consciousness that the author displays about having selected this medium as an alternative to others. The evidence analyzed in these chapters attests in multiple ways to devotees constructing and being in varied relationships with the Great Goddess. What is not always clear is how much those relationships are also the construction of the scholars who are writing about them.[3]

Fourth, regardless of whether there turn out to be distinctive features of Hindu deity when conceived as female—our first question above—we need also to reflect on the narrower question of whether there are common features of Mahādevī, the Great Goddess, as she is constructed in the different contexts examined in this book. It is tempting to take the Goddess's "core identity" as the cosmogonic principles of *śakti*, *prakṛti*, and *māyā* that Tracy Pintchman finds persisting through complex sectarian mutations in the Purāṇas and to see if it also persists in other contexts. But in beginning to do so, I found myself drawn back into fundamental questions about basic terminology, to which my remarks on the relational quality of our language for deity are a partial response. But, beyond that, it seems necessary to revisit the question of one or many Goddess(es) and the appropriateness of using the article "the" in speaking of Her/them. In the essays in this book, the most common way of referring to deity seems to be with a proper noun, a name that captures the requisite personality and intimacy. But thereafter *śakti* appears at least as often as Devī or Mahādevī as a designation of deity, and this prompts me to wonder whether we might imagine our book's subtitle to be Constructing the Identities of Śakti, rather than Constructing the Identities of the Hindu Great Goddess. Such a shift would force us to move beyond the conceptualization of "goddesses" that pervades the literature cited in these essays. But it also has the virtue of avoiding the choices that English forces on us: whether or not to use the singular or plural, or to capitalize, or to use the article. Moreover, as Kathleen Erndl notes, "*sakti* is such a fluid concept that it seems to transcend distinctions of singular and plural" (199), and it therefore comes much closer to the actual experience and conceptualization of devotees. It is therefore more apt than speaking of devotees as worshipping "the Goddess." To think of what we are studying as *śakti* also does not highlight the gender issue in the way that English "goddess" does, but simply takes it for granted. *Everybody* (everybody familiar with Indian usage) knows that *śakti* is a fluid, powerful, female sort of thing, capable of taking infinite forms, but essentially one. Everybody also knows that *śakti* is both a subjective and immanent phenomenon, latent within each individual, but also an objective and transcendent phenomenon, beyond the ken of anyone. Central to its mystery is that those two poles are, in fact, on a continuum, are in complex, mutually implicating relationship. We have long accustomed ourselves to using certain Indic terms without translation: *karma*, *saṃsāra*, *dharma*, *ātman*, *bhakti*, and so forth. Has the time now come for us to use *śakti* in most cases when we might hitherto have been tempted to use "goddess," "Goddess," or "the Goddess?"

Finally, let us return to the heuristic diagram we have been using to think about the relational quality of religious subject matter. Let us note that the arrows point in *both* directions. They do not just move from left to right, from human beings to the religious datum or deity, for that would imply that the "construction" process was mere projection. As we have seen, the authors of the essays in this book are consistently concerned to understand the religious life of Goddess devotees on the devotees' own terms. Some particularly emphasize the dialectical, reciprocal nature of the devotees' relationship with the Goddess and the reality of her appearance and presence in their lives. The Devī-Māhātmya, the earliest crystallization in text of Great Goddess theology, which has often been cited in these essays, itself emphasizes the mutuality involved in construction of the Goddess. When the gods learn of the depradations of the demon Mahiṣa, it is from the congealed splendor *(tejas)* of their anger that the Great Goddess arises or, we might say, is constructed, along with her weapons. But, as important, thus constructed, she then continues to be an ongoing, active, consequential presence in their lives. Similarly, at the very end of the story, having learned of the glories of the Great Goddess, the king and merchant "constructed (*sic*) an image of the Goddess, fashioned of earth, on the riverbank, and they worshipped her for three years," at the end of which time, "much delighted, she appeared in front of their very eyes" (Coburn 1991, 83). In the long run, the evidence for the mutual construction of the Goddess and her devotees forces the thoughtful student to take a stance on the metaphysical issues involved in worshipping the Great Goddess or in religious life more broadly. Sarah Caldwell does this gently at the end of her essay, with the image of the Goddess as sunlight, refracting at various angles. Jeffrey J. Kripal does this more overtly at the end of his essay, with his wonderful metaphor of how diamonds, like divinity, are both discovered and polished. And in an earlier essay, Kathleen M. Erndl reports on how an impulsive "Yes" answer to the question of whether she "ever believed that it really was the Goddess possessing those women" led her to a deeper reflection:

> I realized that it was the experience of observing possession, of coming face-to-face with this impressive manifestation of the Goddess's power *(śakti),* that brought home to me in a very concrete fashion the immediacy with which devotees experience the Goddess's presence. This in turn led me to take seriously the notion of the Goddess as an agent herself, rather than simply a symbol or projection. (Erndl 1996, 174)

Not everyone, of course, will wish to take matters this seriously, to pursue construction of the Great Goddess to this level of self-reflexiveness or engagement. And that, of course, is fine. There is plenty of work still to do, with all kinds of motivation, beyond the new ground that these essays break. At the same time, it would be dishonest to ignore the deep questions of meaning—and intimations of answers—that have engaged many, not just Hindu devotees, but others who are either in or seeking relationship to deity.

Notes

1. Particularly relevant, by way of contrast with our ensuing discussion of deity as a relational-interactive concept, is the early "religion is merely a projection" of Xenophanes: "... if cattle or lions had hands, so as to paint with their hands and produce works of art as men do, they would paint their gods and give them bodies in form like their own—horses like horses, cattle like cattle" (Nahm 1962, 109). I am indebted to Philip Larson for this reference.

2. I deliberately choose to make this point with the second order relationship between aunts/uncles and nephews/nieces, rather than the primary order of siblings, because it emphasizes the extrinsic quality of relationships. Notice with regard to primary relationships, for instance, how much easier it is to think and say—"I have *X* brothers and *Y* sisters"—rather than—"I am *brother to* *X* males and *Y* females" even though the latter captures more precisely the mutually implicating nature of brother and sisterhood.

3. I have reflected further on the media selected for study of the Great Goddess in chapter four of Coburn 1991.

Glossary

Abhaya Mūdra: "Fear not" gesture, a gesture of protection.
Advaita Vedānta: The orthodox Hindu philosophical school, based on the teachings of the Upaniṣads (Vedānta), that affirms ultimate reality to be the non-dual Brahman.
Asura: Demon.
Avatāra: Incarnation of the Divine.
Bhakti: Devotion.
Brahman: Ultimate reality; the Godhead.
Darśan: Exchange of vision between devotee and deity. Darśan provides a direct connection between the worshiper and the deity worshipped.
Devī Māhātmya: "Glorification of the Goddess;" a text from approximately the sixth century C.E. that forms part of the Mārkaṇḍeya Purāṇa. The Devī-Māhātmya recounts Devī's victory over the buffalo demon Mahiṣāsura.
Dharma: Religious duty or obligation; righteousness.
Dharmśālā: Religious rest house, often set up to accommodate pilgrims on a pilgrimage journey.
Guṇa: See *prakṛti.*
Kaḷam: Colored powder drawing of a deity in a temple.
Kalkī Avatāra: The tenth and future incarnation of Viṣṇu who will bring an end to Kali Yuga, the current age, and initiate Sat Yuga, the golden age of the next cycle of creation.
Kalpa: A period of time measuring 432 million years; considered to be one day in the life of the deity Brahmā and encompassing 1,000 cycles of the four *yugas* (see *yuga*, below).
Lajja: Modesty, deference, respectful self-restraint.
Liṅga: "Mark" or "characteristic"; an aniconic representation of the deity Śiva that symbolizes his transcendent, formless nature; also a term for the male sex organ.

Mahas: "Greatness, power, light, luster"; an Upaniṣadic term descriptive of Brahman applied to the Goddess in the Devī Gītā.

Mahāvidyās: "The (ten) Great Knowledges"; aspects or emanations of the Great Goddess, especially important in Tantric circles.

Mantra: A sound or formula generally believed to embody sacred energy or potency; mantras are used in a variety of ritual and meditative contexts.

Mātṛkās: "Mothers," a group of female deities (usually seven).

Māyā: The creative, projecting power of the Goddess and part of her essential nature; sometimes associated with the idea of "world-illusion," *māyā* is also equated with *prakṛti* and/or *śakti* in some contexts.

Mokṣa: Liberation from the cycle of birth and death.

Mudrā: A hand position or gesture that has religious significance.

Mūlaprakṛti: "root" *prakṛti; prakṛti* in its most basic, unformed state.

Muṭiyēṟṟu: Ritual dance drama performed as an offering to the fierce goddess Bhagavati in Kerala temples.

Nāyar: Martial caste of Kerala.

Nirguṇa: Having no qualities or transcending all particular qualities; a term for designating the formless, unmanifest dimension of Brahman.

Piṇḍi: A rounded stone or outcropping of rock identified as a manifestation of a deity, usually a goddess.

Pradhāna: Another term for *prakṛti.*

Prakṛti: Matter, the material principle from which the world evolves. Prakṛti is said to consist of three constituent qualities or parts called "*guṇas*": *sattva* (purity), *rajas* (activity), and *tamas* (lethargy).

Prasāda (Hindi: *Prasād*): Food first offered to a deity and then distributed to devotees as sacred or blessed food.

Pūjā: Hindu ritual worship of a deity that includes the offering of particular items, including flowers, food, incense, lights, and pleasing sounds.

Purāṇa: Hindu scriptures recorded in written form in Sanskrit from about the third to the seventeenth centuries. The Purāṇas encompass a wide range of materials, including a great deal of traditional mythological and ritual lore.

Puruṣa: In the Ṛg Veda, a cosmic being who is sacrificed at the beginning of creation; in the Sāṁkhya school of philosophy, the principle of pure consciousness; in the Purāṇas, often the male counterpart of *prakṛti.*

Rajas: See *prakṛti.*

Sādhana: Ascetic or religious practice.

Sādhu: An ascetic or world renouncer.

Saguṇa: "With qualities"; a term for designating the manifest dimension of Brahman.

Śaiva: Pertaining to the schools, texts, and devotees who view the deity Śiva as the Ultimate.

Śākta: Pertaining to the schools, texts, and devotees who view the Goddess, Śakti (energy or power), as the Ultimate.

Śakti: "Power" or "energy"; Śakti is both an epithet of the Goddess and one of her attributes.

Śakti Pīṭha (Hindi: *Pīṭh)*: "Seat" of the Goddess; pilgrimage sites associated with the Goddess and believed to enshrine portions of the goddess Sati's body.

Saṁsāra: The cycle of birth, death, and rebirth that living beings endure.

Sattva: See *prakṛti.*

Sat Yuga: See *yuga.*

Tamas: See *prakṛti.*

Tantric: Referring to a broad range of doctrines and practices that consistently emphasize the positive nature of physical embodiment as a means of ultimate transformation.

Tapas: Literally "heat"; the term "*tapas*" refers to the austerities undertaken by ascetics, as well as the power that ascetic performance is said to generate.

Tattvas: The basic constitutents of the world; the *tattvas* flow forth from the three *guṇas* of *prakṛti.*

Tejas: Power or fiery energy.

Triguṇā: Consisting of the three *guṇas*; see *prakṛti.*

Vaiṣṇava: Pertaining to the schools, texts, and devotees who view the deity Viṣṇu or one of his incarnations (e.g., Rāma, Kṛṣṇa) as the Ultimate.

Vētāḷam: Forest-dwelling female ghost who drinks Dārika's blood.

Yantra: A symbolically potent diagram used in meditation or worship. *Yantra*s embody different realms of reality in geometric form and generally represent both the human person and the cosmos, a dimension of the cosmos, or a particular deity.

Yuga: "Age"; traditional Hindu cosmology posits the existence of four progressively degenerating ages or *yuga*s. The first, Sat Yuga, is considered a kind of golden age; the last, Kali Yuga, the most degenerate age, is the age in which we currently live.

References

Allen, M. R. 1976. "Kumari or 'Virgin' Worship in Kathmandu Valley." *Contributions to Indian Sociology* 10: 293–315.

Alter, Joseph. 1992. *The Wrestler's Body*. Berkeley: University of California Press.

Ashley, W. 1993. "Recodings: Ritual, Theatre, and Political Display in Kerala State, South India." Ph. D. diss., Performance Studies, New York University.

Ayer, V. A. K. 1988. "Mother Bhuvaneswari." In *Tattvaloka: The Splendour of Truth* 11, No. 4: 45–46.

Babb, Lawrence A. 1975. *The Divine Hierarchy: Popular Hinduism in Central India.* New York: Columbia University Press.

Banerjee, P. 1986. *Rama in Indian Literature, Art and Thought.* Vol. 1. Delhi: Sundeep Prakashan.

Bayly, Susan. 1989. *Saints, Goddesses and Kings.* Cambridge: Cambridge University Press.

Beck, Brenda E. F. 1974. "The Kin Nucleus in Tamil Folklore." In *Kinship and History in South Asia,* edited by Thomas Trautmann. Michigan Papers on South and Southeast Asia, no. 7, pp. 1–28. Ann Arbor: Center for South and Southeast Asian Studies, The University of Michigan.

———. 1981. "The Goddess and the Demon: A Local South Indian Festival and Its Wider Context." In *Autour de la Deesse Hindoue,* edited by Madeleine Biardeau. *Puruṣārtha* 5: 83–136.

Beck, Guy. 1993. *Sonic Theology: Hinduism and Sacred Sound.* Columbia, SC: University of South Carolina Press.

Berger, Peter L. 1967. *The Sacred Canopy: Elements of a Sociological Theory of Religion*. New York: Doubleday.

Berger, Peter L., and Thomas Luckmann. 1966. *The Social Construction of Reality: A Treatise in the Sociology of Knowledge*. New York: Doubleday.

Bhattacaryya, Narendra Nath. 1974. *History of the Śākta Religion*. New Delhi: Munshiram Manoharlal.

Biardeau, Madeleine. 1982. *Hinduism: The Anthropology of a Civilization*. New York: Oxford University Press.

———. 1989. "Brahmans and Meat-Eating Gods." In *Criminal Gods and Demon Devotees: Essays on the Guardians of Popular Hinduism*, edited by Alf Hiltebeitel, 19–33. Albany: State University of New York Press.

Blackburn, Stuart. 1985. "Death and Deification: Folk Cults in Hinduism." *History of Religions* 24: 255–274.

Bolon, Carol Radcliffe. 1992. *Forms of the Goddess Lajja Gauri in Indian Art*. University Park, PA: Pennsylvania State University Press.

The Brahmāṇḍa Purāṇa. 1983–1984. Translated by Ganesh Vasudeo Tagare. 5 Vols. Ancient Indian Tradition and Mythology Series. Vols. 22–26. Delhi: Motilal Banarsidass.

The Brahma-Vaivarta Purāṇam. [1920-22] 1974. Translated by R. N. Sen, Sacred Books of the Hindus. Vol. 24, parts 1 and 2. Reprint, New York: AMS Press.

Brahmavaivartapurāṇam. 1935. Edited Vināyaka Gaṇeśa Āpte. 2 Vols. Ānandāśrama Sanskrit Series, no. 102. Poona: Ānandāśrama Press.

Brooks, Douglas Renfrew. 1990. *The Secret of the Three Cities: An Introduction to Hindu Śākta Tantrism*. Chicago: University of Chicago Press.

———. 1992. *Auspicious Wisdom: The Texts and Traditions of Śrīvidyā Śākta Tantrism in South India*. Albany: State University of New York Press.

Brown, C. Mackenzie. 1974. *God as Mother: A Feminine Theology in India; An Historical and Theological Study of the Brahmavaivarta Purāṇa*. Hartford, VT: Claude Starke and Co.

———. 1990. *The Triumph of the Goddess: the Canonical Models and Theological Visions of the Devī-Bhāgavata Purāṇa*. Albany: State University of New York Press.

———. 1998. *The Devī-Gītā; The Song of the Goddess: A Translation, Annotation, and Commentary*. Albany: State University of New York Press.

Brubaker, Richard Lee. 1978. "The Ambivalent Mistress: A Study of South Indian Village Goddesses and Their Religious Meaning." Ph.D. diss. University of Chicago.

Caldwell, Sarah. 1994. "Surrender, Transformation, and Cognitive Love: Approaches to the Anthropological Study of Religious Experience." Paper presented at the American Academy of Religion Annual Meeting, Chicago, IL.

———. 1996. "Bhagavati: Ball of Fire." In *Devī: Goddesses of India*, edited by John S. Hawley and Donna M. Wulff, 195–226. Berkeley: University of California Press.

———. 1999. *Oh Terrifying Mother: Sexuality, Violence, and Worship of the Goddess Kāḷi*. Delhi: Oxford University Press.

Chakravarti, Chintaharan. 1963. *Tantras: Studies on Their Religion and Literature*. Calcutta: Punthi Pustak.

Charak, Sukhdev Singh, trans. 1980. *History and Culture of Himalayan States: Jammu Kingdom, Part I (Ancient and Medieval, up to 1800 A.D.)*. New Delhi: Light and Life Publishers.

———. 1991. *Ganeshdas Badehra's Rajdarshani: A Persian History of North Western India from earliest times to A.D. 1847*. Jammu: Jay Kay Book House.

Choondal, C. 1981. *Muṭiyēṯṯu: Study in Folk Theatre*. Trichur, Kerala: Kerala Folklore Academy. [*In Malayalam*]

Coburn, Thomas B. 1982. "Consort of None, Śakti of All: The Vision of the Devī-Māhātmya." In *The Divine Consort: Rādhā and the Goddesses of India*, edited by John S. Hawley and Donna M. Wulff, 153–165. Berkeley: Graduate Theological Union.

———. 1985. *Devī Māhātmya: The Crystallization of the Goddess Tradition*. Delhi and Columbia, MO: Motilal Banarsidass and South Asia Books.

———. 1991. *Encountering the Goddess: A Translation of the Devī-Māhātmya and a Study of Its Interpretation*. Albany: State University of New York Press.

———. 1996. "Devī the Great Goddess." In *Devī: Goddesses of India*, edited by John S. Hawley and Donna M. Wulff, 31–48. Berkeley: University of California Press.

Cohn, Bernard S. 1955. "The Changing Status of a Depressed Class." In *Village India*, edited by McKim Marriott, 53–57. Chicago: University of Chicago Press.

Daniel, Sheryl B. 1980. "Marriage in Tamil Culture: The Problem of Conflicting Models." In *The Powers of Tamil Women*, edited by Susan Wadley, 61–92. Syracuse: Syracuse University.

Dāsa, Sāralā. *Caṇḍī Purāṇa.* 1993. Cuttack, Orissa: Dharma Grantha, Alisha Bazaar.

Dasgupta, Surendranath. 1922. *A History of Indian Philosophy*. Vol. 1. Cambridge: Cambridge University Press.

Datta, Ram Chandra. 1935. *Śrīśrīrāmakṛṣṇa Paramahaṁsadever Jīvan-avṛttānta.* 5th ed. Calcutta: Swami Yogavimala. Originally published in 1890.

Devī Gītā (constitutes chaps. 31–40 of the 7th Skandha of the *Devī-Bhāgavata Purāṇa*, for which see under *Srimad Devi Bhagavatam* and *Śrimaddevībhāgavatam*)

The Devī-Māhātmyam or Śrī Durgā-Saptaśatī (700 Mantras on Śrī Durgā). 1969. Translated by Swami Jagadisvarananda. 3d ed. Madras: Sri Ramakrishna Math.

Devyupaniṣat [Devī Upaniṣad]. 1950. In The *Śākta Upaniṣads, with the Commentary of Śrī Upaniṣad-Brahma-Yogin*, edited by A. Mahadeva Sastri, 53–60. Adyar Library Series, no. 10. Madras: Adyar Library.

Dirks, Nicholas B. 1990. "History as a Sign of the Modern." *Public Culture Bulletin* 2, No. 2: 25–32.

———. n.d. "The Policing of Tradition: Colonialism and Anthropology in Southern India." Unpublished manuscript.

Doniger, Wendy. 1995. "'Put a Bag Over Her Head': Beheading Mythological Women." In *Off With Her Head! The Denial of Women's Identity in Myth, Religion, and Culture*, edited by Howard Eilberg-Schwartz and Wendy Doniger, 15–31. Berkeley: University of California Press.

———. 1998. "Mother Goose and the Voices of Women." In *The Implied Spider*, chap. 5. New York: Columbia University Press.

Dubois, Abbe J. A. 1906. *Hindu Manners, Customs and Ceremonies.* Oxford: The Clarendon Press.

Elmore, Wilbur Theodore. 1915. *Dravidian Gods in Modern Hinduism: A Study of the Local and Village Deities of Southern India*. Lincoln: University of Nebraska.

Erndl, Kathleen M. 1989. "Rapist or Bodyguard, Demon or Devotee? Images of Bhairo in the Mythology and Cult of Vaiṣṇo Devī." In *Criminal Gods and Demon Devotees*, edited by Alf Hiltebeitel, 239–250. Albany: State University of New York Press.

———. 1993. *Victory to the Mother: The Hindu Goddess of Northwest India in Myth, Ritual, and Symbol*. New York: Oxford University Press.

———. 1996. "Śerāṅvālī: The Mother Who Possesses." In *Devī: Goddesses of India*, edited by John S. Hawley and Donna M. Wulff, 173–194. Berkeley: University of California Press.

———. 1997. "The Goddess and Women's Power: A Hindu Case Study." In *Women and Goddess Traditions in Antiquity and Today*, edited by Karen L. King with an introduction by Karen Jo Torjesen, 17–38. Studies in Antiquity and Christianity. Minneapolis: Fortress Press.

Farquhar, J. N. [1920] 1967. *An Outline of the Religious Literature of India*. Reprint, Delhi: Motilal Banarsidass.

Freeman, J. R. 1991. "Purity and Violence: Sacred Power in the Teyyam Worship of Malabar." Ph.D. diss. University of Pennsylvania, Philadelphia.

Gambhirananda, Swami. 1986. *Holy Mother: Śrī Sarada Devī*. Mylapore: Sri Ramakrishna Math.

The Garuḍa Purāṇa. 1978–80. Translated by a board of scholars. Ancient Indian Tradition and Mythology Series. Vols. 12–14. Delhi: Motilal Banarsidass.

Gatwood, Lynn E. 1985. *Devī and the Spouse Goddess: Women, Sexuality, and Marriages in India*. Riverdale, MD: The Riverdale Company.

Gopinatha Rao, T. A. 1985. *Elements of Hindu Iconography*. Vol. 1, part 2. Delhi: Motilal Banarsidass.

The Gospel of the Holy Mother. 1986. Madras: Śrī Ramakrishna Math.

Graham, William A. 1986. "Scripture." In *The Encyclopedia of Religion*, edited by Mircea Eliade. Vol. 13: 133–145. New York: Macmillan.

Gross, Rita M. 1983. "Hindu Female Deities as a Resource for Contemporary Rediscovery of the Goddess." In *The Book of the Goddess Past and Present: An Introduction to Her Religion*, edited by Carl Olson, 217–230. New York: Crossroad.

Gupta, Mahendranath [M]. 1987. *Śrīśrīrāmakṛṣṇakathāmṛta.* 31st ed. Calcutta: Kathamrita Bhaban.

Haberman, David. 1994. *Journey through the Twelve Forests: An Encounter with Krishna.* New York: Oxford University Press.

Hacking, Ian. 1999. *The Social Construction of What?* Cambridge, MA: Harvard University Press.

Hardy, F. 1983. *Virāha-bhakti: the early history of Kṛṣṇa devotion in South India.* Oxford: Oxford University Press.

Harper, Edward B. 1969. "Fear and the Status of Women." *Southwestern Journal of Anthropology* 25: 81–95.

Harper, Katherine Anne. 1989. *The Iconography of the Saptamatrikas.* Lewiston, NY: Edwin Mellen Press.

Hart, George L., III. 1973. "Woman and the Sacred in Ancient Tamilnad." *Journal of Asian Studies* 32, No. 2 (February): 233–250.

———. 1975. *The Poems of Ancient Tamil.* Berkeley: University of California Press.

———. 1980. "The Theory of Reincarnation Among the Tamils." In *Karma and Rebirth in Classical Indian Traditions*, edited by Wendy O'Flaherty, 116–133. Berkeley: University of California Press.

———. 1988. "Early Evidence for Caste in South India." In *Dimensions of Social Life: Essays in Honor of David G. Mandelbaum*, edited by Paul Hockings, 467–491. Berlin: Mouton de Gruyter.

Hawley, John S. 1982. "Preface." In *The Divine Consort: Rādhā and the Goddesses of India*, edited by John S. Hawley and Donna M. Wulff, xi–xviii. Berkeley: Graduate Theological Union.

———. 1996. "Prologue: The Goddess in India." In *Devī: Goddesses of India*, edited by John S. Hawley and Donna M. Wulff, 1–28. Berkeley: University of California Press.

Hawley, John S., and Donna M. Wulff, eds. 1996. *Devī: Goddesses of India.* Berkeley: University of California Press.

Hazra, R. C. 1963. *Studies in the Upapurāṇas.* Vol. 2. Calcutta: Sanskrit College.

———. 1975. *Studies in the Purāṇic Record on Hindu Rites and Customs.* 2d ed. Delhi: Motilal Banarsidass.

Heesterman, J. C. 1967. "The Case of the Severed Head." *Wiener Zeitschrift zur Kunde des Sud- und Ostasiens* 11: 22–43.

Hiltebeitel, Alf. 1988. *The Cult of Draupadī, Vol. 1: Mythologies: From Gingee to Kurukṣetra*. Chicago: University of Chicago Press.

———. 1991. *The Cult of Draupadī, Vol. 2: On Hindu Ritual and the Goddess*. Chicago: University of Chicago Press.

Holy Mother: Being the Life of Sri Sarada Devi Wife of Sri Ramakrishana and Helpmate in His Mission. See Nikhilananda, Swami.

Holy Mother: Sri Sarada Devi. See Gambhirananda, Swami.

Hudson, Dennis. 1978. "Śiva, Mīnākśī, Viṣṇu—Reflections on a Popular Myth in Madurai." In *South Indian Temples*, edited by Burton Stein, 107–118. Delhi: Vikas.

Humes, Cynthia Ann. 1996. "Vindhyavāsinī: Local Goddess yet Great Goddess." In *Devī: Goddesses of India*, edited by John S. Hawley and Donna M. Wulff, 49–76. Berkeley: University of California Press.

Ilankovatikal. 1993. *The Cilappatikaram of Ilanko Atikal: an Epic of South India*, translated by R. Parthasarathy. New York: Columbia University Press.

Jagmohan. 1991. *My Frozen Turbulence in Kashmir*. New Delhi: Allied Publishers Limited.

Jones, Clifford. 1982. "Kaḷam Eḻuttu: Art and Ritual in Kerala." In *Religious festivals in South India and Sri Lanka*, edited by Guy R. Welbon and Glenn E. Yocum, 269–94. New Delhi: Manohar.

Jung, C. G. 1938. "Psychological Aspects of the Mother Archetype." In C. G. Jung, *The Archetypes and the Collective Unconscious*, translated by R. F. C. Hull, 75–110. Princeton: Princeton University Press.

Kapadia, Karin. 1995. *Siva and Her Sisters: Gender, Caste, and Class in Rural South India*. Boulder: Westview Press.

Kena Upaniṣad. 1965. In *Eight Upaniṣads, with the Commentary of Śaṅkarācārya* [with Sanskrit text of the Upaniṣad], Vol. 1: 33–96. Translated by Swāmi Gambhīrānanda. 2d ed. Calcutta: Advaita Ashrama.

Khare, R. S. 1982. "From *Kanyā* to *Mātā:* Aspects of the Cultural Language of Kinship in Northern India." In *Concepts of Person: Kinship, Caste, and Marriage in India*, edited by Ákos Östör, Lina Fruzetti, and Steve Barnett, 143–171. Cambridge, MA: Harvard University Press.

Kinsley, David R. 1982. "Blood and Death Out of Place: Reflections on the Goddess Kālī." In *The Divine Consort: Rādhā and the Goddesses of India*, edited by John S. Hawley and Donna M. Wulff, 144–152. Berkeley: Graduate Theological Union.

———. 1986. *Hindu Goddesses: Visions of the Divine Feminine in the Hindu Religious Tradition*. Berkeley: University of California Press. Indian edition, 1987. Delhi: Motilal Banarsidass.

———. 1997. *Tantric Visions of the Divine Feminine: The Ten Mahāvidyās*. Berkeley: University of California Press.

Kosambi, D. D. [1963] 1983. *Myth and Reality: Studies in the Formation of Indian Culture*. Reprint, Bombay: Popular Prakashan.

Kripal, Jeffrey J. 1998. *Kālī's Child: The Mystical and the Erotic in the Life and Teachings of Ramakrishna*. 2d ed. Chicago: University of Chicago Press.

Krishna Sastry, V. V. 1983. *The Proto and Early Historic Cultures of Andhra Pradesh*. Hyderabad: Government of Andhra Pradesh.

The Kūrma Purāṇa (With English Translation). 1972. Edited by Anand Swarup Gupta; translated by Ahibhushan Bhattacharya et al. Varanasi: All-India Kashiraj Trust.

Kurtz, Stanley N. 1992. *All the Mothers Are One: Hindu India and the Cultural Reshaping of Psychoanalysis*. New York: Columbia University Press.

Lamotte, Etienne. 1988. *History of Indian Buddhism*. Louvain: Peeters Press.

The Liṅga Purāṇa. 1973. Translated by a Board of Scholars. Ancient Indian Tradition and Mythology Series. Vols. 5–6. Delhi: Motilal Banarsidass.

Lutgendorf, Philip. 1994. "My Hanuman is Bigger than Yours." *History of Religions* 33, No. 3: 211–45.

———. 1997. "Monkey in the Middle: The Status of Hanuman in Popular Hinduism." *Religion* 27: 311–332.

Mackay, E. 1935. *Early Indus Civilization*. 2d ed. London: L. Dickson and Thompson.

Madan, T. N. 1987. *Non-Renunciation*. Delhi: Oxford University Press.

The Mahābhāgavata Purāṇa (An Ancient Treatise on Śakti Cult). 1983. Critical editor Pushpendra Kumar. Delhi: Eastern Book Linkers, 1983.

Mahapatra, M. 1981. *Traditional Structure and Change in an Orissa Temple Town.* Calcutta: Punthi Pustak.

Marglin, Frederique Apffel. 1985. "Female Sexuality in the Hindu World." In *Immaculate and Powerful: The Female in Sacred Image and Social Reality,* edited by Clarissa W. Atkinson, Constance H. Buchanan, and Margaret R. Miles, 39–60. Boston: Beacon Press.

Māriyammaṉ Kaliveṇpā, D–306. Government Library, Madras.

Māriyammaṉ Tālāṭṭu, D–171. Government Library, Madras.

Marshall, John. 1931. *Mohenjo-daro and the Indus Civilization.* 3 Vols. London: A. Probsthain.

Masilamani-Meyer, Eveline. 1989. "The Changing Face of Kāttavarāyan." In *Criminal Gods and Demon Devotees: Essays on the Guardians of Popular Hinduism,* edited by Alf Hiltebeitel, 69–103. Albany: State University of New York Press.

McKean, Lise. 1996. *Divine Enterprise: Gurus and the Hindu Nationalist Movement.* Chicago: University of Chicago Press.

Mehandru, Saurabh. 1996. "Be happy, don't go touristy." *Times of India,* 6 May.

Menon, C. A. [1943] 1959. *Kāḷi Worship in Kerala.* 2d ed. Reprint, Madras: University of Madras. [*In Malayalam*]

Menon, Usha, and Richard A. Shweder. 1994. "Kali's Tongue: Cultural Psychology and the Power of 'Shame' in Orissa, India." In *Emotion and Culture,* edited by S. Kitayama and H. Markus, 241–284. Washington DC: American Psychological Association.

Meyer, Eveline. 1986. *Aṅkāḷaparamēcuvari: A Goddess of Tamilnadu, Her Myths and Cult.* Stuttgart: Steiner Verlag Wiesbaden GMBH.

Michell, George. [1977] 1988. *The Hindu Temple.* Reprint, Chicago: University of Chicago Press.

Mishra, N. 1980. "Rāmāyaṇa in Oriya Literature and Oral Tradition." In *The Ramayana Tradition in Asia,* edited by V. Raghavan, 617–635. New Delhi: Sahitya Akademi Press.

Mitra, Satyacharan. 1897. *Śrī Śrī Rāmakṛṣṇa Paramahaṁsa—Jīvana o Upadeśa.* Calcutta: Great Indian Press.

Muṇḍaka Upaniṣad. 1966. In *Eight Upaniṣads, with the Commentary of Śaṅkarācārya* [with Sanskrit text of the Upaniṣad]. Vol. 2: 77–172. Translated by Swāmi Gambhīrānanda. 2d ed. Calcutta: Advaita Ashrama.

Nahm, Milton, ed. 1962. *Selections from Early Greek Philosophy*. 3rd ed. New York: Appleton-Century Crofts.

Nambissan, A. N., comp. 1978. *Brāhmaṇippaṭṭukaḷ*. Trichur, Kerala: Amina Book Stall.

The Nārada Purāṇa. 1980–1982. Translated by G. V. Tagare. 5 vols. Ancient Indian Tradition and Mythology Series. Vols. 15–19. Delhi: Motilal Banarsidass.

Nargis, Narsingdas. 1967. *Tarikh-i-Dogra Desh*. Jammu: Chand Publishing House.

Nikhilananda, Swami. 1963. *Holy Mother: Being the Life of Śrī Sarada Devī Wife of Śrī Ramakrishna and Helpmate in His Mission*. London: George Allen and Unwin.

Nirmohi, Shiv. 1988. *Duggar ke Devsthān*. Pakka, Danga, Jammu: Vinod Book Depot.

Obeyesekere, Gananath. 1984. *The Cult of the Goddess Pattini*. Chicago: University of Chicago Press.

———. 1992. *The Work of Culture*. Chicago: University of Chicago Press.

Obeyesekere, Gananath, and Richard Gombrich. 1988. *Buddhism Transformed: Religious Change in Sri Lanka*. Princeton, NJ: Princeton University Press.

Oddie, G. A. 1986. "Hook-Swinging and Popular Religion in South India during the Nineteenth Century." *The Indian Economic and Social History Review* 23, No. 1 (Jan.–Mar.): 93–106.

———. 1995. *Popular Religion, Elites and Reform: Hook-Swinging and its Prohibition in Colonial India, 1800–1894*. New Delhi: Manohar.

O'Flaherty, Wendy Doniger. 1980. *Women, Androgynes, and Other Mythical Beasts*. Chicago: University of Chicago Press.

———. 1988. *Textual Sources for the Study of Hinduism*. Totowa, NJ: Barnes and Noble Books.

Oppert, Gustav. [1893] 1986. *On the Original Inhabitants of Bharatavarṣa or India*. Reprint, New Delhi: Unity Book Service.

Paden, William E. 1994. *Religious Worlds: The Comparative Study of Religion*. 2d ed. Boston: Beacon Press.

Pal, Pratapaditya. 1981. *Hindu Religion and Iconology According to the Tantrasāra*. Los Angeles: Vichitra Press.

Pañcīkaraṇam: Text and the Vārttika with Word for Word Translation, English Rendering, Comments, and the Glossary. 1976. 3d rev. ed. Calcutta: Advaita Ashrama.

Pandit, Baljinnath. 1983. *Vaiṣṇavī Devī Rahasya.* Kulgam, Kashmir: Yambak Prakashan.

Pathik, Jyoteshwar. 1990. *Glimpses of History of Jammu & Kashmir.* Jammu: Jay Kay Book House.

Pintchman, Tracy. 1994. *The Rise of the Goddess in the Hindu Tradition.* Albany: State University of New York Press.

Prasad, Jwala Chaturvedi, editor. n.d.a. *Śrī Vaiṣṇo Devī kī Sampūrṇ Kahānī.* Jammu: Pustak Sansar.

———. n.d.b. *Nau Devīyoṅ kī Amar Kahānī.* Jammu: Pustak Sansar.

Preston, James J. 1980. *Cult of the Goddess.* Prospect Heights, IL: Waveland Press.

Raheja, Gloria G., and Ann G. Gold. 1994. *Listen to the Heron's Words: Reimagining Gender and Kinship in North India.* Berkeley: University of California Press.

Rajeswari, D. R. 1989. *Śakti Iconography.* New Delhi: Intellectual Publishing House.

Rajiv, Rajendra Kumar. 1988. *Hamāre Pūjya Tīrṭh.* Delhi: Khari Bavali.

Ramanujan, A. K. 1986. "Two Realms of Kannada Folklore." In *Another Harmony: New Essays on the Folklore of India,* edited by Stuart Blackburn and A. K. Ramanujan, 41–75. Delhi: Oxford University Press.

———. 1990. "Is there an Indian way of thinking?" In *India through Hindu Categories,* edited by M. Marriott, 41–58. New Delhi: Sage.

———. 1993. "On Folk Mythologies and Folk Purāṇas." In *Purāṇa Perennis,* edited by Wendy Doniger, 101–120. Albany: State University of New York Press.

Rao, Velcheru Narayana. 1991. "A Ramayana of Their Own: Women's Oral Tradition in Telugu." In *Many Ramayanas,* edited by P. Richman, 114–136. Berkeley: University of California Press.

Reynolds, Holly Baker. 1980. "The Auspicious Married Woman." In *The Powers of Tamil Women,* edited by Susan Wadley, 35–60. Syracuse: Syracuse University.

Rohe, Mark. 1994. "Becoming Mothers: Origin Stories of Female Gurus." Paper presented at the Conference on South Asia, Madison, Wisconsin.

Śāradā-Tilaka Tantram: Text with Introduction. [1933] 1982. Edited by John Woodroffe [Arthur Avalon]. Tantrik Text Series, vol. 17. Reprint, Delhi: Motilal Banarsidass.

Saradeshananda, Swami. 1994. *Śrī Śrī Māyer Smṛtikathā*. Calcutta: Udbodhan Karjalay.

Satyanarayana Murty, Kundurti. 1989. *Prachīnāndhra Mahā Kavula Devī Pratipatti*. Vijayawada: Bhuvana Vijayam Publications.

Saundarya Lahari of Sri Sankaracarya. 1987? Translation and notes by Swami Tapasyananda. Madras: Sri Ramakrishna Math.

Saundarya Laharī (The Ocean of Beauty) of Śrī Śaṁkara-Bhagavatpāda. 1977. Translation and commentary by Pandit S. Subrahmanya Sastri and T. R. Srinivasa Ayyangar. Madras: Theosophical Publishing House.

Sax, William S. 1991. *Mountain Goddess: Gender and Politics in a Himalayan Pilgrimage*. New York: Oxford University Press.

———. 1994. "Gender and Politics in Garhwal." In *Women as Subjects: South Asian Histories*, edited by Nita Kumar, 172–210. Charlottesville: University of Virginia Press.

Searle, John R. 1995. *The Construction of Social Reality*. New York: The Free Press.

Seymour, S. 1983. "Household Structure and Status and Expression of Affect in India." *Ethos* 11: 263–277.

Sharma, Balkrishan. n.d. *Mātā Vaiṣṇo Devī kī Janm Kathā*. Jammu: Bhavani Pustak Mahal.

Shastri, B. K. 1991. *Mātā Vaiṣṇo Devī: 'Itihās aur Kathā.'* Jammu: Rajesh Prakashan.

Shastri, Jagdish Chandra. 1976. *Vaiṣṇavī Siddh Pīṭh*. Jammu: Shastri Prakashan.

Shulman, David Dean. 1980. *Tamil Temple Myths: Sacrifice and Divine Marriage in the South Indian Śaiva Tradition*. Princeton: Princeton University Press.

———. 1985. *The King and the Clown in South Indian Myth and Poetry*. Princeton: Princeton University Press.

Shweder, Richard A. 1991. *Thinking through Cultures*. Cambridge, MA: Harvard University Press.

Sil, Narasingha P. 1991. *Rāmakṛṣṇa Paramahaṁsa: A Psychological Profile*. Leiden: E. J. Brill.

Sircar, D. C. 1973. *The Śākta Pīṭhas*. 2d rev. ed. Delhi: Motilal Banarsidass.

The Śiva Mahāpurāṇa. 1981. Critical editor Pushpendra Kumar. NP Series no. 48. Delhi: Nag Publishers.

The Śiva Purāṇa. 1969–1970. Translated by a Board of Scholars. 4 vols. Ancient Indian Tradition and Mythology Series. Vols. 1–4. Delhi: Motilal Banarsidass.

Śivapurāṇam. 1906. Bombay: Veṅkaṭeśvara Press.

Smith, Jonathan Z. 1982. *Imagining Religion: From Babylon to Jonestown*. Chicago: The University of Chicago Press.

Śrīgaruḍamahāpurāṇam [Garuḍa Purāṇa]. [1906] 1984. Edited by S. N. Sharma. Reprint, Delhi: Nag Publishers.

Śrī Lalitā Sahasranāma. 1987? Translated and edited by Swami Tapasyananda. Madras: Sri Ramakrishna Math.

The Srimad Devi Bhagavatam [Devī-Bhāgavata Purāṇa]. [1921–1923] 1977. Translated by Hari Prasanna Chatterji [Swami Vijnananda]. Sacred Books of the Hindus. Vol. 26. Reprint, New Delhi: Oriental Books.

Śrīmaddevībhāgavatam [Devī-Bhāgavata Purāṇa]. 1919. Bombay: Veṅkaṭeśvara Press.

Śrīmaddevībhāgavatam (mahapuranam) [Devī-Bhāgavata Purāṇa]. 1969. Edited by Rāmatejapāṇḍeya. Kāśī: Paṇḍa-Pustakālaya.

Śrīnāradīyamahāpurāṇam. [1923 or 1924] 1984. Reprint, Delhi: Nag Publishers.

Śrī Śrī Māyer Kathā. 1995. Calcutta: Udbodhan Karjalay.

Śrī Śrī Māyer Smṛtikathā. See Saradeshananda, Swami.

Śrī Vaiṣṇo Devī kī Sampūrṇ Kahānī. n.d. Haridwar: Randhir Book Sales.

Srivastav, C. M. 1988. *Mātā Vaiṣṇo Devī kī Sampūrṇ Kahānī Jagrātā aur Bheṇṭ*. Ishwarpuri, Merath: Newton Pocket Press.

Taittirīya Upaniṣad. 1965. In *Eight Upaniṣads, with the Commentary of Śaṇkarācārya* [with Sanskrit text of the Upaniṣad]. Vol. 1: 231–416.

Translated by Swāmi Gambhīrānanda. 2d ed. Calcutta: Advaita Ashrama.

Thurston, Edgar. [1906] 1989. *Ethnographic Notes in Southern India.* Reprint, New Delhi: Asian Educational Services.

———. [1909] 1975. *Castes and Tribes of Southern India.* Reprint, Delhi: Cosmo Publications.

———. [1912] 1979. *Omens and Superstitions of Southern India.* Reprint, London: T. Fisher Unwin.

Tirumump, T. Subrahmanian. 1975. *Śrī Bhadrakāḷīmāhātmyam (Dārukavadham).* Trichur, Kerala: Geetha Press.

Trawick, Margaret. 1990. *Notes on Love in a Tamil Family.* Berkeley: University of California Press.

Tripurā-Rahasya (Jñānakhanda): English Translation and a Comparative Study of the Process of Individuation. 1965. Translated by A. U. Vasavada. Chowkhamba Sanskrit Series Office.

Uddhārakośa. [1941] 1985. In *Devī Rahasya with Pariśishṭas,* edited by Ram Chandra Kak and Harabhatta Shastri, 522–74. Reprint, Delhi: Butala.

Urban, Hugh B. 1998. "The 'Poor Company': Secrecy and Symbolic Power in the Kartabhaja Sect of Colonial Bengal." Ph.D. diss., The University of Chicago.

Vaudeville, Charlotte. 1982. "Krishna Gopālā, Rādhā, and the Great Goddess." In *The Divine Consort: Rādhā and the Goddesses of India,* edited by John S. Hawley and Donna M. Wulff, 1–12. Berkeley: Graduate Theological Union.

Venu, G. 1984. "Mudiyettu: Ritual Dance-Drama of Kerala." *Quarterly Journal of the National Centre for the Performing Arts* 13(4): 5–12.

Vidyarthi, G. 1976. "Mudiyettu: Rare Ritual Theatre of Kerala." *Sangeet Natak* 42: 41–63.

Wadley, Susan. 1980. "The Paradoxical Powers of Tamil Women." In *The Powers of Tamil Women,* edited by Susan Wadley, 153–170. Syracuse: Syracuse University.

Whitehead, Henry. [1921] 1980 and 1988. *The Village Gods of South India.* Reprint, New York: Garland Publishing Company; New Delhi: Asian Educational Services.

Winternitz, Maurice. 1927. *A History of Indian Literature*. Vol. 1. Translated by S. V. Ketkar and rev. by the author. Calcutta: University of Calcutta.

Woodroffe, John. 1922. *The Garland of Letters (Varnamālā): Studies in the Mantra-Shāstra*. Madras: Ganesh.

Ziegenbalg, B. [1869] 1984. *Genealogy of the South Indian Gods*. Reprint, New Delhi: Unity Book Service.

Zimmer, Heinrich. 1946. *Myths and Symbols in Indian Art and Civilization*, edited by Joseph Campbell. Princeton: Princeton University Press.

Contributors

C. MACKENZIE BROWN is professor of religion at Trinity University. His writings on the Goddess include *The Devī Gītā; The Song of the Goddess: A Translation, Annotation, and Commentary,* and *The Triumph of the Goddess: The Canonical Models and Theological Visions of the Devī-Bhāgavata Purāṇa,* both published by State University of New York Press, as well as *God as Mother: A Feminine Theology in India; An Historical Study of the Brahmavaivarta Purāṇa.*

SARAH CALDWELL is assistant professor of religious studies at California State University, Chico. She has completed a book, *Oh Terrifying Mother: Sexuality, Violence, and Worship of the Goddess Kāḷi* (Oxford University Press, 1999), a film, and several articles based on her field research on Kali possession rituals in Kerala, south India.

THOMAS B. COBURN is Charles A. Dana Professor of Religious Studies at St. Lawrence University, where he also currently serves as vice president of the university and dean of academic affairs. His publications include *Encountering the Goddess: A Translation of the Devī-Māhātmya and a Study of Its Interpretation* (State University of New York Press, 1991) and numerous articles on Hindu goddesses and comparative topics.

ELAINE CRADDOCK is associate professor in the Department of Religion and Philosophy at Southwestern University. Her current research interests include the modernization of Hindu goddess traditions in South India, the connections between goddesses and women in India, and feminist and cross-cultural theories of the body.

KATHLEEN M. ERNDL, associate professor of religion at Florida State University, is the author of *Victory to the Mother: The Hindu Goddess of Northwest India in Myth, Ritual, and Symbol* (Oxford University Press, 1993), along with a number of articles on Hindu goddesses and the role of women in Hinduism. She is coeditor with Alf Hiltebeitel of *Is the Goddess a Feminist? The Politics of South Asian Goddesses* (New York University Press, 2000) and is currently working on a book entitled *Playing with the Mother: Women, Goddess Possession, and Power in Kangra Hinduism.*

JEFFREY J. KRIPAL is the Vira I. Heinz Associate Professor of Religion at Westminster College. He is the author *of Kālī's Child: The Mystical and the Erotic in the Life and Teachings of Ramakrishna* (University of Chicago Press 1995), which won the American Academy of Religion's History of Religions Prize for the best first book of 1995, and the coeditor (with T. G. Vaidyanathan) of *Vishnu on Freud's Desk: A Psychoanalysis and Hinduism Reader* (Oxford University Press, 1999). He is presently working on a psychohistorical monograph on the academic study of mysticism in the twentieth century.

USHA MENON, an anthropologist, is a member of the Department of Psychology, Sociology, and Anthropology at Drexel University in Philadelphia. She has lived in Orissa for over twenty years and works in the temple community around the Liṅgarāj temple located in the older part of Bhubaneshwar. She has written extensively on the goddess Kālī and gender relations in Oriya Hindu society. She is currently completing a book on the life experiences of Oriya Hindu women.

SREE PADMA is currently administering the Inter-Collegiate Sri Lanka Education (ISLE) program, a study abroad program in Sri Lanka. She has been a research associate in the Department of History and Archaeology at Andhra University in Visakhapatnam, Andhra Pradesh, where she completed her Ph.D. She has taught at Harvard University as a lecturer and research associate in women's studies and history of religions and at Bowdoin College as assistant professor of history. She is the author of *Costume, Coiffure, and Ornament in the Temple Sculpture of Northern Andhra* (Agam Kala Prakasan, 1991). In addition to her research on village goddesses, she has also published several articles on the cultural links between the Andhra coast and South and Southeast Asia.

TRACY PINTCHMAN is director of the program in Religion, Culture, and Society and associate professor of Hindu studies at Loyola University of Chicago. Her publications include *The Rise of the Goddess in the Hindu Tradition* (State University of New York Press, 1994) and a number of articles and book chapters. She is currently working on a book on Hindu women's rituals.

MARK EDWIN ROHE is visiting assistant professor in the Department of Anthropology and Sociology at Sweet Briar College, Virginia. His current interests include female gurus, spontaneous *darśan*, and Hindu concepts of history. His recently completed dissertation is entitled, "Where the Śakti Flows: The Pilgrimage and Cult of Vaiṣṇo Devī."

Index

abhaya mūdra, 127–28
Ādikumārī, 68, 70
ādiśakti/Ādyaśakti, 70, 171
Ādiśeṣa, 161–62
Advaita Vedānta philosophy, 78
  birth of Devī and, 9, 21–24, 29–30, 34
Agni, 22, 31
aiśvarya (sovereignty), 25–26
Allen, M. R., 42
All the Mothers Are One (Kurtz), 200–1
Alter, Joseph, 7
Ambēdkarnagar, 163
Annapūrṇa, 171
Aṟipakkam, 163
Ashley, W., 112 n.1
asuras (demons), 39, 103–4
aṭittaṇṭam (ritual of prostration), 157
Ātman/Brahman, 33, 84, 220
avatāras, 39, 189, 194
  Kalkī Avatāra, 68, 73
axis mundi, 161, 162
Ayer, V. A. K., 24, 32

Babb, Lawrence A., 20, 212 n.3
Badehra, Ganeshdas, 55–56
Bagala, 187–88
Baishno Devī. *See* Vaiṣṇo Devī
Banerjee, P., 54 n.8
Bavāṉiyammaṉ, 13, 145–69. *See also* Māriyammaṉ
  festival of, 163–66
  as Mahādevī, 166, 167
  transformation through suffering and rage, 159–66
Beck, Brenda E. F., 164, 168 n.7
Beck, Guy, 32
Berger, Peter L., 4–5, 196 n.12
Bhadrakāḷī. *See* Bhagavati.
Bhadrakāḷi Māhātmyam/Bhadrōḷpati, 93, 94–95, 96, 100–1, 103, 105
Bhadrōḷpati. *See* Bhadrakāḷi Māhātmyam
Bhagavata Kaḷam Pāttu, 93, 96, 97–100
Bhāgavata Purāṇa, 7
Bhagavati, 11–12, 93–114
  Bhadrakāḷi and, 93, 100–1
  Bhagavati Kaḷam Pāttu and, 93, 96, 97–100
  Brahmaṇi Pāṭṭu, 93, 96, 107–10
  Dārikavadham and, 93, 94–95, 96, 102–7
  Kālī and, 100
  Śiva and, 102–3, 108–10
Bhairo, 58, 60, 65, 69, 70
Bhañja (Oriya poet), 49–50
Bhārat Mātā (Mother India), 74
Bhattacaryya, Narendra Nath, 35 n.5
Bhīḍādevī, 25
Bhubaneshwar (Orissa), 9–10, 37–54
Bhuvaneśvarī (Ruler of the Universe), 9, 24–34
Biardeau, Madeleine, 136, 168 n.5
Blackburn, Stuart, 149
Brahmā, 23, 27, 38–39, 87, 106, 161

Brahman dimension of Devī, 9, 21–24, 29–30, 78, 79–80, 89
Brahmaṇi Pāṭṭu (Songs of Brahmin Women), 93, 96, 107–10
Brahmavaivarta Purāṇa, 7, 84–86
Brahmavidyā, 23, 29
Brahmins
  construction of Goddess and, 12, 96, 100–1, 102, 110–11
  mixing with other castes, 154
Braj Vaiṣṇavism, 7
Bṛhadāraṇyaka Upaniṣad, 116
Brooks, Douglas Renfrew, 32, 35 n.5, 112 n.11
Brown, C. Mackenzie, 3, 5, 6–10, 19–36, 35 n.5, 47–48, 71, 74 n.3, 75 n.14, 79, 85, 89, 92 n.8, 92 n.10, 92 n.12, 200, 214
Brubaker, Richard Lee, 150
buffalo, as sacred, 153–54

Caldwell, Sarah, 7, 8–9, 11–12, 15, 93–114, 112 n.1, 112 n.2, 112 n.10, 112 n.12, 114 n.29, 114 n.30, 114 n.32, 221
Cāmuṇḍā, 60, 69, 200, 204, 207–10, 212
Caṇḍī Purāṇa, 47, 48, 69
celibacy, 68–69, 70, 126–27, 148–51
Chakravarti, Chintaharan, 35 n.6
Chāndogya Upaniṣad, 116
Charak, Sukhdev Singh, 55
Choondal, C., 102, 112 n.1, 112 n.17
Cilappatikāram, 154
Coburn, Thomas B., 1–3, 4, 8, 16, 47, 56, 68, 78–79, 86, 200, 212 n.2, 213–22, 222 n.3
Cohn, Bernard S., 143 n.9
cosmogenesis, 3, 6, 11, 29–31, 77, 78–91
Craddock, Elaine, 6, 7, 8–9, 13, 145–69, 215

Daniel, Sheryl B., 165
Dārika, 99, 100–101, 103, 105–7, 109, 111
Dārikavadham (The Killing of Dārika), 93, 94–95, 96, 102–7
darśan, 146, 206–7, 211
  Vaiṣṇo Devī and, 59, 60–62, 72
Dasgupta, Surendranath, 35 n.5
Datta, Ram Chandra, 180, 186
Dev, Raja Jas, 55–56
Devī: Goddesses of India (Hawley), 8, 199–200
Devī-Bhāgavata Purāṇa, 3, 47–48, 88–89, 94–95
  cosmogenesis in, 77
  manifestation of the Goddess in, 23, 26, 56–57, 69
  origin story in, 20–21, 22, 89–90
Devī Gītā (Song of the Goddess), 6, 89
  as alternative birth story of Goddess, 9, 20–21, 28–29
  and Goddess as infinite being, 21–24
  world-mother status and, 10
Devī-Māhātmya (Glorification of the Goddess), 1–2, 47, 69, 88–89, 94–95
  birth of Great Goddess, 9, 19–21
  cosmogenesis in, 77, 79, 86
  as early literary conception of Goddess, 3
  importance of, 13
  influence on portrayals of Māhadevī, 3, 116–17
Devī Upaniṣad, 24, 27–28
dharma, 14, 24, 52, 67, 111, 190–91, 193, 220
Dharmarth Trust, 57, 67
Dhyānū Bhagat, 158–59
Dirks, Nicholas B., 73, 155
Doniger, Wendy, 113 n.25, 162, 168 n.3
Dubois, Abbe J. A., 155
Durgā, 11–12, 25, 26, 42, 47, 83, 84, 141–42, 147, 163, 200, 201, 206
  Bhagavati and, 103
  as Mahādevī, 116–17
  as Parameśvarī Śakti, 64
  Pyḍamma as, 125–27
  Rādhā and, 85–86
  Sharada Devi and, 171, 172
  Śiva and, 63, 86

Vaiṣṇo Devī as, 61, 62–66, 68, 70, 71–72, 74
Durgālamma, 61, 127–28

Ellamma, 136–38, 141, 147
Elmore, Wilbur Theodore, 155, 160, 161
Erndl, Kathleen M., 5, 8–9, 14–16, 64, 74 n.4, 75 n.7, 75 n.9, 147, 158, 168 n.10, 169 n.14, 199–212, 212 n.5, 213, 220, 221
Erukamma, 121–24

Farquhar, J. N., 35 n.5
female sexuality, 148–51
Four-Armed Mātā, 200, 204, 207–10, 212
Freeman, J. R., 95–96, 98, 112 n.1, 112 n.8
Freud, Sigmund, 180

Gaṅgamma, 147, 162
Garuḍa Purāṇa, 63–64, 81–83, 89
Gatwood, Lynn E., 212 n.3
Giri, J. C., 66, 71
Golap-Ma, 172, 176, 177, 188
Gold, Ann G., 113 n.25
Gombrich, Richard, 120
Gopinatha Rao, T. A., 131
Graham, William A., 216
Gross, Rita M., 42
Gulab Singh, Maharaj, 57
guṇas, of *prakṛti*, 80, 82, 84–85, 87
Gupta, Mahendranath, 182, 185, 188, 192

Haberman, David, 7
Hacking, Ian, 17 n.1
Hanumān, 7, 70
Hardy, F., 112 n.3
Hāriti, 121–24
Harper, Edward B., 150
Harper, Katherine Anne, 143 n.5
Hart, George L., 112 n.3, 150, 160, 168 n.4, 168 n.8
Hawley, John S., 2, 6, 7, 8, 38–39, 199–200, 212 n.1
Hazra, R. C., 35 n.9, 91–92 n.4
head shaving, 158–59
Heesterman, J. C., 160–61, 169 n.12
Hiltebeitel, Alf, 162, 169 n.12
Himālaya, 20
hookswinging, 154–56
Hrīṃ (Hrīllekha; mantra), 6, 9, 23, 24, 28, 29–33, 214
Hudson, Dennis, 165
Humes, Cynthia Ann, 74 n.4, 114 n.31

Ilankovatikal, 112 n.17
Indra, 22, 31
Īśāna, 27
Īśvara (Lord), 86–87
Īśvarī (Ruler/Queen), 31

Jagmohan, Shri, 57–58, 73
Jamadagni, 136, 148, 149, 162–63, 165
Jeweled Island, 6, 33
Jñāna Yoga (Knowledge Yoga), 33
Jones, Clifford, 112 n.1
Jung, C. G., 212 n.3
Jvālājī/Jvālā Mukhī/Jvālāmukhī, 25, 200, 201, 204–5, 207, 212
Jyotir-liṅga, 23

Kākatiyas, 138
kaḷam (portraits of the Goddess in colored powders), 11–12, 94, 97, 99, 107–8
Kālī/Kāḷi, 8, 11–12, 15, 20, 100–101, 147, 153. *See also* Bhagavati, Mahākālī
  anger of, 42–43, 46–47, 110
  facial expressions of, 43–44
  lajjā and, 44, 46–47, 48
  Mahādevī (Great Goddess) as, 42–50, 86
  manifestations of, 60, 200, 201, 204, 206, 207–10
  as mother, 10, 49–50
  Sharada Devi and, 171, 172
  Śiva and, 10, 38, 43–46, 47, 50–52, 104–5
  Vaiṣṇo Devī as, 60, 61, 65, 67–68, 69, 71–72

Kālīkā Purāṇas, 47
Kāḷi Worship in Kerala (Menon), 95
Kali Yuga, 59, 68, 73
Kalkī Avatār, 68, 73
Kanaka Durgā/Kanakamma, 132–35
Kanaka Durgā temple, 116–17, 132–35, 142
Kanaka Mahālakṣmī, 133–34, 138–39, 142
Kannada creation myth, 39–40
Kaṇṇaki, 154
kanyā, 56, 68–70
Kapadia, Karin, 112 n.6, 114 n.32
Kartyāyini, 103, 105–7
Kena Upaniṣad, 22–23
Khare, R. S., 75 n.15
Kinsley, David R., 2, 3–4, 6, 25, 30, 32, 35 n.6, 35 n.9, 42–43, 52, 56, 63, 69, 75 n.13, 169 n.15
Koṟṟavai, 94, 100, 111
Kosambi, D. D., 122
Kripal, Jeffrey J., 8–9, 13–14, 15, 171–97, 195 n.5, 214–15
Kṛṣṇa, 7, 83–86, 194
Kṣatriya/Nāyar, 12, 96, 97–100
Kunchamma, 130, 131
Kuṇḍalinī Yoga, 32
Kūrma Purāṇa, 87–88
Kurtz, Stanley N., 75 n.11, 200–1

lajjā, 44, 46–47, 48
Lakṣmī, 2, 3–4, 20, 25, 83, 84, 187, 201. *See also* Mahālakṣmī
  Durgālamma as form of, 61, 128
  māyā and, 81–82
  Vaiṣṇo Devī as, 61–64, 66–68, 71–72, 74
  Viṣṇu and, 64, 77, 81, 128
Lalitā, 27–28
Lamotte, Etienne, 143 n.4
Larson, Philip, 222 n.1
Laya Upāsanā (a meditative practice), 33
liṅga, 23, 47, 160, 161, 162
Liṅga Purāṇa, 23
Liṅgarāj/Liṅgarāj temple, 37, 38, 49
local goddess cults, 4, 5, 12–13, 115–43
  Bavāṉṉiyammaṉ, 13, 145–69
  context for studying, 118–19
  Durgālamma, 61, 127–28
  Ellamma, 136–38, 141, 147
  Erukamma, 121–24
  general changes in, 119–21
  Kanaka Durgā, 116–17, 132–35, 142
  Kanaka Mahālakṣmī, 133–34, 138–39, 142
  Mariḍamma, 135–36, 138, 141, 142
  Māriyammaṉ, 13, 145–69
  Polamma, 129–31, 134–35, 142
  Pyḍamma, 124–27, 142
  Sharada Devi, 13–14, 171–97
lower castes
  construction of Goddess and, 12, 96, 102–7
Luckmann, Thomas, 196 n.12
Lutgendorf, Philip, 7

Madan, T. N., 53
Mahābhāgavata Purāṇa, 25
Mahādevī (Great Goddess), 2–9, 200
  as Bhagavati, 11–12, 93–114
  birth of, 9, 19–21, 24–33, 34
  as both male and female, 31
  Brahman dimension of, 9, 21–24, 29–30, 78, 79–80, 89
  characteristics central to nature of, 5–7
  and complementarity of male and female, 50–52
  creation and, 6, 78–91
  as Divine Mother, 6–7, 8, 9, 13, 29–30, 37, 49–50, 52–54, 90
  form and identity of, 11–12
  identification with ultimate reality, 3
  independence from male control, 3, 8
  and Kuṇḍalinī energy, 6
  localized portrayals of, 4, 5, 12–13, 115–43
  manifestations of, 6, 9, 10–11, 23, 26, 42–50, 56–57, 60, 69, 199

Māriyammaṉ as, 13, 145–69
multiple identities of, 5, 95
nature of, 2–3
as nowhere and everywhere, 16–17
Oriya Hindus and, 37–54
and principles of *prakṛti*, *māyā*, and *śakti*, 3, 8, 11, 77–91, 219–20
as *śakti*/Śakti, 6–7, 38–41, 79, 150–53, 219–20
Sharada Devi as, 13–14, 171–97
as supreme female deity, 4, 95
Tantric identity as Bhuvaneśvarī, 9, 24–34
Vaiṣṇo Devī as, 56, 70–72
Vedāntic identity as Brahman, 9, 21–24, 29–30, 78, 79–80, 89
Mahākāla, 40
Mahākālī, 10–11, 58–59, 60–61, 71, 199
Mahālakṣmī, 10–11, 58–59, 60–61, 67, 68, 71, 199
Mahāmāyā (great *māyā*), 79, 95
Mahapatra, M., 37
mahas, 22, 23
Mahāsarasvatī, 10–11, 58–59, 60–61, 71, 199
Mahāvidyā (Great Wisdom), 25–26
Mahayana Buddhism, 121–24
Maheśvara/Maheśwar (Śiva), 23, 38–39
Mahiṣāsura, 46, 47–48, 126
Mahiṣāsuramardinī, 68
Mahishamangalan, 107
Māṇḍūkya Upaniṣad, 33
Manōdari (Dārika's wife), 105–7, 109–10
mantras, 180, 182
Hrīṁ, 6, 9, 23, 24, 28, 29–33, 214
Oṃ, 9, 23, 29–33, 39
Marar, Krishnan Kutty, 97, 112 n.9
Marglin, Frederique, 148–51
Mariḍamma, 135–36, 138, 141, 142
Māriyammaṉ, 13, 145–69
as Mahādevī, 151, 167
Reṇukā myth and, 13, 148–51, 154, 158, 161, 162–63, 165–67
smallpox and, 145–46, 153, 156–57, 159–60, 166–67
Māriyammaṉ Kaliveṇpā, 168 n.6
Māriyammaṉ Tālāṭṭu, 168 n.6
Mārkaṇḍeya Purāṇa, 19, 56–57, 94–95, 100
Masilamani-Meyer, Eveline, 162
Mātaṅgī/Mātañki/Mātañkiyammaṉ, 25, 149, 161, 162
māyā (cosmic illusion), 3, 8, 11, 29–30, 31, 78–91, 219–20. *See also* Mahāmāyā
McKean, Lise, 186–87
meditative practices, 33, 126
Mehandru, Saurabh, 76 n.17
Menon, C. A., 95, 113 n.23
Menon, Usha, 6, 8–9, 10, 15, 37–54, 43, 214, 218
Meyer, Eveline, 160
Mishra, N., 54 n.8
Mitra, Satyacharan, 192, 194, 195–96n. 7
mokṣa, 24, 52–53, 126–27, 177, 193
Mukherjee, Ram, 172
Mulāprakṛti Īśvarī, 84–85
Muṇḍaka Upaniṣad, 31–32
muṭiyēṯṯu, 102

Nahm, Milton, 222 n.1
Nambissan, 107
Nandimahākālan, 104–5
Nārada Purāṇa, 82–84, 89
Narayanan, Vasudha, 8
Nārāyaṇī, 67, 68
Nargis, Narsingdas, 60
Nath, Gorakh, 60, 75 n.5
Nath, Prem, 67
Nāyars
construction of Goddess and, 12, 96, 97–100
neem sari ritual. See *vēppañcelai*
Nīlamma, 130–31
Nirmohi, Shiv, 67

Obeyesekere, Gananath, 120, 212 n.3
Ocean of Nectar, 26
Oddie, G. A., 154–55

O'Flaherty, Wendy Doniger, 69, 212 n.3
Oṃ (mantra), 9, 23, 29–33, 39
Oppert, Gustav, 154–55
Oriya Hindus, 6, 9–10, 15, 37–54

Paden, William E., 217–18
Padma, Sree, 8–9, 12–13, 15, 115–43
Pal, Pratapaditya, 35 n.6
Pañca-Pretāsana (Seat of Five Corpses), 27, 32–33
Pāncarātra school, 3–4
Pañcīkaraṇa, 33
Pandit, Baljinnath, 64
Paramahamsa, Ramakrishna, 13–14
Paraśurāma, 136, 148–49, 162, 165, 167
Pārvatī, 2, 20, 24, 38, 206
  association of Vaiṣṇo Devī, 64–66
  Erukamma and, 123–24
  Kanada Durgā as incarnation of, 133
  Śiva and, 123
  Viṣṇu and, 164–65
pāthana (offering of crops to the Goddess), 135
piṇḍis, 6, 10–11, 56, 58–62, 64–65, 67, 68, 72, 208–9
Pintchman, Tracy, 1–17, 8–9, 53, 77–92, 91 n.2, 202, 212 n.2, 213, 214, 219–20
Polamma/Polamāmba, 129–31, 134–35, 142
Prajāpati, 69–70
prakṛti (materiality), 3, 8, 11, 30, 31, 78–91, 111, 219–20
  defined, 78
  guṇas of, 80
  māyā and, 79
  as *nirguṇā*, 85, 89
  śakti/Śakti as, 80, 83, 87
Prasad, Jwala Chaturvedi, 68, 70
pulikudy (tamarind-drinking) ceremony, 104
Purāṇas
  Brahmavaivarta Purāṇa, 7, 84–86
  Caṇḍī Purāṇa, 47, 48, 69
  creation and, 6, 11, 77–91
  Garuḍa Purāṇa, 63–64, 81–83, 88
  Kālīkā Purāṇas, 47
  Kūrma Purāṇa, 87–88
  Liṅga Purāṇa, 23
  Mahābhāgavata Purāṇa, 25
  Mārkaṇdeya Purāna, 19, 56–57, 94–95, 100
  Nārada Purāṇa, 82–84, 89
  Śiva Purāṇa, 23, 25, 26, 38–41, 86–87
  See also Devī-Bhāgavata Purāṇa
Puruṣa/*puruṣa*, 39, 69–70, 80, 83, 84–85, 88, 150, 161
Puruṣa Sūkta, 7
Pyḍamma, 124–27, 142

Rādhā, 8, 83–86
Radhu (niece of Sharada Devi), 172, 174, 177–78, 183, 186, 192, 193
Raheja, Gloria G., 113 n.25
Rajagopalan, L. S., 113 n.23
Rajeswari, D. R., 134, 139
Rajiv, Rajendra Kumar, 65
Rājñī, 25
Raktadantikā, 26
Rāllapāṭi, 163
Rāma, Lord, 59–60, 65, 66–67, 73–74, 194
Ramakrishna Paramahaṁsa, 171, 189–90
  death of, 179, 181–82
  and deification of Sharada Devi, 175–77
Rāmakṛṣṇa-Puṅthi, 185–86
Ramanujan, A. K., 39–40, 52, 113 n.25, 154, 168 n.8, 212 n.3
Ranbir Singh, Maharaja, 67
Rao, Veldheru Narayana, 113 n.25, 113 n.27, 114 n.32
Reṇukā, 13, 148–51, 154, 158, 161, 162–63, 165–67
Reynolds, Holly Baker, 165
Ṛg Veda, 7, 28, 69, 150, 160–61
Rohe, Mark Edwin, 6, 8–11, 15, 55–76, 212 n.5, 214
Rudra, 27, 87

Sabaro, 40–41
Sacred Canopy, The (Berger), 4–5
sacrifice/sacrificial themes, 13, 68–69, 145–67
sādhana, 172, 180, 189
Sagūr Mātā, 207–10
Śakambharī, 26
Śāktas, 6, 25, 28, 97, 101
Śākta Tantrics, 30, 88–90
Śākta Upaniṣad, 27–28
śakti pīṭhas, 7, 65–66, 200
śakti/Śakti, 3, 8, 9–10, 11, 13, 30, 78–91, 110, 116
  defined, 78
  as female side of Śiva, 87–88
  Great Goddess as, 6–7, 38–41, 79, 150–53, 219–20
  local goddess cults and, 115–16, 141, 147–51
  as *prakṛti*, 80, 83, 87
  Vaiṣṇavī and, 56
  Viṣṇu and, 82, 87
Sāṁkhya philosophy, 80, 85
Sanskritization, 117–18, 120, 127, 129, 141
Saradananda, Swami, 185
Śāradā-Tilaka Tantra, 24
Sāralā Dāsa, 47, 48–49, 54 n.8
Sarasvatī/Saraswatī, 61, 67–68, 84, 171, 201
Sarayabula Devi, 180–81
Śārikā, 25
Satī, 25, 64–65
Satyanarayana Murty, Kundurti, 116
Saundarya Laharī, 93, 96, 97–100
Sāvitrī, 84
Sax, William S., 5, 162, 201
Searle, John R., 17 n.1
Sen, Akshay Kumar, 185–86
Śeraṇwālī
  Vaiṣṇo Devī as, 59, 63, 71–72
Seven Mothers (*saptamātṛkā)*, 66, 147
Seven Sisters, 66, 147, 162
Seymour, S., 37
Sharada Devi/ Śāradā Devī, 13–14, 171–97, 203
  devotees of, 178–79, 190–94
  dreams and deification of, 179–83
  life of, 174–78, 190–94
  and Radhu (niece), 172, 174, 177–78, 183, 186, 192, 193
  silence of, 173, 183, 184–94
Shastri, B. K., 68
Shastri, Jagdish Chandra, 65
Shastri, Shri Kaka Ram, 67
Shri Mata Vaishno Devī Shrine Act, 57–58
Shulman, David Dean, 112 n.3, 112 n.16, 160, 161, 164, 169 n.13
Shweder, Richard A., 37, 43
Sil, Narasingha P., 195 n.5
Singh, Karan, 57
Singh, Suraj, 72
Singh, Y. B., 66
Sircar, D. C., 169 n.14
Sītā
  association of Vaiṣṇo Devī with, 65, 66–67
Śiva, 9–10, 161
  Bhagavati and, 102–3, 108–10
  Dārikavadham and, 94–95
  Durgā and, 63, 86
  Kālī and, 10, 38, 43–46, 47, 50–52, 104–5
  as male rival of the Goddess, 23, 32
  Pārvatī and, 123
  as Sadāśiva (eternal śiva), 27, 86–87
  Śakti as female side of, 87
Śivā, 87
Sivananda, Swami, 186–87
Śiva Purāṇa, 23, 25, 26, 38–41, 86–87
Śiv Khoṛī, 65
smallpox, 13, 145–46, 153, 156–57, 159–60, 166–67
Smith, Jonathan Z., 219
ṣoḍaśīpūjā ("worship of the sixteen-year-old"), 174, 175, 184
Sofa of Five Corpses, 27, 32–33
sonic energy, 24, 28–34
Śrī Cakra, 97–100
Srivastav, C. M., 68
Śrī Vidyā cult, 7
Śudra
  construction of Goddess and, 96

Suresh Kumār, 207–10, 211–12
Sureśvara, 33

Taittirīya Upaniṣad, 22, 23
Taṇṭamānagar, 163
Tantric philosophy
  birth of Devī and, 9, 24–33, 34
  Vaiṣṇo Devī and, 64
tapas, 154
  Vaiṣṇo Devī and, 61, 65, 67, 68, 70
Tārā, 25–26, 172
Tāraka, 20–21, 24
tattvas, 80, 82, 87
tejas (power), 22–23, 59, 60, 63, 68, 221
teyyam, 95–96
Thurston, Edgar, 153, 154–55, 157–58
Tirumump, T. Subrahmanian, 113 n.19
toliyērlu (ploughing rite), 135
Trawick, Margaret, 164, 165
Trikta Devī. *See* Vaiṣṇo Devī
trimūrti, 38–39
Tripurā, 25–28
Tūlaja Bhavānī, 133–34

Umā Haimavatī, 22–23, 31
Untouchables
  mixing with other castes, 154
Urban, Hugh B., 196 n.11

Vāgdevī, 25
Vaiṣṇava, 3, 25, 62–63, 79, 88–89
Vaiṣṇavī
  Vaiṣṇo Devī as, 62–64, 66, 68
Vaiṣṇo Devī, 10–11, 55–76, 200, 214
  ambiguous nature of, 68–72
  appearance to Shri Dhar, 60–72
  association with Pārvatī, 64–66
  association with Sītā, 65, 66–67
  cave shrine of, 55–59, 62–65, 73
  as Durgā, 61, 62–66, 68, 70, 71–72, 74
  as Kālī, 60, 61, 65, 67–68, 69, 71–72
  as Lakṣmī, 61–64, 66–68, 71–72, 74
  as Mahādevī, 56, 70–72
  origin of, 59–61, 65
  piṇḍis of, 56, 58–62, 64–65, 67, 68, 72
  Lord Rāma and, 59–60, 65, 66–67, 73–74
  as Satī, 64–65
  as Śeraṇwālī, 59, 63, 71–72
  triguṇā nature of, 63, 67–68, 70
  as Vaiṣṇavī, 62–64, 66, 68
  Viṣṇu and, 59–60, 66–68
Varadā Tantra, 30–31, 32
Vaudeville, Charlotte, 86
Vāyu, 22, 31
vegetarianism, 68–69, 70
Venu, G., 112 n.1
vēppañcelai (neem sari ritual), 157
Vētāḷam, 103, 106
Vidyarthi, G., 112 n.1
virginity, 68–69
vīrya, 81–82
Visakhapatnam (Andhra Pradesh), 12–13, 115–43
Viṣṇu, 23, 25, 27, 38–39, 40, 70, 161–62
  Lakṣmī and, 64, 77, 81, 128
  Pārvatī and, 164–65
  śakti/Śakti and, 82, 87
  Vaiṣṇo Devī and, 59–60, 66–68
Viṣṇu-Māyā, 67, 68

Wadley, Susan, 165
Winternitz, Maurice, 35 n.5
Woodroffe, John, 36 n.16
Wulff, Donna, 8

yakṣa, Brahman as, 22–23
Yama, 156–57
Yoga
  Jñāna (Knowledge Yoga), 33
  Kuṇḍalinī, 32
Yogin-Ma, 172, 177, 183, 189

Ziegenbalg, B., 136
Zimmer, Heinrich, 40

4088209R10149

Printed in Great Britain
by Amazon.co.uk, Ltd.,
Marston Gate.